GW00503215

Gregory Doran

Gregory Doran is the Chief Associate Director of the Royal Shakespeare Company. Described by the *Sunday Times* as 'one of the great Shakespearians of his generation', Doran has directed over half the canon of Shakespeare's plays at Stratford, including *Hamlet* with David Tennant (filmed for the BBC/Illuminations); *Antony and Cleopatra* with Patrick Stewart and Harriet Walter; *Coriolanus* with Janet Suzman and William Houston; *Timon of Athens* with Michael Pennington; *Henry VIII* with Jane Lapotaire and Paul Jesson; *The Taming of the Shrew* with Jasper Britton and Alexandra Gilbreath; *Twelfth Night* with Nancy Carroll and Richard Wilson; and *All's Well That Ends Well* with Judi Dench. He also directed a puppet masque of *Venus and Adonis* in a co-production with the Little Angel Theatre.

He has directed his partner, RSC Associate Artist Antony Sher, many times, including as the title role in *Macbeth* (filmed for Channel 4 /Illuminations); as Iago in *Othello*; as Leontes in *The Winter's Tale*; and as Titus Andronicus at the Market Theatre in Johannesburg, the subject of his book *Woza Shakespeare!* (co-written with Sher).

He has also directed Derek Walcott's adaptation of Homer's *Odyssey;* Mike Poulton's adaptations of Malory's *Morte d'Arthur* and Chaucer's *The Canterbury Tales*; a new play *Anjin: The English Samurai*, about William Adams, the first Englishman in Japan (co-written by Poulton and Sochiro Kawaii) in Tokyo; and the *York Mystery Plays* in York Minster to celebrate the Millennium.

In 2003 he directed a season of rare Jacobean plays which won the Olivier Award for Outstanding Achievement. He is author of *The Shakespeare Almanac*.

Shakespeare's Lost Play

In Search of *Cardenio*

Gregory Doran

NICK HERN BOOKS
London
www.nickhernbooks.co.uk

A Nick Hern Book

Shakespeare's Lost Play
first published in Great Britain in 2012
by Nick Hern Books Limited,
14 Larden Road, London W3 7ST

Front cover image based on a costume design by
Niki Turner from Gregory Doran's production of
Cardenio (RSC, 2011), using a detail from El Greco's *The Burial of the
Count of Orgaz*. Back cover photograph by Ellie Kurttz of Oliver Rix in
the title role of the same production of *Cardenio*.
Cover design by Ned Hoste, 2h Design

Typeset by Nick Hern Books, London
Printed and bound in Great Britain by
Ashford Colour Press, Gosport, Hampshire

A CIP catalogue record for this book
is available from the British Library

ISBN 978 1 84842 208 7

MIX
Paper from
responsible sources
FSC® C011748

Illustration on page ii: 'A Youthful Mendicant' (sketched at the Venta de Cardenas), from Gustave Doré's *Spain* (1876)

To my loved siblings
Mark, Jo and Ruth

Contents

Illustrations   ix

Synopsis   xi
The Story of *Cardenio*

Introduction   xv

Part One   1
Cardenna, 1612–13

Part Two   61
The History of *Cardenio, 1613–66*

Part Three   121
Researching and Designing the Production

Part Four   149
Re-imagining *Cardenio*

Epilogue   251

Acknowledgements   255

Index   257

Illustrations

The author and publishers gratefully acknowledge permission to reproduce the following illustrations:

John Rich as Lun by an unknown artist © The Art Archive/ Garrick Club

Wood engraving of the Covent Garden Theatre Fire by an unknown artist © The Trustees of the British Museum

Illustrations by Gustave Doré from *Dore's Illustrations for Don Quixote* (first published in two volumes by L. Hachette, Paris, in 1869; original printing in 1863; first published by Dover Publications Inc., Mineola, NY, in 1982), and *Doré's Spain* (written by Baron Davillier; published by Sampson Low, Marston, Low, and Searle, London, in 1876; first published by Dover Publications Inc., Mineola, NY, in 2004)

The Burial of the Count of Orgaz by El Greco © Mary Evans Picture Library/Aisa Media

Sir William Davenant by John Greenhill after William Faithorne; *John Fletcher* by an unknown artist; *Henry, Prince of Wales* by Robert Peake the Elder; and *Alexander Pope* by William Hoare © National Portrait Gallery, London

Cardenio rehearsal and production shots by Ellie Kurttz © 2011 Royal Shakespeare Company

Set and costume designs for the RSC production of *Cardenio* © 2011 Niki Turner

Engraving by Jacques de Gheyn II © Harry Beard Print Collection/V&A Images/Victoria and Albert Museum, London

'Luscinda gives a passing stranger a clandestine letter for Cardenio', from Gustave Doré's *Illustrations for Don Quixote* (1863)

The Story of *Cardenio*

The following is the synopsis of the RSC production of *Cardenio* as it was performed in the Swan Theatre, Stratford-upon-Avon, in 2011.

Part One

In the town of Almodovar, in Andalucía, young Cardenio is in love with Don Bernardo's daughter, Luscinda. But her father will not allow the match until Cardenio's father, Camillo, makes his approval known. Before Cardenio has the chance to ask his father, he is invited to Court to attend on the Duke's wayward younger son Fernando. Cardenio and Fernando become close friends.

Fernando, meanwhile, is obsessed with Dorotea, the daughter of a wealthy farmer, but she repulses his advances. Eventually he bribes her maid to let him into Dorotea's room. He promises to marry her, and, swearing before the statue of the Virgin Mary that he will be faithful to her (a binding oath, witnessed by Dorotea's maid), Fernando finally persuades Dorotea to yield to him.

However, overcome by guilt, Fernando immediately abandons Dorotea, and persuades Cardenio to join him on a visit back to Almodovar on the pretext of buying horses. Back in his home town, Cardenio takes Fernando to show him his beloved Luscinda. Fernando is immediately smitten with her beauty. He claims he will put in a good word for Cardenio with her father, and sends his friend back to Court to fetch money for the new horses.

With his rival out of the way, Fernando pays suit to Luscinda. Her father, despite his daughter's protestations, insists that she marry Fernando, given that he's the Duke's son. Luscinda sends word to Cardenio of the impending wedding, and he arrives just as the ceremony is about to take place.

Luscinda conceals him behind an arras. She has a knife hidden about her person, and intends to use it if need be, but under the pressure of the ceremony, when asked by the priest if she consents to be Fernando's wife, she faints, murmuring her assent as she swoons.

Devastated by what he thinks is Luscinda's betrayal of their love, Cardenio runs away.

The dagger is discovered in Luscinda's clothing along with a note revealing her rejection of Fernando. He attacks her in a fury, and is bustled out by Don Bernardo's men.

Dorotea has run away from home, so as not to bring shame on her father's house. When she hears that Fernando's marriage to Luscinda has been aborted, she determines to seek him and demand that he acknowledge the wrong he has done her.

Part Two

In the aftermath of the wedding, Cardenio has fled into the mountains and lost his wits. Dorotea, disguised as a shepherd boy, has fled the town, and followed Fernando into the mountains of the Sierra Morena. Here, calling herself Florio, she has taken refuge among the shepherds. The Master Shepherd, realising that this Florio is a woman in disguise, tries to rape her, but Dorotea manages to escape.

Cardenio overhears Dorotea lamenting her woes, and recognises that she is Fernando's abandoned mistress. He reveals his identity, and they take comfort in each other.

Fernando, meanwhile, has learnt that Luscinda has hidden herself in a convent, from which he intends to abduct her. His brother Pedro assists him with reluctance. When Dorotea reveals her identity to Pedro and asks for his help, he determines to bring all parties together at an inn to resolve the situation once and for all.

Pedro has sent word for his father the Duke to meet him at the inn, along with the fathers of both Cardenio and Luscinda. Fernando is surprised at being faced with all the people he has wronged, in particular Dorotea, who protests she is his lawful wife and admits the love she still bears him. Fernando is overcome with remorse, and begs forgiveness of his father, asking formally to be allowed to marry Dorotea. The Duke agrees and all are reconciled.

'The travellers [Don Quixote and Sancho Pança] see a ragged man [Cardenio] leaping among the rocks', from Gustave Doré's *Illustrations for Don Quixote* (1863)

Introduction
'Built upon a Novel in Don Quixot'

'Fantastico!' cried the King of Spain when I told him that Shakespeare may have written a play based on Cervantes. England's greatest writer inspired by Spain's greatest: an irresistible combination. *Cardenio* is named after a character in Cervantes' great novel, *Don Quixote*. If only the play hadn't been lost for the last four centuries...

In 2006, the Royal Shakespeare Company was awarded one of Spain's highest honours, a 'Bellas Artes' gold medal for excellence in the fine arts. I was dispatched to receive it from His Majesty, King Juan Carlos. The RSC had toured a number of productions to Spain in recent years: a whole season of Spanish Golden Age plays (supervised by Laurence Boswell) which played in the Teatro Español in Madrid in 2004, and Mike Poulton's adaptation of *The Canterbury Tales* which I had co-directed earlier that year. The medal ceremony was to be held in the magnificent mosque in Cordoba, La Mezquita.

The train from Madrid climbed from the flat arid planes south of the capital into the steep impenetrable hill country of Andalucía. I had a copy of *Don Quixote* on my knee, and realised that this desolate terrain was the very wilderness into which Cardenio escapes in his madness, the wild, un-peopled mountains of the Sierra Morena. This was the place where the whole story starts. Here were the crags among which Don Quixote and Sancho Pança first find a dead mule with a curious letter in its saddlebag. Here where they encounter the hero of our story, leaping from rock to rock, his face 'toasted by the sun'. Here in a hollow cork tree, the madman made his shelter. And here the wronged Dorotea, dressed as a herdsboy, sang her lament as she bathed her feet in a mountain stream.

The Sierra Morena (literally, 'dark-haired mountain') forms a natural border between Andalucía and the rest of the country. In medieval times it was the frontier between Muslim and Christian Spain.

On the first evening in Cordoba, a reception for all the 'medallistas' took place in a huge seventeenth-century man-sion in the Santa Marina district, called the Palacio de Viana, a grandly aristocratic edifice with endless arcaded patios and courtyards leading one into another, each more lush and beautiful than the next, heavy with the scent of jas-mine and oleander, twinkling with lanterns, and loud with the chatter of fountains and pools: a townhouse worthy of Luscinda's wealthy father, Don Bernardo.

My twin sister Ruth has joined me for the trip, with the RSC producer, the fastidiously stylish Jeremy Adams.

Emilio Hernandez, then director of the Almagro Festival (a classical theatre festival in La Mancha), is there to wel-come us. Emilio has been instrumental in inviting the RSC to Spain, and is a key player in inspiring closer connections between our two countries. *Cardenio*, therefore, is for him the perfect project to further that relationship.

Over dinner, in one of the larger courtyards, he points out some of the famous celebrity guests who are to be honoured with a Bellas Artes medal the following day. An elderly gen-tleman, with a look of Salvador Dalí, with waxed moustache and oiled hair, who is wearing a suit jacket and a tangerine sarong, turns out to be a famous fashion designer. The fiercely handsome señor who holds his square-cut jaw high in the air is, inevitably, a great toreador; and the lady in the pink crape with a sweeping black shawl is, Emilio tells us, one of Spain's great flamenco dancers. And there is an historian, a philosopher, a pop star and a film director among others.

Emilio is Cuban by birth and makes up for his shortness of stature by the size of his gestures. He ignores his plate of lubina in tomato and capers, and concentrates on mapping out an entire future co-production of *Cardenio* while I try and finish my dinner. Suddenly with an emphatic sweep of his hand, he tips his entire glass of vino tinto over me. I wish I hadn't worn a white jacket: I look as if I have been shot.

The following morning we all arrive by coach at La Mezquita, the great mosque of Cordoba. The huge golden walls are studded with great Arabic arches, tiles and stone fretwork. Inside, a forest of columns support double tiers of horseshoe arches in stone and ochre brick. It is a reminder of how the city was once a world centre of knowledge, with enormous libraries and colleges where the study of mathematics, science and architecture flourished.

The mosque has stood for over a millennium. And yet for more than half that time, it has had a Catholic cathedral imposed at its very heart. Monsignors in their black cassocks and pink sashes are sweeping about. Although one of the speeches during the ceremony refers to the Mezquita representing a fusion of East and West, I can't help feeling rather that it bears witness to the fanatical attempts of Christian Europe to dominate its Islamic neighbours.

As I sit on the platform with the rest, awaiting the arrival of the King and Queen, I look out across the baroque vandalism of the cathedral recalling the words of the Holy Roman Emperor, Charles V, who is reputed to have said on viewing the church, 'You have built here what you or anyone might have built anywhere else, but you have destroyed what was unique in the world.'

A gentleman seated next to me, representing the Hispanic Society of America, points out the late arrival of a very distinguished elderly lady with a shock of white hair tinged with fuchsia. 'Juan Carlos and his wife may be the King and Queen of Spain, but that,' he whispers, 'that is the Duchess of Alba.' Apparently the Duchess is the grandest grandee in Spain. Her family stretches back to the Hapsburg dynasty, making the present Bourbon rulers look like newcomers. 'She has more titles than Juan Carlos, and he's got a few. He's still King of all the Sicilies,' he says, 'and King of Jerusalem, which is a claim I'd like to see him try asserting in Israel.'

Then suddenly we are all on our feet and the Royal party arrive.

After the award ceremony is over, we process out to have our photograph taken with the King among the orange trees in the Patio de los Naranjos. Chris Hickey, the head of the British Council here, steers me expertly to have my few words with the King, explaining the importance of the award as we go. It is a sign that Spain regards the RSC very highly and would like to emulate us by establishing their own properly funded classical theatre company. He insists I tell the King about *Cardenio*. I am delighted with the King's reaction to the very idea that Cervantes and Shakespeare are somehow linked through this story.

Later on in a little bodega in the Calle Linares, over some bull's tail stew and a glass of Pedro Ximénez, we try and work out how we can make *Cardenio* happen with some sort of Spanish connection. There is so much goodwill here to make such a project work. I now have the inspiration I need to pursue a production. We could even have a Royal endorsement on the poster: 'Fantastico! – *The King of Spain.*'

'But I thought you said this play has been lost for four centuries,' Jeremy Adams reminds me.

'A-ha,' I grin, 'but I think I know where it is.'

Five years before our trip to Spain, I had received a parcel from Jarndyce Booksellers in Great Russell Street, London. I was inordinately excited. When I opened it up, a slim volume with a plain blue-grey paper cover slipped into my hand. It looked like an old school exercise book. On the inside cover someone had scribbled in pencil 'THEOBALD. Based on Shakespeare? £65.' Opposite on the title page, I read the words:

'DOUBLE FALSHOOD
OR, THE
DISTREST LOVERS.
[Price One Shilling and Sixpence.]

The next page elaborated further:

A PLAY
As it is now Acted at
The Theatre Royal in COVENT-GARDEN
Written ORIGINALLY
By W. SHAKESPEARE;
And REVISED
By Mr. THEOBALD

There followed a quotation from Book Nine of Virgil's *Aeneid*:

— *Quod optanti Divum promittere nemo*
Auderet, volvenda Dies, en! attulit ultro.

['What the Gods themselves could not promise to accomplish, revolving Time has brought to light.']

This was the third edition of the play, printed in London for 'T. Lowndes, in Fleet Street'. The roman numerals then spelled out the date: 1767.

It was the closest I was ever going to get to owning a Shakespeare quarto. I have been obsessed with this play for a number of years. Somehow, now that I possess my own copy, in a genuine eighteenth-century edition, I feel a little closer to understanding its extraordinary story.

What I held in my hand was what the author, Lewis Theobald (pronounced 'Tibbald'), claimed was a lost play by William Shakespeare. The quotation from *The Aeneid* which he chose to put on the frontispiece acknowledges just how unlikely that claim seemed to be. It was nothing short of miraculous.

To lend weight to his claim, on the very opening page of the script, Theobald printed the licence he had acquired from the King himself to publish his play. This Royal decree outlines Theobald's petition to the new monarch:

> He having, at a considerable Expence, Purchased the Manuscript Copy of an Original Play of WILLIAM SHAKSPEARE... and with great Labour and Pains, Revised and Adapted the same to the Stage... (we) grant him Our Royal Privilege and Licence for the sole Printing and Publishing thereof for the Term of Fourteen Years... Given at Our Court at St James, the Fifth Day of December, 1727, in the First Year of Our Reign.

Just under three weeks later *Double Falshood* opened at the Theatre Royal in Drury Lane and ran for ten consecutive performances, a successful run in those days. Theobald himself writes of 'the Universal Applause which crowns this Orphan Play'. My third edition, printed forty years later, demonstrates that the play was thought worthy enough (or had sufficient curiosity value) to warrant a revival, this time at Covent Garden.

The question that has been debated by scholars for many years now is simply this: did Lewis Theobald really have the manuscript copy of a Shakespeare play, or was *Double Falshood* an elaborate forgery? And if he did have such a rarity, what happened to the original manuscript?

Theobald writes a rather defensive editor's preface to his edition, in which several things caught my attention, requiring further exploration. The tale, he writes, is 'built upon a Novel in Don Quixot'. In tracing the play's lineage he says:

> There is a Tradition (which I have from a Noble Person, who supply'd me with One of my Copies) that this Play was given by our Author, as a Present of Value, to a Natural Daughter of his, for whose Sake he wrote it, in the Time of his Retirement from the Stage.

One of the manuscript copies he has is 'of above Sixty Years Standing, in the Hand-writing of Mr Downes, the famous

Old Prompter' and used to belong to the great Restoration actor Thomas Betterton, 'and by Him design'd to have been usher'd into the World'.

Theobald also provides some intriguing details about the circumstances of that first production at Drury Lane Theatre, and his dealings with the management, which have an all-too-familiar ring about them.

So it was that in 2001 I joined the fray and began to consider Theobald's adaptation from a theatrical standpoint. I started to delve into the play's fascinating history, with the result a decade later that we mounted a production at Stratford for the Royal Shakespeare Company. We described it as: 'Shakespeare's "Lost Play" Re-imagined'. This is an account of that often surprising journey of exploration, and of my growing admiration for the literary chancer, and bardolator *par excellence*, Lewis Theobald.

'Chapel of the Zancarron, Mosque of Cordoba', from Gustave Doré's *Spain* (1876)

Part One

Cardenna, 1612–13

1

'Cardenna'

How do we know that there was play called *Cardenio* in the first place? I travelled to Oxford to start my quest.

My arrival at the Admissions Office of the Bodleian Library caused a little stir. I had forgotten to bring my relevant application papers for admission, so my assistant, Amanda, had phoned ahead to ask if they would allow them to be faxed through. When I walked into the rather imposing office at the corner of Broad Street and Catte Street, a cry went up: 'Are you Greg?', 'Ah, here's Greg,' 'Hi Greg.' For some reason the flurry of phone calls about this mysterious 'Greg' had brightened up a slow morning.

I was on the trail of the first written evidence that a play called *Cardenio* actually existed, and had been told I would find that here in Oxford.

I was perched on a chair in the corner, while Helen, the admissions officer, went through my papers and decided how to process my application. I stared out of the window at the bright-blue early September morning. Oxford looked beautiful. The heads of the Roman Emperors glaring down from their pedestals on the railings around the Sheldonian next door, looked as startled as when Zuleika Dobson's landau rolled by in the opening pages of Max Beerbohm's Oxford love story.

Eventually my papers were passed to another lady, who informed me that the book I wanted was held in the Special Collections at the Radcliffe Science Library while the Bodleian itself was being renovated, and she gave me a map. The rules meant I could not use pens, not take in a bag, and of course no food. She suggested I ate my banana on my way up the road.

She passed me a laminated card, and asked me to read the oath it contained out loud, which I duly did. 'I hereby undertake not to remove from the Library, or to mark, deface, or injure in any way, any volume, document, or other object belonging to it or in its custody; nor to bring into the Library or kindle therein any fire or flame, and not to smoke in the Library; and I promise to obey all rules of the Library.'

The first reference to an oath goes back to the 1400s, she said, and ran through a brief history of how the oath had changed over the years. It used to be in Latin, and since 1609 has been declared out loud, and more recently any reference to Almighty God was removed, due to the widening of the readership among different faiths, and the secular.

Eventually, after about half an hour, and having paid my fiver, and clutching my new photo-ID reader's card, I headed back into the sunshine and off up Parkes Road.

The Special Collections Room is on the second level underground at the Radcliffe. I felt I was entering some special secret bunker, and settled at a table with my precious loan, a grey box folder containing the Treasurer's accounts for 1612–13. With some trepidation, and feeling a bit of a fraud among all this scholarly hush, I opened the box. The large vellum account book had lettering inked on the front. Inside, each page was marked up with two parallel lines, down the centre of which were itemised the various expenditures of the Court of King James I.

I suddenly realised just how unprepared I was. I am no scholar, and I had no idea where, in this large book, two simple accounts would be, and furthermore I couldn't even read

the handwriting, a swirling looping copperplate, called secretary hand, which scriveners used in this period.

The penmanship was beautiful – brown ink in extravagant
flourishes – but I couldn't read it. The abbreviations used
and the odd spelling were hard to work out. What seemed
to read 'Spoon' I eventually realised was 'upon', although
spelled with double 'p'. And 'the' seemed to bear no sem-
blance to the actual word, or indeed any word I recognised.

But as I pored through the book, page by page, the words
started to come into focus, and a brave new world appeared.
Here were payments to His Majesty's watermen, to the
Venetian Bassano family for music, to the keeper of His
Majesty's gardens at Theobald's Palace, wages for messen-
gers, for apparelling and the like. Occasionally a word is
written in a particular clear hand. For example, one of the
grooms of the chamber is paid for keeping and feeding an
ARMADILLO. Presumably it was a gift to His Majesty from
one of the early trips to Virginia.

I began to imagine those Court performances: perhaps the
first performance of *Cardenio*, with the Bassanos playing
chamber music by Alfonso Ferrabosco, or Robert Johnson,
footmen scurrying here and there, and one of the grooms of
the chamber standing at the back, struggling with a wriggly
armadillo.

Then suddenly at the bottom of one page, in accounts for
the Court at Greenwich, I read an item paid to John Hemings,
'for himself and the rest of his fellowes... his majesties players...
for presenting a playe... before the Duke of Savoyes embas-
sador... on the 8th daye of June 1613.' And then in the most
extraordinary script the word '*Cardenna*'. The initial C looks
like a hot cross bun, a sort of O with a cross through it. The
word seemed to have its own enigmatic calligraphic flourish.

The Duke of Savoy's Ambassador is referred to on the next
page, too, where there is a payment for bear baiting in his
honour in July. Who was he? And why is he honoured with
a special performance of our play?

At the top of the next page there are two items paid to
John Hemings, the first for presenting fourteen several

plays, at Whitehall. There are references to *Philaster*, one called *The Knot of Fools*, here's *Much Ado About Nothing*, *The Maid's Tragedy*, *The Merry Devil of Edmonton*, *A King and No King*, *The Winter's Tale*, and *Sir John Falstaff* (*Henry IV, Part Two*?).

I can make out quite clearly the words *The Tempest*. It is wonderful to see the names of these plays which are so familiar and which have gone through so many productions in so many languages in so many parts of the world 'in states unborn and accents yet unknown' written by quill, at the time of the original performance. The direct connection, the rush of immediacy catches my breath.

The next item lists six several plays, one play called *A Bad Beginning Makes a Good Ending*, which is probably a proverbial title for another lost play. Or could it just be *All's Well That Ends Well* badly remembered? There are more familiar titles hidden behind *The Hotspur* (presumably *Henry IV, Part One*) and *Benidicte and Betteris* (a second performance of *Much Ado*). There's Fletcher's *The Captain*, and Ben Jonson's *The Alchemist* and then the next one glows off the page: 'one other *Cardenno*'. 'All played within the tyme of this accompte viz paid forty pounds.' Clearly the King was pleased with the entertainment provided for it then says 'And by way of His Majesty's reward, twenty pounds in all.'

So, a play called *Cardenna*, or *Cardenno* had been performed at Court along with other plays by Shakespeare and Fletcher. Now I needed to know two things: what was happening at Court that Christmas, and why was there a special performance of the play six months later for the Savoy Ambassador?

I drive back to Stratford pondering my new acquaintance with 'Cardenno'. This spelling, in the account book, seems to suggest that King Juan Carlos's pronunciation of the name 'Cardenio' is how the English Jacobeans said the name, and that the play should be called 'Car-den-io', and not 'Car-deen-io' as we had been saying. So at least I've got the title sorted.

The workman was wiring up the particularly splendid five-lantern lamp-post that stands sentinel by the gate to the gardens. It is only recently that this great black pillar of lights has had its label attached, so I was delighted to read, around a painted Spanish flag, the name of its donor, Alcalá de Henares.

Before embarking on the *Cardenio* project, I doubt I would have recognised the name. Alcalá de Henares, a little town, north-east of Madrid, is the birthplace of Don Miguel de Cervantes Saavedra, the author of *The History of Don Quixote of La Mancha*. And indeed, a statue of *El Príncipe de los Ingenios*, or 'The Prince of Wits', as the Spanish call Cervantes, stands on a plinth in the centre of the little town square. He is dressed in doublet and hose, and neat ruff, and holds an inordinately long quill pen. If you did not know you were in Spain, you would assume this was a statue of his exact contemporary, William Shakespeare.

Cervantes seems to me to share the same spirit of compassion and humanity which is evident in the works of Chaucer, Shakespeare and Dickens. But unlike Shakespeare, Cervantes' life was full of adventure. He travelled to Italy, possibly fleeing arrest having wounded a man in a duel. He became a soldier and fought bravely in the Battle of Lepanto, the great triumphant defeat of the Ottoman fleet by the forces of Christian Spain in 1571. During the naval encounter, he was shot three times by a harquebus, and lost the use of his left arm. On his way back to Barcelona, he was captured by corsairs and held prisoner as a slave in Algiers for five years. He made several escape attempts. His accomplice in one such attempt, a gardener, was hanged by the left foot for helping him.

Professor José Manuel González, a professor at the University of Alicante, ponders why Cervantes' captor, the city governor, Hasan Baha, a man with a cruel reputation, should have treated Cervantes so leniently after each of these escape attempts. He suggests that there were homoerotic overtones to their relationship. 'Cervantes' sexuality, like Shakespeare's,' he writes, 'has been the subject of repeated debate.'

When Cervantes returned to Spain, he married a much older woman, Catalina de Salazar, having already fallen in love with a married woman called Ana Franca, and made her pregnant. But he seems to have virtually abandoned Catalina, first to become a purveyor, travelling all over Spain to requisition supplies for the Armada, and later as a tax collector. He even attempted to get a posting to the New World. Cervantes spent most of his life in debt, and suffered bankruptcy. He found himself in prison on at least two occasions.

It was really only during the last nine years of his life that Cervantes settled to write, enjoying a period of relative ease, after the publication and immediate success of *Don Quixote* (considered the first modern novel) in 1605.

Next to Cervantes' action-packed life, what we know of Shakespeare's seems sedentary by comparison.

Anthony Burgess, in a short story called 'A Meeting in Valladolid', imagines a grumpy encounter between the two men, during the visit of the Earl of Nottingham to Spain to ratify the 1604 peace treaty. One hot afternoon, Shakespeare 'and his nut-chewing fellows of the King's Men, all got up for the occasion in their royal livery,' watch the characters of Don Quixote and Sancho Pança parade around the arena of Valladolid to the cheers of the crowd:

> The entertainment began with a tune on a high-pitched
> trumpet, and then there trotted into the ring a long
> elderly man with pasteboard armour, a helmet, broken
> but mended with string, a broken lance dirtily
> bandaged together again, riding a deplorable nag,
> whose bones showed through its mangy skin. He was
> followed by a little fat man astride a donkey, ever and
> anon raising to his shaggily bearded lips a dripping
> wineskin.

As William growls jealously to see these famous characters he is told, 'They are too big for a book. They have escaped from its prison.'

Later, invited by Cervantes to his house, Shakespeare is seated on a lowly saddle stool while his disdainful host reclines in the only chair, and pontificates about the kind of bleak stories beloved by his nation:

> And at the end of a wretched life there is no rest, no peace, only eternal torment. That is the kind of story our nation loves. And that they expected from me when I left the wearying and rewardless world of the theatre for the leisurely narrative. A Don Quixote battered and bruised and broken in God's jape of blood and smashed teeth. But instead I give them comedy.

Shakespeare asks to read the book, and wonders: 'Can it be made into a play?'

He is told: 'It cannot. Its length is its virtue. You cannot encompass so long a journey in your two hours' traffic.'

In the 1920s, in his book of essays *Apes and Angels*, J.B. Priestley conjures up a very different picture of the two great writers, as the very best of friends: 'If those two are not hand-in-glove, then there is no friendship among the shades.' He imagines them looking down from Heaven at half-timbered Stratford, at how everything in the place is 'conscientiously thatched and beamed'; and laughing at the absurdity of the whole Shakespeare industry. What would they have made of the lamp-post from Alcalá de Henares in the Avonbank Gardens, I wonder?

Cervantes claimed to have written some twenty or thirty plays, of which only a few are extant. Imagine. Here I am spending all this time and effort wondering what Shakespeare's lost play might have been like, and nearly every play Cervantes ever wrote is missing. Were they any good? In his prologue to eight plays and interludes that he published at the end of his life, he writes with appealing self-deprecation, that they were not all that bad, 'at least people didn't throw cucumbers'.

Shakespeare and Cervantes died on the same date. I say date, rather than day, because the calendars of England and the rest of Europe were out of sync by ten days.

But why did Shakespeare choose to adapt an episode from Cervantes in the first place?

4

The First Night of *Cardenio*, 1612

In 1612, London was full excitement at the prospect of a Royal wedding. The Bohemian Prince Frederick, Elector Palatine, was to marry King James's beloved daughter, Elizabeth.

A painting of the sparkly eyed bride to be, by Robert Peake, now hangs in the Metropolitan Museum of Art in New York. It shows Elizabeth as the beautiful young woman that the Elector Palatine would have encountered on his arrival in 1612. She is dressed in the highest Jacobean fashion, in a silver farthingale sprigged with brightly coloured flowers and foliage and butterflies, with a high lace standing collar. A diamond-studded chain hangs from her shoulders, and she wears a pearl necklace around her neck. Her hair, adorned with drop pearl and diamond ornaments, is backcombed into what resembles a sixties beehive.

Elizabeth spent much of her childhood at Coombe Abbey, not far from Stratford-upon-Avon, in the care of Sir John Harington. On Queen Elizabeth's death, when the family came down from Scotland for her father's coronation, the young Elizabeth (who had been named after her godmother, the late Queen) was brought here to be educated. It may seem strange to us that the Royal children were brought up separated from their parents, but nevertheless it was so.

But the country retreat nearly proved most dangerous for Elizabeth, for in 1605 the Gunpowder Plotters planned to abduct the Princess from Coombe Abbey. Having assassinated King James and his Parliament in London, they intended to place the little girl on the throne as a puppet monarch. She would have been Queen Elizabeth II.

In that chilly October of 1612, as sixteen-year-old Frederick, Elizabeth's husband-to-be, sailed up the Thames, crowds thronged the banks to meet the handsome young Prince, despite the cold. Some one hundred and fifty boats arrived in his flotilla, and were joined by many more. They were saluted by a great peal of ordnance as they passed the Tower, and were met at the water gate of Whitehall by the Duke of York. It was to be a very grand Royal wedding indeed.

As the happy couple, Frederick and the admired Elizabeth, sat in the Banqueting House at Whitehall to watch the King's Men perform *The Tempest*, there must have been a frisson of recognition as the goddesses in the masque bless the union of Prince Ferdinand and the admired Miranda (both bride and groom had turned sixteen that August).

But Frederick was one of the staunchest Protestant princes in Europe: what on earth was Shakespeare doing adapting the latest hit novel from Catholic Spain for such an occasion? Well, it seems a double wedding was proposed that winter.

King James had a master plan. Not only would he marry his daughter to a Protestant prince, but he would also marry his elder son, Henry, to a prominent European Catholic princess. This was a progressive foreign policy, and accounts for the presence in Court of the Savoyard Ambassador, Giovanni Battista Gabaleone.

Savoy was a small Duchy in Northern Italy, ruled by Duke Carlo Emanuelle, known as Testa di Feu, or 'Fire Head', because of his rash temperament. His father, Emanuele Filiberto (known as Testa di Ferro – 'Iron Head'), had moved the capital of the Duchy from Chambery to Turin, and had brought with it the family's most sacred possession, the shroud of Christ, regarded as the most holy relic in Catholic Christendom. This ducal family were profoundly Catholic. And Gabaleone was charged with negotiating Britain's second Royal marriage between the heir to the throne Prince Henry and the Savoyard Infanta, Maria Apollonia.

Despite the French Queen Marie de Medici's displeasure at the prospect of such a match, and indeed some Spanish disapproval that King James was not promoting a marriage directly with a Spanish princess, it seemed certain that the announcement of a Catholic marriage was on the cards.

Clearly what was wanted that Christmas were plays celebrating the new rapprochement with Catholic Europe. Shakespeare and his younger collaborator, John Fletcher, put their heads together.

Some time that year, it seems, they were collaborating on *All is True*, a play about the most famous Spanish Queen ever to have married into the English Royal Family, Henry VIII's first wife, Katherine of Aragon. The play is at pains to argue the needs of Henry's conscience, in divorcing Katherine, but nevertheless also manages virtually to canonise the saintly Queen. And if that play was performed in the Blackfriars Theatre over that same winter season, then it would have been played in the very room where Katherine's Blackfriars trial had taken place over eighty years before.

Then, it seems, Fletcher and Shakespeare alighted on the new hit novel from Spain, *Don Quixote*, translated by Thomas Shelton. The character of the deluded Don himself and his tireless companion Sancho Pança would have made a play in themselves (and surely Shakespeare would have been enticed by the Falstaffian size of the characterisation to write a play just about him), but they chose instead to unwind the story of the mad Cardenio and his faithless friend Fernando.

We can presume that they presented their new play to the Master of the Revels, well in advance for presentation that Christmas, and having received his approval, began to rehearse their new Spanish play.

Until now Shakespeare had only had one Spanish character in his plays, the fantastical Don Adriano de Armado in *Love's Labour's Lost*. Some think that in an earlier private performance, the character was a satire on Sir Walter Ralegh, and to disguise the portrait for public presentation Shakespeare had made him a Spaniard.

Previously Spaniards had been easy targets on the stage. Indeed it is thought that Fletcher had had to adapt *Philaster*, one of his plays which were presented at Court that Christmas, in case of upsetting the new international relationship, as the villain, Pharamond, was originally a Spaniard.

So, preparation for the Christmas season of festivities would include a flattering nod to Britain's new friends in Catholic Europe. And Gabaleone, the Savoyard Ambassador, was getting very close to some sort of settlement of the marriage between the Infanta and Prince Henry.

Some of the other ambassadors at Court were suspicious of Gabaleone. Antonio Foscarini, the Venetian Ambassador, writing home to his serenity, the Doge of Venice, said that some 'declare that the King should keep his eye on this Savoyard Ambassador called Gabaleone, or "Trick-the Lion" for the Lion is the cognizance of England'.

James already had assurances that if she became the wife of the heir apparent, the Infanta would conduct her own religious observance very privately, so by late October, Gabaleone was merely awaiting the final approval of the dowry to be set, and as he had indicated that the King could more or less state his sum, that did not seem to be a major obstacle. All seemed set for King James's dream of a double wedding to secure Britain's ties with both Catholic and Protestant Europe.

But there was an unforeseen problem. Prince Henry did not want to comply with his father's wishes. He did not want to marry the Catholic Infanta from Savoy.

'Fernando abducts Luscinda from the convent', from Gustave Doré's *Illustrations for Don Quixote* (1863)

5

Other *Cardenios*

Since the reading of *Double Falshood* in the Swan Reading Room back in 2003, I can't leave it alone. I keep coming back to the idea of it containing Shakespeare's lost play. Wouldn't there be some way of supplying the scenes which are missing from Theobald's play?

Shortly after the reading, I was intrigued to receive an email from a scholarly friend in Madrid, alerting my attention to another seventeenth-century stage adaptation of the Cardenio story besides the putative Shakespeare/Fletcher version. The RSC Literary Department helped me to track it down.

Guillén de Castro (1569–1631) was a playwright in the Golden Age of Spanish drama. A Valencian, de Castro had written the play which inspired Corneille's *Le Cid*. Another of his works, *Fuerza de la Costumbre*, tells the story of a young girl, who is brought up from birth as a boy, and of a boy who is brought up from birth as a girl. John Fletcher adapted it into an extraordinary play called *Love's Cure*. But de Castro also wrote the *Comedia de Don Quijote*, in which the Cardenio story appears.

In de Castro's version, both Dorotea and Cardenio secretly attend the wedding of Luscinda to the Marquis (Fernando).

A housekeeper informs them that Luscinda's father has practically dragged his daughter to the marriage by her hair. Cardenio runs away when he sees Luscinda give her hand to the Marquis, but Dorotea stays. Luscinda, having recovered from her faint, berates herself for cowardice for not using her hidden dagger upon herself, and when the Marquis in a fury calls her a peasant, and swears he should kill her 'a thousand times', Luscinda begs him to do so. Threatening to throw everyone out of the windows, the Marquis summons his men, and Luscinda's father summons his, and in the ensuing confusion, Dorotea ushers Luscinda away.

That's quite a radical rewrite of Cervantes, far more so than *Double Falshood*. But then we discovered another adaptation of *Don Quixote*, which forefronts the Cardenio story.

In France, in 1639, there was a Quixote trilogy written by Guyon Guérin de Bouscal (1613–57) and later adapted by Molière's company. It begins with the Cardenio story. In Act Three of the Bouscal play, having sprung Luscinda from the convent, Fernando attempts to persuade her to be his. Rather surprisingly, however, Luscinda manages to win over her abductor, and overwhelmed by remorse, Fernando surrenders her to Cardenio, at which point (according to a stage direction) 'violins strike up a joyful air to express Luscinda's happiness'.

And then some time later, we came across yet another Cardenio play. A French writer called Pichou wrote *Les Folies de Cardenio* (*The Madness of Cardenio*) in 1628. Pichou (who seems only to be known by that single name) wrote three other tragicomedies, but *Les Folies* was the most successful. The play is in such stilted French that even the RSC Literary Assistant, Réjane Collard, who is French herself, has difficulty in understanding it. However, there are some startling bits of rejigging here too. Dorotea flees into the mountains in search of exile when she hears about Fernando's marriage to Luscinda; whereas in *Double Falshood*, when Dorotea hears the marriage has been abandoned, she spies 'a little spark of hope' and pursues Fernando in order 'to wound his conscience'.

Fernando and his henchmen spring Luscinda from the convent, and after encountering Don Quixote in the wood, they all end up in the inn. Then there is a distinct departure from the Cervantes which particularly catches my attention. When Cardenio and Fernando finally face each other, a fight breaks out; and Dorotea, risking her life, intervenes to stop them. Her misery prompts Fernando into a change of heart and he drops his weapons.

Les Folies de Cardenio later re-emerged as a comedy-ballet by Charles-Antoine Coypel, performed at Christmas in the Grand Hall of the Tuileries in 1720, for the Court of the young King Louis XV, with music by Michel Richard de Lalande. It was described in the journal, *Le Mercure*, as follows:

> This spectacle is the most beautiful and most magnificent ever seen, both for the number of actors and actresses, and the quantity of instruments and voices. The king danced with all imaginable grace and propriety.

The versatile and talented Coypel also designed a series of tapestries for the Gobelins factory in Paris, depicting the story of Don Quixote.

So there are a surprising number of continental *Cardenio* plays. I begin to wonder if I can supply the missing scenes in *Double Falshood* from some of these extant versions. I am looking forward to plundering them for ideas, and we commission literal translations of selected scenes.

But I then discovered that when Lewis Theobald mounted *Double Falshood* in 1727, it was not the first time (since the performance of Shakespeare and Fletcher's play for the Savoyard Ambassador in 1613) that the character of the madman Cardenio had appeared on the London stage.

Thomas D'Urfey had had a huge success with *The Comical History of Don Quixote* in 1694. Indeed it was so popular that there soon followed not one but two sequels. D'Urfey was renowned not only for his plays, and his poems and songs, but for his jokes. He produced several volumes of a book called *Pills to Purge Melancholy*. A song called 'The Fart' was one of his biggest hits. He is reputed to have said, 'All animals, except man, know that the principal business of life is to enjoy it.'

In his *Don Quixote* adaptation, Cardenio (played by Mr Bowman) makes his late arrival into the play in Act Four of Part One. D'Urfey's stage direction reads rather abruptly: 'Cardenio enters in ragged clothes, and in a wild Posture sings a Song. Then exit.' The song is by the great baroque composer Henry Purcell, who wrote all the incidental music for the plays. It is a magnificent baritone aria, and it begins:

> Let the dreadful engines of eternal will,
> The thunder roar, and crooked lightning kill.

In the late eighteenth century, George Colman the Younger used the original Cardenio story, interwoven with another tale from *Don Quixote*, and transposed it to Granada, and the period of the expulsion of the Moors from Spain. His melodramatic play, called *The Mountaineers*, was performed at the Haymarket Theatre in 1793.

But perhaps the most surprising incarnation of Cardenio on the stage was a puppet show in 1733 by a Brazilian known as 'the Jew'. *Vida do Grande D. Quixote de la Mancha e do Gordo Sancho Pança* by António José da Silva was a play for marionettes. It stands as a little tragic coda to this list of adaptations.

António's parents were Marranos, Portuguese Jews, who had emigrated to colonial Brazil to escape the Inquisition. António was born in Rio de Janeiro in 1705, but came back to Portugal at the age of eight. That summer, his mother figured among the reconciled in an auto-da-fé in 1713. António was able to go to university to study law, but in 1726 (as Theobald was adapting *Cardenio* in London), he was imprisoned by the Inquisition. He and his mother were interrogated, tortured and forced to attend the great auto-da-fé as penitents, in the presence of the fanatical King Joao V and his Portuguese Court.

On his release, António began to write plays for the marionettes at a theatre in the Bairro Alto District of Lisbon. I
find it moving that he should have chosen *Don Quixote* as
one of his subjects, a story of such life-affirming power.

His career was short-lived, as he and his wife were
denounced by a slave of theirs to the Holy Office. António
was condemned to death on trumped-up charges, and
protesting his Catholic faith to the end, he was publically
strangled and his body burnt at an auto-da-fé on 18 October
1737.

By now, I have assembled an entire library of *Cardenio*
plays. Working through them, it strikes me that I should just
commission a writer to do a new adaptation of Cervantes'
original story, applying as broad a licence to change the plot
as de Castro, Bouscal, Pichou or even Thomas D'Urfey.

6

'Thus Much of Turin':
Impressions of Savoy

In researching any play, you are led off down many interesting side roads, and can find yourself chasing many an odd trail and tangent. *Cardenio* offers a whole map of intriguing and potentially irrelevant possibilities, and who better to travel those byways with than the irrepressible Jacobean traveller, Thomas Coryate.

I keep wondering why *Cardenio* was given a special command performance for the Savoy Ambassador, the summer after the Whitehall performance. Indeed, where is Savoy? And what impressions might the young Prince Henry have had of the Dukedom of Savoy, the home of the Infanta his father proposed for his bride? He might have turned to a book published the previous year in 1611, by the indefatigable Thomas Coryate, who was a sort of court jester to Prince Henry's circle. Ben Jonson said of Coryate, 'He is always Tongue-Major of the company,' which captures something of the lively spirit of this gossipy traveller, so evident in his book.

The lengthy title says it all: 'Coryate's Crudities hastily gobbled up in five months travel, and newly digested in the hungry air of Odcombe in the county of Somerset, and now dispersed to the nourishment of the travelling members of his kingdom'. Coryate dedicated the book to Prince Henry, calling him, with ingratiating hyperbole, 'the orient pearl of the Christian world'.

His 'Observations of Savoy' are contained in the first volume. At ten o'clock in the morning on Wednesday 8 June 1608, Coryate arrived at the foot of his first Alp. He describes how he was carried shoulder high on a precarious chair litter up the mountains at the start of his week in the dukedom. He complains of the terrible roads,

> which were as bad as the worst I ever rode in England
> in the midst of winter, in so much that the ways of
> Savoy may be proverbially spoken of as the Owls of
> Athens, the Pears of Calabria, and the Quails of Delos.

He shudders at the steepness of the roads through the mountain passes: 'if my horse had happened to stumble, he had fallen down with me four or five times as deep in some places as Paul's Tower in London is high.'

He shivers in this chilly damp Alpine pocket. 'The country of Savoy is very cold and much subject to rain by reason of those clouds that are continually hovering about the Alps.' Once he has passed through the Alps, Coryate admires the vineyards and the fine meadows, the chestnut, walnut, and hazel trees, and he marvels at the 'admirable abundance of Butter-flies in many places of Savoy, by the hundredth part more than ever I saw in any country before'.

Oddly he notices how many of the population seem to be afflicted with terrible goitres, which he ascribes to the common drinking of snow water. 'Yea some of their bunches are almost as great as an ordinary football with us in England.'

Coryate always has an eye for the detail of the national costume he sees. In Savoy, he wonders at the high-girdled dress of the women, and admires the quaintness of their headgear:

> For they wrap and fold together after a very seemly
> fashion, almost as much linen upon their heads as the
> Turks do in those linen caps they wear, which are called
> Turbents.

A little further along in his journey to Turin, he observes

> the most delicate straw hats, which both men and
> women use in most places in that province, but
> especially the women. For those that the women wear
> are very pretty, some of them having at least an
> hundred seams with silver and many flowers, borders
> and branches very curiously wrought in them, in so
> much that some of them were valued at two duckatons,
> that is eleven shillings.

When he arrives in Turin, he has to apologise that his observations of 'so flourishing and beautiful a city' are so brief, because like many a traveller, he became ill. He warns his fellow tourist:

> I found so great a distemperature in my body by
> drinking the sweet wine of Piedmont that caused a
> grievous inflammation in my face and hands, so that I
> had but a small desire to walk much abroad in the
> streets. Therefore I advise all Englishmen that intend to
> travel into Italy to mingle their wine with water as soon
> as they come into the country.

He is very impressed with the Duke's palace, and his new gallery. 'Truly it is incomparably the fairest that ever I saw, saving the King of France's at the Louvre in Paris.'

But if Tom Coryate had been allowed to venture into that Royal palace he may have seen a portrait of his Royal master. Robert Peake, the Prince's picture-maker, had painted this portrait of the young Prince of Wales, the hope of the nation, to be sent abroad as a gift to the Duke. Perhaps it was conveyed in the diplomatic bag of Gabaleone himself.

It still hangs in the Palazzo Chiablese in Turin, where it was recently rediscovered. Henry, dressed in a suit of deep-green silk, stands with his left foot on an impressa bearing the triple plume of his office. He is just about to unsheathe his sword, which hangs from a belt adorned with a jewelled George and the Dragon. It is the pose of a Roman hero. The young Prince, his hair worn cropped to his skull, stares at the viewer with a steady gaze, his chin set in youthful defiance, his hat tumbling with a panache of green feathers, and pinned with a glittering black pin set against a bright-scarlet feather.

I wonder what the young Infanta Maria Apollonia thought of the handsome boy, proposed as her husband. Perhaps Gabaleone introduced her to the painting, and watched her stare at the dashing Prince and imagine what he was like. They were the same age.

Maria Apollonia's mother was a beauty. Her portrait by El Greco hangs in the National Gallery of Scotland. It used to be referred to as *The Lady in Furs*. But this is the Princess Catalina Micaela, daughter of King Philip II and his second wife Elizabeth of Valois. Her alluring dark eyes and pale face are wrapped in a white-silk scarf, and she wears a luxurious lynx-fur collar. If it were not for the little silk ruffle at her wrist you could imagine it was a painting of a dark-haired Grace Kelly. If Maria Apollonia inherited any of her mother's looks then she would be a prize indeed for the Prince of Wales.

In his travel diary, Coryate mentions a recent great occasion in Turin. In February 1608 the Duchy of Savoy had seen its own double wedding as Maria Apollonia's two older sisters were married. Marguerite had wed Francesco Gonzaga, the Duke of Mantua, and Isabella became the wife of Alfonso d'Este, the hereditary Prince of Modena.

Marguerite's wedding portrait by Frans Pourbus shows a quite attractive young woman, with a dimpled chin and her eyebrow arched, encased in a silk ruff of quite enormous size. Her huge bell-shaped Spanish farthingale must have been extraordinarily difficult to walk in. When her grandmother Elizabeth became Queen of Spain she complained how impossible they were to wear without swinging about, and was told by her chamberlain that by the punctilious court etiquette, she had to be seen to glide, as 'the Queen of Spain has no legs'.

Perhaps Maria Apollonia dreamed of the wedding dress she would wear and of the splendid double wedding of King

James of England's son and daughter which would surely be the talk of Europe.

But, as Coryate writes, 'Thus much of Turin.'

Back in London, Shakespeare and Fletcher are preparing their new play, *Cardenio*. Savoy's links with Spain make the Spanish subject highly appropriate for the imminent Catholic alliance which King James is busy preparing for the Prince of Wales. The Court is buzzing with rumours of an imminent announcement. The King's ambitions of uniting Catholic and Protestant Europe in the weddings of his children is a political coup to be celebrated. But Henry, Prince of Wales, is not going to play ball.

7

Modest John Fletcher

The prospect of a wedding of not just one, but of two of the Royal children must have set all London in a spin. Shakespeare's company, the King's Men, must surely have started preparing their material to catch the public mood. If, as is often said, their greatest playwright had by that time retired to put his feet up back home in Warwickshire, then the burden of finding suitable material would have fallen to his successor, John Fletcher.

But who was this John Fletcher? I realised that although I had done three of his plays, I knew very little about the real man. So one Saturday morning, having finished our final run of *The Tamer Tamed* at the RSC rehearsal rooms in Clapham, I decided to go in search of clues. This is my diary account of that day:

February 2003

The one fact I know for certain about Fletcher is that he is buried in Southwark Cathedral, still known in his day by its curious pre-Reformation name, St Mary Overie (a corruption of 'over the river'). I park in Distaff Lane, just below St

Paul's Cathedral on the north bank, and back over the 'rie' I go, on the silver sliver of the wobbly Millennium Bridge, to seek him out.

I suppose Fletcher is best known for his famous collaboration with Francis Beaumont. Only the names of Hemings and Condell, the two actors who collated the First Folio of Shakespeare's works in 1623, are perhaps as commonly linked together. Hemings and Condell, who were neighbours in Aldermanbury, were a philoprogenitive pair. They shared not only friendship but a love of large families, having fourteen and nine children respectively. Beaumont and Fletcher on the other hand (according to the frankly unreliable gossip John Aubrey) shared not only a house together in Bankside, but a bed.

Now, I don't somehow think these playwrights shared a bed in the Eric and Ernie sense. One Edwardian editor chooses to disregard any other implication by saying, 'Of the life they led while working together we know nothing positive. I shall therefore refrain from all conjecture...' – thus contributing to the usual refusal to allow any unorthodox relationships to be celebrated on the pages of history without scandal or disapprobation. Aubrey attributes the 'dearnesse of friendship' between them to 'a wonderful consimilty of phansey'. He also suggests that Fletcher was the true writer and that Francis Beaumont's function was 'to lop the overflowings of Mr Fletcher's luxuriant fancy'.

Entering Southwark Cathedral, I pick up the 'welcome' pamphlet, and scan the sheet for the whereabouts of the grave. There is the gaudy tomb of that dry stick John Gower, the first English poet, who appears as the chorus in *Pericles*. And of course Shakespeare himself is represented.

He's actually buried in Holy Trinity Church, Stratford-upon-Avon, but here he has a frankly silly Edwardian monument showing him reclining uncomfortably in a Bankside meadow. Indeed there is an entire window dedicated to Shakespeare which was unveiled by Dame Sybil Thorndike in the early fifties.

Apparently the stained-glass windows in the south aisle used to depict a whole series of Elizabethan dramatists, but they were all blown out by a bomb in Borough Market in 1940. Only Shakespeare made it back, a telling physical demonstration of how his genius has overshadowed the reputation and the fine talent of his contemporaries.

In the seventeenth century, Shakespeare received no such pre-eminence. Dryden tells us that two Beaumont and Fletcher plays were performed for every one of Shakespeare's. Indeed Fletcher and Jonson share the limelight equally with Shakespeare as the 'great triumvirate of wit'.

Having strolled around the church I still can't find John Fletcher's tomb. I know the great entrepreneur, Philip Henslowe, the Cameron Mackintosh of his day, is buried here in an unmarked grave, but surely Fletcher's tomb is marked. One of the guides, a helpful lady with a soft Irish burr, points me towards the chancel.

'I think you'll find him on the left in front of the choir stalls, with Shakespeare's brother, and the other dramatist fellow.'

Edmond Shakespeare strikes me as a sad case. He obviously followed his successful older brother to London, but seems to have had little luck as an actor. The parish records indicate that he was 'buried with a forenoon knell of the great bell'. It was usual to be buried in the afternoon, when it cost a couple of shillings, but Edmond's funeral took place in the morning and cost twenty. Presumably, his brother forked out for a morning event so that it could be attended by his fellow actors who would be busy onstage in the afternoon.

The ledger slab indicates that Edmond died aged twenty-seven in 1607, the same year that Fletcher's name is first associated with Beaumont, in commendatory verses attached to the quarto of Ben Jonson's *Volpone*.

But to my surprise, the 'other dramatist fellow' buried alongside Fletcher is not Beaumont at all, but Philip Massinger. Massinger succeeded Fletcher as chief dramatist of the King's Men. He is the author of *The Roman Actor* and

The City Madam. Again the parish records indicate that Massinger's funeral cost twenty shillings, not for a morning funeral, but because he was 'a stranger', i.e. not a member of the parish. So why did Massinger pay so much to be buried in the same tomb as his fellow playwright?

In a poem which some have suggested was intended to be cut on their joint tomb, as an epitaph, Sir Aston Cockayne writes:

> In the same grave Fletcher was buried, here
> Lies the stage poet Philip Massinger.
> Plays they did write together, were great friends
> And now one grave includes them at their ends.
> So whom on earth, nothing did part, beneath
> Here in their fames, they lie in spite of death.

Compare that with the foreword to the collected edition of Beaumont and Fletcher that appeared in the dark days of 1647, 'in this silence of the stage' when the theatres had been closed for five years. The publisher, one Humphrey Moseley, tells his readers why he has chosen a joint edition:

> ...since they were never parted while they lived, I conceived it not equitable to separate their ashes.

Oddly enough, of the fifty-two plays indiscriminately ascribed to Beaumont and Fletcher by Moseley in this edition, only a dozen are collaborations between them; whereas Fletcher wrote at least fifteen with Massinger. (Humphrey Moseley will come back into our story later.)

Fletcher came to prominence just as Shakespeare was completing his great series of tragedies, *Othello*, *King Lear* and *Macbeth*. His work was something new, taking a new form, the tragi-comedy. And Shakespeare was certainly influenced by this new wave of writing. He seems, around this time, to have attempted collaborating with other writers, Middleton perhaps in *Timon of Athens* and George Wilkins in *Pericles*. His mastery of this new genre takes flight in the late plays *The Tempest* and *The Winter's Tale*. After which it is supposed that he largely retired to

Stratford-upon-Avon. And it is at this point that Fletcher writes *The Tamer Tamed*.

Why? To attract the attention of the senior writer and lure him back to the theatre? If so, it's a pretty cheeky move.

The play ends with an epilogue which calls for equality between the sexes; thus demonstrating that in the twenty years since the original, the role of women in society had changed, and was now a matter of intense debate.

And what did Shakespeare think of it? We don't know for sure, but I think he can't have borne a grudge, for within a year or so he was back in London collaborating with Fletcher on three plays (*The Two Noble Kinsmen*, *All is True* or *Henry VIII* and *Cardenio*).

Was this a new lease of life for Shakespeare? We know he finally bought his first London property at that time, above the Blackfriars gatehouse, having always rented lodgings before. And it was, I suspect, a momentous year for Fletcher too. Beaumont decided to leave the theatre, and the house he shared with Fletcher on Bankside, and marry a wealthy widow.

And then in June during a performance of their new play, *All is True*, a fire breaks out at the Globe, and the theatre burns down. What effect did the fire have on Shakespeare? By the end of that year his writing career was over, and within three years he was dead. And three weeks before his death, Francis Beaumont died.

And where is Beaumont's body? Within three days of his death, he was buried in Westminster Abbey. Shakespeare didn't get a memorial there until 1741 (and Christopher Marlowe not until 2002). Jonson, although fond of Beaumont, felt a little put out by his elevation above Shakespeare:

> My Shakespeare rise, I will not lodge thee by
> Chaucer or Spencer, or bid Beaumont lie
> A little further to make thee a room,
> Thou art a monument without a tomb.

And what of Fletcher? How did he react to the deaths of both his collaborators within a little month? He takes over from Shakespeare as the chief dramatist of the King's Men and begins a new partnership with a poor, young writer, new to town, called Philip Massinger.

Fletcher died of the plague in the hot August of 1625. He had stayed behind in London to collect a new suit of clothes from his tailor, instead of fleeing to the country. It was another thirteen years before Massinger passed away, and yet in St Mary Overie, he still secured his reunion with his 'great friend'.

Perhaps I am falsely appropriating Fletcher. Perhaps I see in his perspective on male–female relationships an outsider's objectivity, which I assign to his sexuality, because I am gay. Perhaps I want to counter what Katherine Duncan-Jones, writing about Shakespeare's sonnets, describes as 'a determination to heterosexualise'. And if I claim Fletcher's place among the pantheon of writers who share my sexuality, will that alter the audience's perceptions of his work at all?

At the same time, I'm not going to inflate the nature of his talent. It is true that, within that era of doubt, of dark Jacobean incertitude and instability, Fletcher's work has a contrary lightness of tone; he is measured and occasionally sentimental where Shakespeare is hectic and clamorous. His plays are well made and delightful where Shakespeare's are surprising and unpredictable. They overflow with wit, where Shakespeare's investigate the hurt behind the smile; and they sparkle with intellect where Shakespeare's throb violently with pain. Shakespeare dissects the human condition where Fletcher can only describe it. Nevertheless, both have a compassion and humanity which still resonate, and which presumably allowed them to contemplate collaboration.

Down on one knee, I stroke the worn inscription on Fletcher's tomb. I sense he was a passionate man, who formed profound and intimate attachments, but after all we can know so little about him. There is one detail which has come down from two of his friends which I enjoy. One of his most successful plays was called *The Wild Goose Chase*.

It was published by two actors who knew the writer very well: John Lowin (probably the original Henry VIII in *All is True*), and Joseph Taylor (the next Hamlet after Richard Burbage). Both men had appeared together in Massinger's *The Roman Actor* as Domitian Caesar and Paris, the eponymous role.

'In despite of his innate modesty,' they write in the foreword, he could not refrain from joining with the crowded audience in 'applauding this rare issue of his brain'. It's a charming image, this prolific writer, so delighted by the response to his comedy that despite himself, he joins in.

I leave the cathedral and head back to the river, pondering if my speculations about Fletcher are correct. A deep crimson sun is fast disappearing in the winter sky.

And then a funny thing happens. When I get home a parcel is waiting for me; a mid-Victorian edition of Massinger's plays which I have ordered on the internet from somewhere in Ohio. In the introduction by one Lieutenant Colonel F. Cunningham, I read that in the 1830s the Southwark church had become so damp and derelict that there was a vote to demolish it, a vote which was ultimately reversed. Repairs were begun, during which the floor was levelled. According to the Lieutenant Colonel the dust of Fletcher and Massinger

> most probably has found its last resting-place under the kitchen floor of some house in Doddington Grove, Kennington SW which is built, we are told, on the three feet of surface earth removed from Southwark Cathedral.

And with that piece of information, the one certain fact I knew about Fletcher, the location of his grave, is thus, like so much in this story, thrown into question.

So did Fletcher come across Thomas Shelton's new translation of the Spanish book, *Don Quixote*, as he was browsing through the bookstalls and stations in St Paul's Churchyard one day? Did he take it to his new collaborator, and suggest that one of the plots within it might make a good play, particularly with the prospect of a double Royal wedding within the year? And did Shakespeare read it and say, 'All right, John, I'll help you unwind the story and plot it out, but you must do all the dialogue'?

Fletcher was, above all, a collaborator. Maybe that is a key note if I am to reinvent *Cardenio*. I need my own collaborator.

8

The Future King Henry IX

Prince Henry had played Oberon. Not in Shakespeare's *A Midsummer Night's Dream*, but at a masque in Court in 1611 written by Ben Jonson. The Prince of Wales, attired *a l'antique*, had arrived onstage 'to loud triumphant music', in a chariot 'drawn by two white bears'.

Henry was a great patron of the arts and a popular prince. He had proved himself a remarkable horseman too, and wanted to combine his interests by mounting 'a masque on horseback', but the King would not allow it. Henry did not always see eye to eye with his father.

When Prince Henry was thirteen his mother, Queen Anne, had taken the Prince to meet the famous Sir Walter Ralegh, who had been locked up in the Tower of London on trumped-up charges of treason early in James's reign. 'No one but my father would keep such a bird in a cage,' he said.

Ralegh wrote the Prince a long letter advising him to refuse the match with Savoy. He reminds him that Queen Mary tried to get her sister (the future Queen Elizabeth) married off to Savoy, 'which though they failed to get, yet thereby we failed not to lose Calais'. And he lists a gruesome series of examples of treacherous marriages with their terrible consequences: a catalogue of treachery which reads like a play by John Webster. 'There is a kind of noble and royal deceiving in marriages between kings and princes,' Ralegh warns. 'It is the fairest and most unsuspected trade of betraying.' And if that didn't frighten off the young Prince then Ralegh moved on to what he regarded as the insidious relationship between Savoy and Spain.

He declared that Spain was inseparable from Savoy and therefore irreconcilable with England. Not surprising perhaps from a man whose memory of the Spanish Armada was so clear. The English victory had been a close shave. 'If the Queen would have believed her men of war, as she did her scribes,' he wrote bitterly,

> we had in her time beaten that great empire in pieces, and made their kings, kings of figs and oranges as in the old times... Yea, in '88, when he [King Philip of Spain] made his great and fearful fleet, if the Queen would have hearkened to reason, we had burnt all his ships and preparations in his own ports.

Ralegh's inveterate hatred of Spain burns through the letter. Savoy would be a useless ally, he argues, trapped as they are between Spain and France and the Pope ('our king hath no enemy so malicious as that prelate'), and we don't want to get saddled with them as we are with Ireland, he argues, yet 'Ireland is near to us, and in our sight, and yet we have often wished it at the bottom of the sea... it has served us as a grave to our best captains and soldiers.'

He ends his passionate appeal to young Prince Henry advising him to wait:

> Seeing His Majesty is yet but young, and by God's favour like to live many years... Seeing therefore we have nothing yet in hand, seeing there is nothing moves; seeing the world is yet in a slumber, and that this long calm will shortly break out in some terrible tempest, I would advise the prince to keep his own ground for a while, and no way engage or entangle himself.

But God's favour was not to be extended to the Prince. On 6 November 1612, just three weeks after the joyful arrival of the Elector Palatine, his sister's husband-to-be, and while Fletcher and Shakespeare were putting the finishing touches to their new play, *Cardenio*, for the Christmas celebrations, Henry suddenly died.

9

Constructing the Missing Scenes:
The Shelton Version

My favourite shop in Stratford-upon-Avon was a rare-book establishment called Robert Vaughan's on Chapel Street. I used to spend far too much money in Robert Vaughan's. I rarely go into second-hand bookshops in search of a particular book, but I invariably find one that I need and decide I must have. These days I go online to find something specific and thus never browse, and lose the pleasure of the chance encounter, and the joy of handling the books themselves. Robert Vaughan's shop is now an estate agent's.

However, one day in the spring of 2004, I came across a handsome 1923 edition of *The History of Don Quixote of the Mancha* privately printed for the Navarre Society in two volumes and bound in white woven cloth and stamped in gilt. But it was the particular translation which caught my eye. The books were reprinted from the first edition of 1612–20, and translated from the Spanish by Thomas Shelton.

This was not only the first English translation of Cervantes' blockbuster, but the first translation into any language. I carried it home and settled down to read the

Cardenio story in the version that Shakespeare and Fletcher must have first read it.

> There lived, not long since, in a certain village of the Mancha, the name whereof I purposefully omit, a gentleman of their calling that used to pile up in their halls old lances, halberds, morions, and such other armours and weapons...

I turn to the most famous scene of all, in Chapter Eight, where the mad Don tilts at the windmills, and he and his horse Rozinante are swept high into the air:

> With this the wind increased, and the mill sails began to run about, which Don Quixote espying, said: 'Although thou movest more arms than the giant Briareus, thou shalt stoop to me.' And after saying this, and commending himself devoutly to his Lady Dulcinea, desiring her to succour him in that trance, covering himself well with his buckler and setting his lance on his rest, he spurred on Rozinante and encountered with the first mill that was before him, and striking his lance into the sail the wind swung it about with such fury that it broke his lance into shivers, carrying him and his horse after it, and finally tumbled him a good way off from it on the field in a very evil plight.

I am not surprised that Jorge Luis Borges, the great Argentinean novelist, himself described Shelton's translation as being the best there could be. But who was this Thomas Shelton?

Experts seem to differ on Shelton, and indeed he is a pretty shady character, with strong and dangerous connections to a Catholic network in Europe. He seems to have been a kinsman of the Earl of Suffolk, and therefore closely allied to the powerful Howard family.

The 1st Earl, Thomas Howard, was made Lord Chamberlain by King James in 1603. He had fought against the Spanish Armada, and was one of the men to uncover the Gunpowder Plot in 1605, having spotted the brushwood which concealed the powder barrels under the Houses of Parliament. So you might have supposed him to be a fierce opponent of the Spanish. But his wife was a Catholic sympathiser and received an annual pension of £1,000 from Spain. Their son, Theophilus, became the 2nd Earl on his father's death. This man, Lord Howard of Walden, was Shelton's patron. The same year that *Don Quixote* hit the stationers' bookstalls in St Paul's Churchyard, Theophilus married Elizabeth (their daughter Margaret comes into the story later).

Thomas Shelton was also a friend of a man called Richard Verstegan, who had published *Don Quixote* in Spanish in Brussels in 1607. It is thought that Shelton translated the book at around this time, for his noble patron as he says, 'in forty days, being thereunto more than half enforced through the importunity of a very dear friend, that was desirous to understand the subject'.

The Catholic Verstegan had secretly published an account of the execution of Edmund Campion, and fled England when this was discovered. He had been imprisoned in Paris at the insistence of the English Ambassador, and settled in Antwerp. He subsequently continued to print information about the sufferings of the Catholic priests in England under Queen Elizabeth: *Theatre of Cruelties of the heretics of our time* (1587). He set up as a publisher in Antwerp from where he smuggled books into England. So Shelton had some pretty dangerous and some very influential friends.

As I settle to read his translation of *Don Quixote*, I am struck with the brilliance of the storytelling. The Cardenio story unwinds like a mystery thriller. Cervantes keeps serving up intriguing details, clues which you have to piece together like a jigsaw puzzle. Don Quixote and Sancho Pança, wandering in the Sierra Morena, 'found a little stream wherein lay dead, and half-devoured by dogs and crows, a mule saddled and bridled'. Later they discover the mad Cardenio.

Dorotea conjures her happy busy country life: 'of the oil mill, the wine presses, the number of great and little cattle, the beehives; in fine, of all that which so rich a farmer, as my father was, had, or could have, I kept the account.' I turn to the moment where she relates her tale, and her seduction by Don Ferdinando (as Fernando is called by Cervantes).

It is all in first-person narrative, and she recalls her assailant's persuasive tactics in great detail, concluding, 'I left to be a maiden and he began to be a traitor and disloyal man.' It occurs to me that I could easily translate this into dialogue, and I begin to sketch it out.

The university wit, Robert Greene, who wrote for a rival company, the Queen's Men, famously attacked Shakespeare in his early days in London, as an 'upstart crow' for 'supposing he is as well able to bombast out a line of blank verse as the best of you'. Now it's my turn to try and bombast out a line or two, and I'm already beginning to feel like a bit of an upstart. I need the advice of another university wit.

It is autumn 2005. I am sitting at John Barton's kitchen table, in his book-laden flat in Marylebone. 'I hear you are working on *Cardenio*,' he says. 'Anne thinks it's a waste of time.' John's wife, the distinguished Cambridge scholar Anne Barton, is a Ben Jonson expert. She came to see my production of *Sejanus* earlier this year, and was very complimentary. She thinks I should be concentrating my attention on genuine Jacobean plays, and not trying to revive eighteenth-century pastiches. And of course she is probably right. John, however, is more open to the idea.

'The trouble is, John, that the *Double Falshood* script has all these missing scenes. I've combed through other seventeenth-century versions of the Cardenio story but they aren't all that helpful, but one of the scenes in the original Cervantes is written in first-person narrative, and I wonder if I couldn't render it in dialogue somehow. What do you think?'

John has a gleam in his eye. This is the man who adapted *The Wars of the Roses* for Peter Hall, one of the seminal productions for the young Royal Shakespeare Company in 1964, adding a number of his own lines. When he directed *King John* in 1974, including lines from Bale's 1535 play *King John* and bits of his own, Michael Billington in the *Guardian* coined the term the 'bartonising of the bard', but declared the result 'one of the best new plays we've seen this year'.

John is enthusiastic about adding in the missing scenes.

'But I'm not a writer, John.'

'If you've got the structure of the scene, and the language, isn't it just a matter of putting that into iambic pentameter? If anyone can do that, you can, by now, surely? It's pretty straightforward after all. "I want to go and have a cup of tea," there, that's an iambic pentameter for you. Nothing very difficult about it.'

I try.

I look at the wedding scene in Thomas Shelton's translation of *Don Quixote*. In *Double Falshood*, Cardenio jumps out from behind the arras where he has been concealed to interrupt the ceremony and challenge his rival, Fernando. But in the Cervantes the action is completely different: Cardenio is frozen in shock when he thinks he witnesses his beloved, Luscinda, betray him and agree to marry Fernando.

Here is how Cardenio tells Don Quixote about his emotional state, in Shelton's rather coagulated prose:

> Now only remains untold the case wherein I was,
> seeing in that 'yea', which I heard, my hopes deluded,
> Luscinda's words and promises falsified and myself
> wholly disabled to recover in any time the good which I
> lost in that instant. I rested void of counsel, abandoned
> (in mine opinion) by Heaven, proclaimed an enemy to
> the earth which upheld me, the air denying breath
> enough for my sighs and the water humour sufficient to
> my eyes; only the fire increased in such a manner that I
> burned thoroughly with rage and jealousy.

And here's my attempt to distil that into roughly iambic pentameters:

> Lost, in an instant, in a little word.
> Abandoned by Heaven, devoid of counsel,

Proclaimed an enemy unto the earth
Which should uphold me: the air denies me
Breath enough for my sighs, the water humour
Sufficient to my eyes; only the fire
Increases in such a manner that I
Burn thoroughly with rage and jealousy.

But what of the scenes that don't appear, even in the *Quixote*, but which are crucial for the storyline: the abduction from the convent, for example? Even if I manage to render the Shelton into serviceable verse, I think I need help. I must find my collaborator.

10

The Death of Princes

Prince Henry's death was mysterious. Some said it was typhoid; others even whispered that it was poison.

I recently visited Westminster Abbey to see if I could find the tomb of the young Prince. I began in the Henry VII Chapel where Queen Elizabeth I lies in chilly marble grandeur in the north aisle. In 'Innocents Corner', at the eastern end of the chapel, lie King James's two infant daughters, who died in childhood. The baby Princess Sophia, who expired within forty-eight hours of her birth, lies pathetically swaddled in a funerary crib; her actual remains rest beneath the stone covers. Next to her, reclining on top of her tomb is her two-year-old sister, Princess Mary. But their elder brother, Henry, isn't here. I wander back towards the south aisle where Henry's grandmother, Mary, Queen of Scots, lies on her magnificent tomb.

When Queen Elizabeth died, King James had a problem: what to do with the body of his mother, the tragic Mary, Queen of Scots, who was interred at Peterborough Cathedral. James decided to have her body exhumed and brought to Westminster. The King's master mason, Cornelius Cure, in his workshop in Southwark, yards from the Globe Theatre, had been carving her image for six years by the time the occupant of the tomb arrived from Peterborough in 1612. The work was finished by his son William, on his death. The Queen's statue was not as we see it today, in cold white alabaster, but would have been painted, in colours we would probably now consider to be gaudy.

When Simon Forman, the astrologer and figure-caster, saw *The Winter's Tale* in May 1611 at the Globe, or when it was performed at Court that Christmas of 1612, the audience must have gasped when Paulina prevented Leontes from moving forward to kiss Hermione's statue, with the line:

> Good my lord, forbear.
> The ruddiness upon her lip is wet:
> You'll mar it if you kiss it, stain your own
> With oily painting.

The spectators can only have thought of that other silent queen, whose painted statue was about to be instated in Westminster near her bitter rival, Elizabeth.

King James had his mother's tomb finally put into position in September 1612. Two months later he was mourning the death of his son. Sir Walter Ralegh, imprisoned in the Tower, gave up writing his great *History of the World* when young Prince Henry died. 'My harp is also turned to mourning and my organ into the voice of them that weep.' The whole country was devastated, and bewailed the loss of their future monarch, King Henry IX.

King James was not present at his son's death. He had fled to Theobald's, his palace in the Hertfordshire countryside. The Queen had been unable to remain in the Prince's sick room, when it became clear that he would not survive.

The Venetian Ambassador, Foscarini, tactfully suggests:

> ... it is thought that they cannot bear the spectacle of
> the Prince their son, dead before their eyes; while the
> King thinks the solitude of the country more fitting
> for grief and tears, than the bustle of London and the
> Court.

The Prince's body lay in state at St James's Palace for a month, and then the funeral took place on 7 December.

There is an engraving by William Hole for an elaborate hearse for Prince Henry, but a monument was never built. This afternoon, in Westminster Abbey, I cannot find any evidence of England's lost prince. He's lost in death too. So I approach one of the Abbey attendants in their crimson gowns. The lady looks quite perplexed, 'Do you know,' she says, 'no one has ever asked me that question before.' She does, of course, know of the Prince but cannot place where he is buried. But she finds a little book and with a moment's cross referencing, she leads me back to the south aisle. Between the catafalque of Mary, Queen of Scots, and the Lady Margaret Beaufort's there is a grey slab on the floor. It reads, 'Henry Frederick, Prince of Wales died 1612'. Henry is interred in the same tomb as his tragic grandmother.

What must Shakespeare and Fletcher have thought? The effort to produce a new play on the occasion of the announcement of a Catholic bride for the young Prince was all in vain. Like Luscinda's aborted marriage in the play, Henry's wedding was not to be. *Cardenio* was nearly lost before it was ever performed.

11

What Would Happen Next?

No one knew what would happen next. Poor Frederick, the Elector Palatine. He had arrived in triumph to marry the Princess Elizabeth, but now would the Royal marriage take place at all? Some said that with the heir to the throne dead, and the second son only ten years old, it would not be appropriate for Princess Elizabeth to leave the country with her new husband.

However, the King hastily announced that the Christmas festivities, with all the attendant celebrations for the Royal betrothal, would still take place. You can't help thinking that his behaviour displays, at the very least, a lack of respect for his eldest son. It is as if he was determined not to be deprived of the splendid party he had organised. The Venetian Ambassador gossiped that 'the 600,000 crowns destined for these fetes have grown to a million and those who know say that even this will not suffice.'

Within a fortnight of Prince Henry's funeral, the Christmas season launched into full swing. John Hemings would be paid £93 6s 8d for mounting fourteen plays, *Cardenio* among them, and then £60 for another six. The wedding, which had been postponed until at least Easter, was then suddenly, and with indecent haste, brought forward to February, so the celebrations would hardly let up until March.

And so the wedding of James's beloved Bessy, with the Elector Palatine of the Rhine, took place on Valentine's Day, Sunday 14 February 1613. Both were dressed in cloth of silver, embroidered in silver thread, and Elizabeth wore an 'exceedingly rich coronet' which her father bragged, rather tactlessly, cost a million crowns. The masques presented for the occasion, which were all published, provide both a context for the first performance of *Cardenio*, and an insight into the extravagance of the Jacobean Court. There were three masques in all, each one 'full of rare invention'.

In *The Lords' Masque*, by Thomas Campion, presented in the Banqueting House in Whitehall on the wedding night itself, Inigo Jones outdid himself, creating dancing lights which moved 'in an exceeding strange and delightful manner'.

The recent colonisation of Virginia had provided George Chapman's *Memorable Masque*, on the Monday night, with its imaginative coup. American Indians would seem to present their congratulations to the bridal pair; and a great rock split open to reveal 'a rich and refulgent mine of gold', representing the sort of El Dorado which the New World seemed to offer to its new colonisers.

In the final wedding masque, by Francis Beaumont (known merely as *The Masque of the Inner Temple and Gray's Inn*), Mercury announced that the Olympic Games were to be revived for the wedding; and as well as dancing statues, there was a rustic anti-masque, which includes a May lord and lady, and a baboon, and which was restaged as part of *The Two Noble Kinsmen* by Shakespeare and Fletcher later that year.

This final masque was meant to have been performed the next night, Shrove Tuesday. An order had gone out that the ladies would not be admitted if they were wearing farthingales, in order to allow more room. But in all the excitement and crush, the hall was not ready for the performers, and the crucial members of the audience could not get to their places. So, at the last minute, His Majesty postponed the masque until the following Saturday.

But the real reason for the postponement was that the irascible King James was worn out with all the festivities, and the idea of sitting through another long masque appalled him.

So it was for these wedding celebrations that *Cardenio* was originally written. But it does seem odd to choose a play in which a wedding is presented where the bride is forced against her will to marry. But then, as we know, *Much Ado About Nothing* was also presented that Christmas. And in that play there is also a wedding scene, in which the groom denounces his bride at the altar as a whore. Perhaps marriage as a theme, whatever its outcome, was thought appropriate fare for such occasions.

The Sunday Times, in April 2011, pronounced the wedding of Kate Middleton and Prince William to be the biggest thing to happen to the monarchy since the funeral of Diana, and declared that the story had a happy ending: Britain was making peace with its past. In 1613, the wedding of Princess Elizabeth with her Bohemian Prince was certainly much anticipated, despite the cloud of her brother's death. This was, after all, the first Royal wedding England had seen since the disastrous union of Queen Mary with the haughty King Philip II of Spain.

Princess Elizabeth's wedding festivities carried on through March, with the usual tilting match on Lady Day, and the couple departed for the continent on 10 April. At the festivities in the groom's home city of Heidelberg they witnessed a knockabout entertainment featuring Don Quixote and Sancho Pança, perhaps just like the one Anthony Burgess described in 'A Meeting in Valladolid'.

But ultimately Princess Elizabeth's story was a sad one. Due to her marriage to Frederick, she became briefly the Queen of Bohemia. He built her a palace at Heidelberg with a monkey house and a garden so beautiful is was described as the eighth wonder of the world. But Elizabeth was to become known to History as the Winter Queen, when her husband's Catholic enemies drove the couple away from their throne, and they found themselves embroiled in what we now call the Thirty Years War, one of the most destructive conflicts in European history. Elizabeth's descendants would become the Hanoverian monarchs of England. She was the grandmother of the future King George I.

12

'Trick the Lion'

I still have not discovered why *Cardenio* was given a special command performance in the early summer of 1613, for the Ambassador from the Duchy of Savoy. What of Gabaleone? What did he do next?

The death of Prince Henry, the intended groom to the Savoyard Infanta, Maria Apollonia, took everyone by surprise. Gabaleone must have thought he was about to secure an enormously important Royal match, coupling the ducal line of his hot-headed master, Testa di Feu ('Fire Head'), with the crown of England.

After the Prince's funeral, the Savoyard Ambassador prepared to return home to Turin. Foscarini writes: 'Last Saturday, Gabaleone took his leave of the King.' Apparently James insisted that Savoy could count on the support of England as if the marriage *had* taken place, and to show his affection for the Ambassador he made him a Knight of the Rose with 'the right to wear the Rose of England and the Thistle of Scotland as crest to his arms'. In a personal gesture of goodwill the King then took off his finger a diamond worth 1,500 crowns and gave it to Gabaleone.

The Ambassador's personal influence can also be marked by the fact that the grieving Queen herself received him, and spent an hour in conversation, 'though living as much retired as possible', and she too gave Gabaleone a ring, a diamond cluster, of a similar value to the King's gift.

It is possible that the Savoy Ambassador may already have considered proposing that, although Prince Henry had unfortunately expired, the Infanta Maria Apollonia was still available, and might be an eligible bride for the new heir to the throne, young Prince Charles. But now was not the time for such a proposition.

When Gabaleone returned in June (with his replacement, the Marquis de Villa), it is not surprising that he should be graciously entertained by their Royal Highnesses, and that the King would command his players to revive the Spanish play *Cardenio* they had written especially for the Christmas season, and which because of sad and unforeseen events and his subsequent departure, the Savoyard Ambassador had missed.

There is no record of the play being registered for publication at this time, so, as far as we know, there is no suggestion that the Savoyard Ambassador returned with a copy of the play to the Court in Turin, and probably little point therefore in launching a search of the ducal libraries for evidence of its survival. But such a thing is possible. We know that of the nineteen or so extant King's Men play manuscripts that have survived, a dozen or so are scribal copies, especially written out for presentation. Indeed Professor Andrew Gurr informs us, in his book *The Shakespeare Company*, that in the 1620s the Globe bookkeeper, Edward Knight, transcribed several Fletcher plays for presentation (including *The Tamer Tamed*); so it is not beyond the bounds of possibility that the Master of the Revels in 1613 paid a few shillings to have *Cardenio* copied out for Gabaleone to take home to Turin. What a tantalising prospect.

And if I am permitted to fantasise a little further, is it possible that Gabaleone might have taken such a copy, for the poor Infanta to treasure? Did she gaze now at the face of her dead Prince in Robert Peake's portrait, and mourn her lost marriage?

We do know, however, from the diplomatic letters of Foscarini, the Venetian Ambassador, that while the new Ambassador presented his credentials, offering congratulations on the marriage of the Princess Elizabeth, and condolences on the death of Prince Henry, Gabaleone remained in London, with 'special instructions' and 'proposals for alliance'.

On 12 July 1613, within a month of the special command performance of *Cardenio*, Foscarini has an audience with Queen Anne. He writes:

> She afterwards spoke of the ambassador of Savoy who has shown a great desire to marry one of the Infanti to the prince... She had replied that there was not conformity of age. He added that the Infanta was not more than fifteen, but she knew that she was... at least nineteen now, and the prince is barely thirteen.

In reality, while Savoy was perceived to be 'truckling' up to Spain, James was no longer going to contemplate an alliance through marriage, and on the death of the Prince had sent the Duke of Lennox – on his way back from accompanying Princess Elizabeth to Heidelberg – to Paris to negotiate a marriage for Charles with the second Princess of 'His Most Christian Majesty', the late King Henri IV of France, the seven-year-old Christine-Marie. James wasn't sure, however, that he could wait that long to be blessed with a grandchild.

In August 1613, the Spanish Ambassador, Sarmiento, began his distinguished embassy in London, and tried to persuade James to marry Charles to one of the Spanish Royal Infantas, offering whatever dowry he asked for.

With France and Spain bidding against each other for an English alliance, poor little Savoy no longer had any hope. Poor Infanta Maria Apollonia. What would become of her?

She never married, but like her sister Francesca (and rather like Luscinda in the play, in a way), she became a nun.

Her older brother, Maurice, had already become a cardinal, and Bishop of Vercelli, aged fourteen. It seems she ended her days making copies of the family's most precious possession, the Turin Shroud, for friends. At least seven are known to exist.

We have no idea if the command performance for Gabaleone on 8 June 1613 represents the last ever performance of *Cardenio*, but it is possible that three weeks later the script was lost for good.

13

Up in Flames

On St Peter's Day, 29 June 1613, three weeks after the Greenwich performance of *Cardenio*, the King's Men were presenting one of the other plays in which Shakespeare had collaborated with John Fletcher, *All is True* (or *Henry VIII*) at their home, the Globe Theatre on Bankside, when a fire broke out.

It happened during the party scene. Cardinal Wolsey is having a banquet; suddenly the young King Henry turns up in disguise among a group of masquers. He is about to have his first fatal encounter with Anne Boleyn. Cannons are discharged. Unfortunately, some of the wadding with which they were packed lands on the thatched roof of the theatre, setting it alight. In an hour the whole building burns down. Sir Henry Wotton writes to his friend Sir Edmund Bacon three days later:

> I will entertain you... with what happened this week at the Bank's side. The King's Players had a new play, called *All is True*, representing some principal pieces in the reign of Henry VIII, which was set forth with many extraordinary circumstances of pomp and majesty, even to the matting on the stage: the Knights of the

Order with their Georges and garters, the guards with their embroidered coats, and the like – sufficient in truth within a while to make greatness very familiar if not ridiculous. Now King Henry making a masque at the Cardinal Wolsey's house, and certain chambers [i.e. cannons] being shot off at his entry, some of the paper or other stuff wherewith one of them was stopped did light on the thatch, where being thought at first but an idle smoke, and their eyes more attentive on the show, it kindled inwardly and ran round like a train, consuming within less than an hour the whole house to the very grounds. This was the fatal period of that virtuous fabric wherein yet nothing did perish but wood and straw and a few forsaken cloaks.

Wotton then adds a colourful little detail:

Only one man had his breeches set on fire that would perhaps have broiled him if he had not by the benefit of a provident wit put it out with bottle ale.

There is a ballad, 'Upon the pitiful burning of the Globe Playhouse', which adds to our picture of the conflagration.

It conjures the Tragic Muse, Melpomene, 'wrapped in a sea-coal robe' to relate the tragic scene, repeating a refrain that presumably puns on the title of the play being performed that afternoon: 'Oh sorrow, pitiful sorrow, and yet all this is true!'

The fire, like death's 'raking brand', tears round the thatch and catches the tiring house:

And burnt down both beam and snag,
And did not spare the silken flag.

The audience flee, losing hats and swords in their panic, followed by Burbage presumably still dressed as Cardinal Wolsey, and perhaps John Lowin as Henry VIII in his masquing costume, and the rest of the actors, with jerkins singed, and periwigs fried 'like buttered firkins'. Meanwhile, in the middle of it all, watching their livelihood go up in flames, 'Distressed stood old stuttering Hemings.' John

Hemings acted as the business manager for the King's Men; and he was also the tapster of the Globe's tavern, and had a house in the grounds: hardly surprising then, that he was spluttering with impotent distress. And in this fine summer weather, there was no prospect of rain to douse the flames:

> No shower his rain did there down force
> In all that sun-shine weather,
> To save that great renowned house;
> Nor thou, O ale-house! neither.
> Had it begun below, sans doubt,
> Their wives for fear had pissed it out.

The author of this doggerel ballad (a Jacobean William McGonagall) then takes a high moral tone, addressing all 'stage strutters':

> Be warned, you stage strutters all,
> Lest you again be catched,
> And such a burning do befall,
> As to them whose house was thatched:
> Forbear your whoring, breeding biles,
> And lay up that expence for tiles.

This ballad was entered in the Stationers' Register on 30 June 1613, the very day after the fire, and must have been written before the flames were properly extinguished. Exactly a year and day after the conflagration, a new Globe opened, with a tiled roof, just as the balladeer had recommended.

Did the King's Men keep their valuable play-scripts at the theatre? If so, it really is no wonder that John Hemings was so distressed.

So did Shakespeare and Fletcher's Spanish play go up in smoke that St Peter's Day? Well, it would seem not. But we hear no more of *Cardenio* for forty years.

'Balconies at Granada', from Gustave Doré's *Spain* (1876)

Part Two

The History of *Cardenio*, 1613–66

14

Preparing a Script of *Cardenio*

The Shakespeare Memorial Theatre in Stratford-upon-Avon, built in 1879, famously burnt down one blustery March afternoon in 1926. Elisabeth Scott's 1932 art-deco theatre which replaced it was in turn closed for redevelopment in April 2007. Whereas the first Globe Theatre had stood for fourteen years, Scott's theatre had done service for five times that long.

I had by now done a considerable amount of work on the text of my version of *Cardenio*, bombasting out my own blank verse, and adding extra scenes that are not in *Double Falshood*; altering some elements, in line with the Cervantes original, and deleting the loose ends of what might have been a subplot.

The closure of the RST site meant that any likelihood of mounting a production of *Cardenio* would have to be shelved for at least four years until the Swan reopened. But at least I could crystallise my thoughts about the project in the meantime, and shape my early experiments into a proper working script with the aid of a collaborator. But who should that be?

My own production of *Coriolanus*, with William Houston, Janet Suzman and Timothy West, was the final production in the Main House before the closure. After the Stratford run we had been invited to take the show to Washington, and to the Teatro Albéniz in Madrid.

While in Madrid at a press conference, I announced that the RSC were working on Shakespeare's lost play, in a new version of *Cardenio*, and, as the project combined both Cervantes and Shakespeare, the two greatest writers the seventeenth century produced, it would only be appropriate to develop the production as an Anglo-Spanish project.

'That was either very brave, or very foolish,' quipped Jeremy Adams. 'Now we just sit back and wait.'

Within twenty-four hours, I was being pursued by American TV stations and Spanish theatre impresarios. I would have to work fast. Emilio Hernandez, the Cuban-born firecracker director of the Almagro Festival in La Mancha, reminded me of the young man he had introduced me to at a conference there, when we brought an adaptation of Chaucer's *Canterbury Tales* to Spain in the previous year, 2006. Emilio had brought together a series of Spanish theatre practitioners to discuss Spanish classical theatre, and one of the participants was a writer and theatre director called Antonio Álamo. 'Antonio would be the perfect guy to work with you,' said Emilio. 'I will ring him now.' Before we left Madrid, I had a Spanish dramaturg.

Perhaps my announcement at the press conference was a good idea after all; it had kick-started the whole project back into life. Perhaps this production could now happen.

At about this time, I got a message that the Shakespeare scholar Gary Taylor wanted to make contact with me. I invited him for lunch opposite the RSC's London offices in Earlham Street.

I don't know what I had expected of the distinguished co-general editor of both the recent Oxford Middleton and Oxford Shakespeare editions. I have several of Taylor's brilliantly provocative books on my shelves from his *Reinventing Shakespeare* to his *Castration: An Abbreviated History of Western Manhood*; so I was delighted to meet a slightly built man from Kansas, in his mid-fifties, with a flowery shirt and a bolas boot-string tie. His long black hair, worn in a ponytail, made his pale complexion seem even paler, and his fingernails, painted Goth black, proclaimed his quondam reputation as an *enfant terrible* of Shakespeare scholarship.

He brought me a gift, his edition of Fletcher's *The Tamer Tamed*, which Manchester University Press had just published, and which focused on my own production in 2003. And here was his pitch. He had done his own reconstruction of *Cardenio* and, having heard that I had embarked on one, suggested that I save myself the trouble and use his version, which had received a successful production at the Victoria University of Wellington, in New Zealand, as part of a seminar on Shakespeare's lost play.

He wouldn't describe his adaptation, but when I asked about his general approach he said, 'I tend to say, my version may not be authentic, but at least it's authentish.' I thought that was rather neat.

He argued that, as I had done more professional productions of Fletcher plays than pretty much anyone else (*All is True, The Island Princess, The Tamer Tamed*); and he was the scholar who probably knew most about Fletcher, this was the ideal match. I admitted that I had already progressed a considerable way down the road by this point, and formed some particular opinions about how our production should proceed. On the other hand, it occurred to me that having someone as distinguished and formidable as Taylor on the team was a fascinating prospect. But how could such a relationship work out in reality? He had been developing his version for some time, and might not be open to different opinions. So I suggested that the most straightforward way to proceed would be for me, without prejudice, to read his version.

His reply stumped me. I could read his version, but only if I agreed to his involvement beforehand. I completely understood his anxiety that I might be tempted simply to steal his ideas, and leave him uncredited, and uninvolved.

But, having gone so far with my own version, I could not agree to his proposition, and subsequently wrote to him to apologise. I would no doubt regret it, but I felt we had to continue down the path we had set out upon. I promised that I would not read his version to remove any danger of my plagiarising his idea inadvertently or otherwise.

I later learnt that Taylor had introduced Don Quixote into the plotline of his *History of Cardenio*, which was the very thing I had determined not to do. My own feeling was that the appearance of the Knight with the Woeful Countenance would unbalance the play, and although two of the three seventeenth-century versions of the play which I had read did, in fact, include him (the French one by Bouscal and the Spanish one by de Castro), they were both essentially dramatisations of the Don Quixote novel. The French version by Pichou, which concentrated on the Cardenio story (*Les Folies de Cardenio*), left Don Quixote out of the picture. In my opinion the play ain't big enough for the both of them.

A few weeks later I get a letter from Terry Hands at Theatr Clwyd. When Terry ran the RSC, I was, at one point, his assistant director. He has heard a rumour that I may be doing *Double Falshood*, and parading it as Shakespeare, and he urges me to resist the temptation, saying he was approached with a version when he was artistic director back in the eighties, and he thinks the claims are all bullshit. 'Please do another play,' he begs, 'this is an irrelevancy. After all, there are plenty of genuine Jacobean classics still to do.'

15

The Magnificent Pomegranate

I have been invited to speak at a conference called 'Staging Shakespeare and Cervantes Today' organised by the University of Alicante. Although I hardly feel qualified, it gives me another opportunity to discuss with Spanish colleagues what we now refer to as *The Cardenio Project*.

I am to be met at the airport by the splendidly titled Professor José Manuel González Fernandez de Sevilla. I am rather expecting a high-chinned grandee, but José Manuel turns out to be rather a cuddly bear of a man, balding and with heavy glasses, and, as we travel into town in his Ford Cortina, he tells me of his excitement at the programme ahead. He talks passionately about the links between Cervantes and Shakespeare, he expounds rather quixotically and grandiloquently about how they represent our challenge for a better future, in a world of crumbling ideologies; how their heritage prevails over human nonsense and disaster, and how the inexhaustible human voice talks through them.

He is excited that the RSC is working on this script, as it will serve as a reminder of the ties that bind our two great writers together, across nations, he says, across centuries, and theatrical styles. I like Professor José Manuel González Fernandez de Sevilla.

When I arrive at the conference the next day, I am handed a copy of a book. It is a Spanish translation of *Double Falshood* by the late Charles David Ley, an Englishman, and Hispanophile scholar, who lived in Spain. There is a paper flash around the book announcing that this has been authenticated as being genuinely by Shakespeare by the Royal Shakespeare Company. And Professor González translates part of the introduction for me: 'A recent discovery of the Royal Shakespeare Company announced by Greg Doran, its director [I've been promoted], has made possible to authenticate the existence of *Cardenio officially*, written in collaboration by Shakespeare and Fletcher, even he advances its staging in 2009 within a common project between Spain and England.'

An expatriate Irishman called Denis Rafter is on the panel with me, talking about *Miguel/Will*, a play he has directed by José Carlos Somoza which imagines the meeting of Cervantes and Shakespeare. Later Denis gives me a copy of the play in Spanish, suggesting it might complement any future production of *Cardenio*.

That afternoon, after the conference, José Manuel takes me to visit nearby Elche. Elche is perhaps most famous for two things: its palm grove which contains 200,000 trees, and its mystery play. In the Basilíca of Santa María de Elche every August on the Feast of the Assumption, an extraordinary performance takes place, a mystery play dating back at least to the 1530s, if not before.

When I directed the York Mystery Plays in York Minster for the Millennium, I was encouraged by the Dean not to revive the three Marian plays at the end of the Corpus Christi cycle. They deal with the death of the Virgin Mother of Jesus, her assumption and her coronation in Heaven. They had been dropped from the cycle at the Reformation, shortly before the cycle itself was banned. As a Catholic by upbringing, I had an urge to resist this High Anglican censorship, but as we had already had to condense forty-eight plays into the three hours' traffic of the stage, I did not. So I was interested to hear how the Spanish dramatised the story, but was not prepared for the astonishing theatrical coup it contained.

At the height of the performance in the Basilíca, when the little boys who play Mary and her companions have walked the whole length of the nave, a trapdoor appears in the linen-cloth ceiling which has been drawn across the whole span of the dome. Through this peephole 'door to Heaven' there then descends a globe. As the choir sings, this suddenly explodes and, grenade-like, its glittering segments fly apart to reveal the tiny figure of a child brave enough play the angel, giddily suspended over the entire congregation below.

Trying to explain this wonderful mechanical globe back home later, I could only describe it as a sort of Terry's Chocolate Orange. In fact, this magnificent piece of aerial stage machinery dates back to the Renaissance, and is called the Pomegranate (*La Magrana*). It is operated by a sophisticated system of ropes and pulleys, and seems to me to rival anything the Medici masques at the Uffizi, or Inigo Jones at the Banqueting House in London, would later produce.

Once the angel has descended with his palm frond, the globe returns to Heaven with Mary on board. I am rather relieved that the little boy dressed in his sky-blue gown is replaced for this journey with a statue of the Virgin in all her glorious robes.

There is a little museum close to the Basilíca which tells the whole history of the origins of the mystery play, and celebrates the status recently conferred upon it by UNESCO as 'a Masterpiece of the Oral and Intangible Heritage of Humanity'. As I stare at some of the examples of the sumptuous robes worn by the statue of the Virgin, I'm reminded just how prominent a part of life the cult of Mary is in Andalucía.

In the Cervantes story of Cardenio, Dorotea tells how Fernando, having smuggled himself into her room, promises to marry her, and swears his faith in front of an image of the Virgin.

Behold, I give thee here my hand to be thine alone; and
let the heavens, from which nothing is concealed, and
this image of Our Lady, which thou hast here present,
be witness to this truth.

Shakespeare and Fletcher, if they did indeed dramatise this
tense scene in *Cardenio*, would have been very unlikely to
introduce any papist image or statue of the Madonna into
Dorotea's room, but as we intend to set the play back in its
original Andalucían setting, we must do so.

José Manuel has one other place to take me before driving
me back to the airport. Set on a rocky outcrop above the bay
is the fortress of Alicante, which, José Manuel reminds me,
is the setting for Middleton and Rowley's play *The
Changeling*. In this play, Beatrice Joanna's father is the governor of the castle, and as we walk up the steep slope to La
Torreta (the upper enclosure), we muse about doing a production of that play here and picture hideous De Flores,
showing the luckless Alonzo around the castle, and stabbing
him in a narrow vault. I can begin to understand what it was
about these Spanish romances that so attracted Jacobean
audiences.

16

As Seville as an Orange

February 2008. Our producer Jeremy Adams has somehow managed to find the money for me to spend a couple of intensive days in Seville with Antonio Álamo, the Spanish writer/director I had first met in 2006.

Antonio is the director of the Lope de Vega Theatre here. It's a grandiose white-and-lemon neo-baroque building, which was in fact built for the 1929 Iberico-American Expo as the Pavilion of Seville, later used as a casino and only converted into a theatre some fifty years later. Antonio tells me it hosts the famous Flamenco Biennale.

Lope de Vega is said to have written over 1,500 plays, so I ask Antonio if he can recommend any for me to read. Other than *Fuente Ovejuna* and *The Dog in the Manger*, I know very few. I can't believe that, churned out at that phenomenal rate, they can be any good at all but, he tells me, there are many which still get done in Spain from time to time.

We work on the original Cardenio story in the Cervantes, untangling the narrative, which is all told in flashback, and then comparing it with the way the story has been modified and adapted in *Double Falshood*.

We don't always agree. Antonio suggests that we must put in the episode where Dorotea is accompanied into the mountains by a herds-boy, who has supplied her with her boy's disguise. Once alone together among the wild rocks of the Sierra Morena, the herds-boy tries to take advantage of Dorotea. But she shows her mettle by pushing him over a precipice.

I argue that the scene is already represented in *Double Falshood*. The Master Shepherd tries to have his way with the hapless Dorotea, once the mad Cardenio has unwittingly revealed her gender. She resists him, although not quite to the extent of shoving him to his death. But I suspect in truth my resistance to Antonio's idea is just because I can't quite work out how I'd stage someone being pushed over a cliff.

Nevertheless, Antonio is going to have a significant influence on how we come to view the text of our version of *Cardenio*, as he encourages me to fortify the Spanish-ness of the story. He emphasises the strict segregation of women at this period, and the importance of the Duenna as a chaperone, or the rigorous rules of courtship, symbolised by the iron grate on the windows, through which Cardenio and Luscinda's relationship must be conducted. He elaborates on the cult of the horse in Andalucían society, as an expression of manhood; or the particular devotion accorded to the Virgin Mary in the region.

After a hard day's brain work, unpicking and comparing plots, Antonio and I take a stroll. Antonio is tall with ash-blond hair, a patrician profile and long fingers which are often fiddling with a rolled cigarette. We pass the university, which used to house the vast old tobacco factory, and wander down along the River Guadalquivir, towards La Plaza de Toros, imagining Carmen, humming the Habanera, smoking a cheroot and flirting her way along the same route. It's warm for February, and to my amazement the orange trees are still laden with fruit; teams of municipal workers are knocking them off and rolling them into piles. 'They do it so that the trees will be back in flower by Semana Santa, for Holy Week,' says Antonio. What a sensual notion, deliberately perfuming the city for Easter, with fragrant orange blossom. Seville is famous for its processions of penitents during this, the greatest festival in the Christian calendar.

The piles of Seville oranges remind me of possibly the worst joke in Shakespeare. In the party scene in *Much Ado About Nothing*, Beatrice describes the irritated young Count Claudio as 'civil as an orange and something of that jealous complexion'. Apparently Seville oranges are famously bitter, which explains the terrible pun.

I am staying in a little tavern by the cathedral, underneath the great Giralda tower. Like La Mezquita in Cordoba, the church was once a mosque and the Giralda was its minaret, from which the local Muslim population would have been called to prayer. Now the cathedral is one of the largest in Spain and the Giralda serves as its bell tower. Inside there is a ramp rather than steps so that the muezzin could ride on horseback to the top.

Watching Spanish TV in my room that evening, I come across coverage of previous Semana Santa celebrations in the city. A slow procession of penitents accompanies the huge pasos (or decorated floats) bearing figures of the crucified Christ, shouldered high through crowded streets. These brotherhoods of masked penitents are commemorating the Passion of Jesus, but the tall steeple-like hoods they wear remind me of the Ku Klux Klan. Occasionally the procession is passionately addressed in song from one of the high balconies overlooking the street. I find myself almost hypnotically drawn to the profoundly Catholic ritual, which stirs childhood memories of my Jesuit upbringing.

By the end of our two days, Antonio and I have dissected the novel, understood more about how Fletcher and Shakespeare perhaps reshaped the story for the theatre, and determined what elements of the original should be retained for our own production. This process in itself helps define what we are actually doing here. This cannot be in any sense a reconstruction of the Jacobean play, but rather our twenty-first-century response to Cervantes' story, using whatever we want from Theobald's play to tell that story for today.

'Penitents Accompanying a Paso [in Seville]', from Gustave Doré's *Spain* (1876)

17

Cardenio Refuses to Fly

Early autumn 2008 in Stratford-upon-Avon. Got up this morning and opened the curtains to find I could not see so far as Holy Trinity steeple. The river is a ghostly grey wall of fog; a hazy silhouette of trees on the other side, and reeds draped with pearly cobwebs on this. A lone heron, the colour of the mist, haunts the far bank, all as beautiful as a Japanese folding screen.

I've spent the week in Stratford preparing the finishing touches to the script we developed in Seville back in February for the workshop which starts today. The play, like the heron on the river, is coming slowly into focus.

Antonio's work on the play has suggested a number of elements, some of which I like, and some of which I reject. I don't, for example, buy the idea of Cardenio delivering a prologue to the play, but I like the shape he has suggested for the convent scene in Act Four. Antonio has delivered his scenes in Spanish, and the literary department have had his work re-translated into English by Duncan Wheeler, but inevitably there is now another whole job to do to render this literal translation back into a language that will sound authentically Jacobean. As Antonio has always found lines from the original Spanish *Don Quixote*, I can usually find them in Shelton's translation. But it is a slow and perhaps (I now think) an overcomplicated process.

This summer in Stratford I have directed an ensemble in three plays in the Courtyard Theatre: a revival of a production of *A Midsummer Night's Dream*, which I did in the RST in 2005; *Hamlet* with David Tennant in the title role; and we have just opened *Love's Labour's Lost*. I have taken advantage of the company's free days in the rehearsal schedule to mount a reading of our *Cardenio* draft in our Arden Street rehearsal rooms.

Ed Bennett (elsewhere our Demetrius/Laertes/King of Navarre) is a witty and moving Cardenio; Peter de Jersey (Oberon/Horatio) a violent Don Fernando; Minnie Gale (Ophelia/Princess of France) is a heart-breaking Dorotea, and Nina Sosanya (Rosaline) a forceful Luscinda.

The workshop goes well, but there are still elements of the play that need a lot of work. I have become more and more convinced that this is a Fletcher play we are dealing with; particularly in the character of the two fathers. Oliver Ford Davies (our Polonius and Holofernes) makes a great Don Bernardo; and Jim Hooper (Starveling/Sir Nathaniel) is a marvellously intemperate Don Camillo.

Cis Berry, the RSC's legendary Head of Voice, has been watching. She's charmed by the play and admits she can't tell which bits are from *Double Falshood*, and what we have constructed from Shelton. 'But,' she says, 'it's the language, isn't it? It's just not Shakespeare. Not surprising enough. It doesn't fly.'

RSC dramaturg, Jeanie O'Hare, has been making notes. On a very practical level, she points out that, as yet, there is not enough of a friendship between Cardenio and Don Fernando, for the Duke's son to betray. In *Double Falshood*, Cardenio and Fernando don't even meet until the last act; and that, though Cardenio's horsemanship is emphasised, nothing is made of it.

Although we have gone as far as we can, extracting from Cervantes' novel the text for the two major scenes which are missing from *Double Falshood*, we now have to take a further imaginative leap.

I discuss with Antonio what possibilities there might be for a co-production with Spain. We had envisaged all sorts of permutations: rehearsing a bilingual company; or starting with a British company, opening in the UK then transferring to Spain and allowing a Spanish company to take over the production. Or even two concurrent productions.

But the timing is bad. The world economic crisis has bitten everyone. And Spain has been hit very hard. Unemployment there is rising to unprecedented levels, and within months the country would officially enter recession. This was not the time to be discussing expensive co-productions. We might have to reign in our horns and concentrate on our home base.

But with the Courtyard Theatre now the RSC's only home until 2011, when the newly developed RST is scheduled to reopen, there would be little hope of doing *Cardenio* for at least another three years. The Swan Theatre is the production's natural home. Perhaps I can persuade Mike Boyd, the RSC's artistic director, to allow me to reopen it with 'Shakespeare's lost play'. The idea provides an extra sense of focus to make this script really fly. But how?

18

Chess Matches:
Both Diplomatic and Dramatic

There is no record of a revival of *Cardenio* after the Globe burned down in 1613. Records for any performances of any plays are scarce. But I suspect any revival in the play's fortunes would have been directly linked with England's political relations with Spain.

The Spanish weren't popular with the English public. Earlier in the summer of 1612, the Spanish Ambassador, Zuñiga, was riding in his *carrosse* with six mules over Holborn Bridge, when a well-dressed cavalier approached, leant through the window, snatched his hat and rode off up the street with it, to the laughter of the crowd. The hat had a rich jewel in it.

A couple of years after that incident, the carriage of the new Ambassador, Sarmiento, was stopped by a mob, but when his attendants wounded a citizen while attempting to clear a path for His Excellency, the riot became so serious that the city gates had to be shut.

In 1623, ten years after the Globe fire, the prospective marriage of the Prince of Wales was again the occasion of a play by the King's Men. In *A Game at Chess*, Thomas Middleton characterised the tricky diplomatic negotiations for Prince Charles to marry the Infanta Maria, the daughter of the King of Spain, as a chess match. King James appears inevitably as the White King, King Philip IV as the Black King. The play centres on the visit to Madrid, earlier that same year, of Prince Charles (the White Knight) with George Villiers, the Duke of Buckingham (the White Duke or Rook).

The Spanish Ambassador, the Count Gondomar, was satirised as the Machiavellian Black Knight, and he didn't like it. He recognised himself in the role and complained to the King, who had the play banned. It had a run of nine performances during which it had become the greatest get-penny (or box-office hit) of the age.

John Chamberlain wrote to his friend Dudley Carleton:

> I doubt not but you have heard of our famous play of Gondomar, which hath been followed with extraordinary concourse, and frequented, by all sorts of people old and young, rich and poor, masters and servants, papists and puritans, wise men etc. ... They counterfeited his person to the life, with all his graces and faces, and had gotten they say a cast suit of his apparel for the purpose, and his litter wherein the world says, lacked nothing but a couple of asses to carry it... They are forbidden to play that or any other play till the King's pleasure be further known; and they may be glad if they can so scape scot free. The wonder lasted but nine days, for so long they played it.

The Globe was shut down and the King's Men fined, and Middleton never wrote another play.

A Game at Chess catches a strong sense of anti-Spanish feeling, and may have been designed to foster the sentiments of a faction that called for war against Spain. It is unlikely that any play with a Spanish subject, like *Cardenio*, would have found favour with the Globe audiences at this period.

The year that Middleton's play enjoyed its Nine Days' Wonder, John Hemings and Henry Condell published their friend Shakespeare's plays. They followed Ben Jonson's example: he had published his own complete works in 1616. Their companion, John Fletcher, a fellow member of the Friday Street Club at the Mermaid Tavern, died two years later, in 1625, without having assembled his own collected works.

Hemings and Condell didn't include *Cardenio* in the First Folio (nor indeed did they include *Pericles*). Perhaps the play did indeed disappear in the Globe fire, or perhaps the play's Spanish subject was thought potentially damaging to sales.

So if the play of *Cardenio* was not revived, and the script survived but was not published, what happened to the manuscript then?

19

In Which We Get Mired in Mystery

August 2009. The press is filled with stories about Fulke Greville, the Elizabethan soldier, statesman, courtier, and spy. Greville, who was a dear friend of Sir Philip Sidney and himself a poet, has been declared the latest in a long line of candidates as the author of Shakespeare's plays. This would make him an alternative 'Man from Stratford', as the Grevilles, like the Shakespeares, were a Warwickshire family who lived in Stratford.

The claims arise from speculation that Greville had several manuscripts buried in his ornate memorial in St Mary's Church, just down the road in Warwick. Radar scans have apparently detected three 'box-like' objects sealed within this 'monument without a tomb', a discovery of *Da Vinci Code* proportions, which Kate McLuskie, director of the Shakespeare Institute in Stratford, says could keep the Shakespeare Industry going for years.

It is thought the box may contain lost manuscripts of his plays, including *Antony and Cleopatra*. Could *Cardenio* also be in there?

Churchill said of Russia in 1939, 'It is a riddle, wrapped in a mystery, inside an enigma.' *Cardenio* seems to me to be much the same. But as Churchill also went on to suggest, 'perhaps there is a key'. For my part, I keep on thinking I have found a key only to lose it in a bunch of speculations.

There is an edition of *Double Falshood* in the Folger Library, in Washington DC. It is marked up as a prompt book. It records a private performance of the play for the Noel family in 1749, and given by a group of relatives and friends, possibly at their home, Luffenham Hall in Rutland. Baptist Noel was the 4th Earl of Gainsborough, and he and his wife Lady Jane Noel took part.

I picture the Noels, husband and wife, as resembling the portrait of Mr and Mrs Andrews in the National Gallery. It was painted by Gainsborough (no relation) around the very same time of the Noel family performance of *Double Falshood*. Mr and Mrs Andrews relax under an oak tree, as the Noels may well have done, in their beautiful parkland.

If you are wondering why the Noel family should decide to mount a private production of 'Shakespeare's lost play', there are plenty of tantalising clues that link the family to Shakespeare. Intriguingly, the 1st Earl of Gainsborough (Baptist was the 4th) had married Elizabeth Wriothesley, the granddaughter of Henry Wriothesley, Shakespeare's patron, the Earl of Southampton (Wriothesley, by the way, is pronounced 'Risley').

And just to add extra spice, the 2nd Earl, who had been christened Wriothesley, had married Catherine Greville, a relative of Fulke Greville.

Did the Noel family inherit a manuscript of *Cardenio* from either the Wriothesleys or the Grevilles? Did they lend Lewis Theobald their copy, and then decide to mount their own production at Luffenham? Did Theobald give them their manuscript back? If so, it's no good my heading off to Rutland with my deerstalker and magnifying glass, as Luffenham Hall was pulled down in 1806. Every time I think I have found a clue to the potential whereabouts of a manuscript of what Theobald called 'this orphan play', it seems to disappear like a lost child.

In Gainsborough's painting too there is a poignant note. Mrs Andrews sits on a lovely twisted rococo bench, confidently expecting that before the painting is finished, she will have a child to complete the family portrait. But her lap is empty, the child was lost, and the painting was never completed.

20

Shakespeare's Natural Son?

In Lewis Theobald's preface to *Double Falshood*, he mentions 'a tradition', handed down from 'a noble person' from whom he obtained one of the three copies of the lost manuscript in his possession, which maintained that the play was written by Shakespeare as a present for his 'Natural Daughter'.

There is no known account of Shakespeare having an illegitimate daughter, but there is a candidate for an illegitimate son. According to the gossipy John Aubrey (1626–97) in his *Brief Lives*, Shakespeare, on his journeys to and from London, would stay at the Crown Tavern in Oxford:

> Mr William Shakespeare was wont to go into Warwickshire once a year, and did commonly in his journey lye at this house in Oxon, where he was exceedingly respected. (I have heard Parson Robert say that Mr William Shakespeare haz given him a hundred kisses.) Now Sir William [Davenant] would sometimes, when he was pleasant over a glasse of wine with his most intimate friends... say, that it seemed to him that he writt with the very spirit that did Shakespeare and seemed contented enough to be thought his Son.

Now as Aubrey actually knew William Davenant, he may be thought to be more reliable than usual in this instance.

William Davenant was born in 1606, and he may be a significant link in our story. He would have been seven years old when *Cardenio* was first performed, and ten when 'godfather' Shakespeare died.

When he was twenty-four, according to Aubrey, Davenant 'got a terrible clap of a black handsome wench that lay in Axe-yard, Westminster... which cost him his nose.' (Axe Yard was a cul-de-sac near present-day Downing Street.) The only image we have of Davenant is an engraving from a lost portrait. It shows an otherwise handsome man with a strong chin in a glossy peruke, crowned with the bays of a poet laureate. But his steady gaze defies you to glance down at his snubby little conk with its apparently extra nostril.

Davenant became a playwright in the footsteps of his godfather, towards the end of King James's reign (1625), and by the 1630s was writing court masques for the young King Charles and his French Queen, Henrietta Maria.

These masques were moved out of King James's great banqueting hall into a temporary timber masking-room, while a new hall (the Banqueting House in Whitehall) was constructed to a design by Inigo Jones. Rubens painted the glorious ceiling we can still see today, depicting the apotheosis of King James, as he is assumed into Heaven, like a baby being lifted to its mother's breast, graphically demonstrating his firmly held belief in the divine right of kings.

The last masque Davenant wrote was called *Salmacida Spolia*. The King and the Queen took part.

The published description sounds spectacular. In the antimasque, which preceded the masque itself, 'a curtain flying up' revealed a horrid scene of storm and tempest. In the midst of all this, the globe of the earth suddenly exploded into a fireball, and turned into a malicious Fury. This is Discord, a hag with snakes in her hair, who invokes malignant spirits to her evil use. But in an instant, the scene is changed to a serene landscape heralding the main body of the masque. Concord attended by 'The Genius of Britain' both descend in a silver chariot to sing, in duet, prophetic words penned by Davenant:

> O who could thus endure
> To live and govern in a sullen age
> When it is harder for to cure
> The people's folly than resist their rage.

As the King himself then appeared in the character of 'Philogenes' (the lover of his people), surrounded by his lords, a chorus sang his praises for having the kingly patience 'to outlast those storms the people's giddy fury raise'.

At which point 'a huge cloud of various colours' descends, within which, among 'a transparent brightness of thin exhalations', sat the Queen environed with her ladies, 'and from over her head were darted lightsome rays... such as are seen in a fair evening sky... that illuminated her seat.'

The King then escorted the Queen in a dance, after which Their Majesties assumed their thrones under the canopy of state, as the scene changed once again to the perspective of a great city. The masque ended with the appearance of the music of the spheres, and a final hymn to the Royal pair, declaring:

> All that are harsh, all that are rude
> Are by your harmony subdued.

This attempt to validate the authority of the King by symbolic means may have been 'generally approved of, especially by the strangers that were present [foreign ambassadors in attendance], to be the noblest and most ingenious that hath ever been done here in that kind', but it was truly an illusion of power.

The date of this masque was Tuesday 21 January 1640. The country was in turmoil, and as Their Majesties danced in the spangled candlelight, few could have guessed that within the decade, in Inigo Jones's splendid new Banqueting House, under Rubens' ceiling depicting the divine right of kings, that same King would be preparing to mount a different kind of stage, and step from the window to the executioner's block.

The following year (1641) King Charles left London only ever to return again for his trial and execution. He raised the standard at Nottingham in August and the Civil War began in earnest.

By September, Parliament had banned all stage plays. The proclamation read: 'Public sports do not agree with public calamities, nor public stage plays with the seasons of humiliation.' By 1642, the Puritans were firmly in control and the theatres were closed permanently. On Monday 15 April 1644 (according to some manuscript additions to a copy of Stowe's *Annales*), 'the Globe was pulled down to the ground, by Sir Matthew Brand... to make tenements in the room of it'.

The same fate awaited the Blackfriars Theatre. William Davenant wrote of its broken shell:

> Poor House, that in days of our grandsires
> Belongst unto the mendicant friars
> And where so often in our fathers' days
> We have seen so many of Shakespeare's plays,
> So many of Jonson's, Beaumont's or Fletcher's
> Until I know not what puritan teachers
> Have made with their rantings the players as poor
> As were the friars and poets before.

The Fortune was pulled down by soldiers in 1649, but the Red Bull Theatre in Clerkenwell survived until just after the Restoration by staging rope-dancing and prizefights, and the occasional illegal play. Finally it too was closed, as Davenant wrote:

> Tell 'em the Red Bull stands empty of fencers
> There are no tenants in it but old spiders.

The saddest fate awaited the bears which were baited at the Hope Theatre on Bankside in Southwark. 'Seven of Mr Godfrey's bears by the command of Thomas Pride the High

Sheriff of Surrey were then shot to death on Saturday the 9th day of February 1655 by a company of soldiers.'

However, a couple of years before Mr Godfrey's bears were put down, there is a surprising twist in the story of our lost play. *Cardenio* was registered for publication.

21

O Rare Sir William Davenant

If you walk past the Town Hall in Stratford-upon-Avon, at the top of Sheep Street, there are two intriguing signs. The first is my favourite. It is a small, round, blue-metal plate, tucked behind a drainpipe. It reads bewilderingly: 'Waiting prohibited on even dates.' It comes from the early days of motoring and refers to the days of the month on which you were allowed to park.

The larger sign is more prominently displayed. It announces that in 1643 the original market hall had been shattered by a gunpowder explosion, when General Monck's parliamentarian forces occupied the town at the height of the Civil War. They had been routed by the King's forces at the Battle of Edgehill, some fifteen miles away.

On 11 July of that year, Charles's Queen, Henrietta Maria, arrived in the town and stayed just along the street from the exploded ruin of the Town Hall, with Shakespeare's daughter Susannah, at New Place. Her visit was 'the occasion of celebration', we are told, with 'bell-ringing and feasting'. Her nephew, the dashing Prince Rupert, met the Queen here and escorted her the rest of the way to Oxford, where Charles had set up his Court.

Whether Shakespeare's 'natural son', William Davenant, was with her or not is unclear. Perhaps he would not have been welcome. But he had accompanied the Queen to France, in a bid to raise money for the Royalist cause. He certainly joined Their Majesties at Oxford and accompanied the King to Gloucester where he was knighted for his services to the crown.

Davenant was in Paris, residing at the Louvre, with the Queen and her eighteen-year-old son, Charles, Prince of Wales, when their husband and father, King Charles I, was executed on 30 January 1649. Davenant's return to London was unexpected. He was sailing for America when he was captured en route, and imprisoned: first on the Isle of Wight and later in the Tower of London, where he spent two years.

In London, various illicit performances had been held during the Commonwealth. But things were in a sorry state. Richard Flecknoe notes

> passing on to Blackfriars, and seeing never a playbill on the gate, no coaches on the place, no door keeper at the Playhouse door with his box like a church warden, desiring you to remember the poor players.

At the Red Bull in Clerkenwell, soldiers had raided several times, arresting the actors, and hauling them from the stage and the tiring house and seizing their stock of costumes too.

But Davenant showed his resilience under the new Lord Protector, Cromwell. He tested the water by presenting new entertainments at an improvised theatre in the back part of his home, Rutland House in Upper Aldersgate Street, near Charterhouse Square. The show he presented was called *The First Day's Entertainment* (1656).

It seems he had managed to persuade Cromwell's Secretary of State of 'the usefulness of entertainments' to divert people's minds from 'that melancholy that breeds sedition'. And it was upon this small beginning that he was to build.

He mounted a production of his own play *The Siege of Rhodes* at the cramped 'cupboard scene' of Rutland House, in 1656. Then two years later, in the autumn of 1658, he moved to the Cockpit (built for Prince Henry in 1609 and now transformed into a theatre).

By the time General Monck, now heading the royalist army, arrived in London in 1660, signalling the imminent restoration of the monarchy, Davenant had positioned himself as one of the major players in the theatre world of the new reign. Among all the feverish manoeuvrings prior to the new King Charles's arrival in London, Davenant, along with the playwright Thomas Killigrew, came out on top.

Charles II entered London on his thirtieth birthday, 29 May 1660. Davenant was fifty-four. By November 1660, he and Killigrew had been granted patents under the great seal to run two theatre companies in London. Killigrew would run the King's company, and Davenant the Duke of York's.

Killigrew performed in a converted space, Gibbon's indoor tennis court in Vere Street near Lincoln's Inn, which held about five hundred, and opened on 8 November with *Henry IV, Part One* (incidentally the same play with which the Shakespeare Memorial Theatre opened in 1932); while Davenant eventually moved to a new theatre nearby in Lincoln's Inn Fields, which could accommodate his new scenery, and with his young company including a twenty-five-year-old Thomas Betterton. He opened with a revival of his play *The Siege of Rhodes*.

Killigrew had sneakily claimed that, as his company were patronised by the King, they should have the stock of plays which his predecessors, the King's Men, had owned before the theatres were closed. This would include the entire Shakespeare canon. Davenant objected and eventually the plays were shared between them. Among the plays Davenant's company got were nine of Shakespeare's, including *Macbeth*, *The Tempest* and *Hamlet*. He also got *All is True* (*Henry VIII*).

Davenant had known the old King's Men actor, John Lowin, who, it is conjectured, had played Henry VIII originally. Lowin was running the company with Joseph Taylor when the theatres were closed, and both men were arrested the following year for playing together in an illegal performance of Fletcher's play *Rollo, Duke of Normandy*. Soldiers dragged them offstage to prison still wearing their costumes. On his release, Lowin went off to Brentford and ran a pub called The Three Pigeons.

Davenant, then, had first-hand information about how *Henry VIII* worked as play, and, according to a contemporary account, was able to instruct Betterton as Henry:

> The part of the king was so right and justly done by Mr
> Betterton, he being instructed in it by Sir William, who
> had it from Old Mr Lowin, that had his instructions
> from Mr Shakespeare himself, that I dare and will aver,
> none can, or ever will come near him in this age, in the
> performance of that part.

Betterton's wife Mary played Queen Katherine, and Henry Harris took the role of Wolsey. We have a drawing of Harris in costume, which makes him the first ever actor in England to be painted in character as a Shakespearian role. The account also describes how 'every part by the great care of Sir William Davenant, was exactly performed... it continued acting fifteen days together with general applause'.

The same account tells us that:

> Hamlet being performed by Mr Betterton, Sir William
> (having seen Mr Taylor of the Blackfriars Company act
> it, who being instructed by the author Mr Shakespeare)
> taught Mr Betterton in every part of it.

Laurence Olivier, in his book *On Acting*, found this information inspiring:

> Burbage created Hamlet and then, sometime after,
> rehearsed a young actor, Joseph Taylor, in the part.
> Taylor played for the King's Company at the Globe and
> the Blackfriars theatres. Being the second Hamlet and
> taught by the first, he must have automatically retained
> some of Burbage's original performance. Thomas
> Betterton played Hamlet and he studied with Sir
> William Davenant, who had seen Taylor.*

---

* Taylor didn't actually join the King's Men until after Burbage's death,
but he would surely have seen the great man play the part.

And Olivier continues:

> Garrick studied and learned from some of the old
> members of the Betterton company, and Kean from the
> survivors of Garrick's Company, and then on to Irving.
> It all sounds very romantic, but looked at this way it
> doesn't make William seem so very far away.

Betterton continued playing Hamlet until he was seventy-five, finally giving his last performance on Tuesday 20 September 1709. There's a record of this actual performance in the *Tatler*:

> Mr Betterton behaved himself so well, that, though
> now about seventy, he acted youth, and by the
> prevalent power of proper manner, gesture and voice,
> appeared through the whole drama a youth of great
> expectation, vivacity and enterprise.

At the same time as Davenant revived *Henry VIII*, he adapted Shakespeare and Fletcher's other collaboration, *The Two Noble Kinsmen*, which he retitled *The Rivals*. One of the actresses playing Celia, 'a shepherdess being mad for love' (the jailer's daughter in the original play), had several 'wild and mad songs' to sing, including one called 'My lodging, it is on the cold ground' performed 'so charmingly, that not long after, it raised her from her bed on the cold ground, to a Bed Royal'. The actress was Mary Davis who briefly became a mistress of King Charles II.

If Davenant revived both *Henry VIII* and *The Two Noble Kinsmen*, is it not likely that he at least considered Shakespeare and Fletcher's third collaboration, *Cardenio*? If Theobald is to be believed, the play was 'in the possession of Mr Betterton and by him designed to have been ushered into the world'.

And what about Theobald's claim that the play had been written as a present for his 'natural daughter'?

Sir William Davenant died on 7 April 1668 (Pepys was backstage at the rival establishment chatting to an actress when he heard the news 'that Sir W Davenant is just now dead'). He was survived by his third wife, a Frenchwoman known as Dame Mary. She had proved a highly capable partner to Davenant in running the theatre.

Perhaps the manuscript of *Cardenio* did belong to Davenant originally. Perhaps he had inherited the play from his 'godfather', and held on to it, which would perhaps explain why it did not make it into the First Folio. Is it possible that after his death it came into the possession of Dame Mary, Shakespeare's 'natural daughter-in-law' as it were?

Pepys saw Davenant's body carried from the Duke's Playhouse to be buried in Westminster Abbey. The whole of the playhouse company attended him. His friend John Aubrey adds the detail that his corpse 'was received at the great west door by the singing-men and choristers who sang the service... to his grave which is in the south cross aisle'.

On my recent visit to Westminster Abbey, I looked around for Sir William Davenant's grave. There is the monument to Ben Jonson on the wall by the exit to the toilets, with the inscription 'O Rare Ben: Johnson', and I search about for Davenant. Dryden has a quite considerable free-standing monument, and of course there is Shakespeare's which arrived very late in the Abbey, not until 1741. The Romantic poets seem to have spirited themselves around his monument in homage. Wordsworth sits looking pensive, Coleridge stares down. And in front of him lie Peggy Ashcroft and Laurence Olivier.

The most ostentatious monument in the entire crowded corner is David Garrick's, who bursts through a pair of curtains as if grabbing one last curtain call, and expecting an ovation from the rest of us below. And then I spot Davenant's name on a marble lozenge on the floor. Like Ben Jonson's and presumably in honour of him the stone reads 'O Rare Sr William Davenant'. But it is cracked and looks a little forgotten. Despite his obscure memorial, Davenant was the greatest impresario of his day. He pulled theatre through the Civil War, and introduced us to theatre practices which are still in use today.

And he plays quite a significant part in our quest for *Cardenio*.

Sir William Davenant, by John Greenhill, after William Faithorne (1672)

22

Adapting Shakespeare

How much of the original lost play of *Cardenio* might there be in *Double Falshood*?

These days we tend to sneer at the way Shakespeare's plays were adapted for the stage after the Restoration. Nahum Tate's happy ending for *King Lear* is the example most often cited, though I don't think it is his most extreme intervention. Take *The Ingratitude of the Commonwealth*, Tate's version of *Coriolanus*, or indeed his *Richard II* which he transposed to Sicily, and renamed *The Sicilian Usurper*.

Lewis Theobald also adapted *Richard II*, which was clearly regarded as a very flawed piece. Theobald attempts to apply the classical unities to the play and cuts over one thousand lines, which makes his later high-handed attack on Pope's emendations in his edition of Shakespeare seem, if not hypocritical, then at least self-righteous. His *Richard II* adaptation was not successful, and ran for only four performances.

William Davenant is perhaps most famous for his 1667 version of *The Tempest*, called *The Enchanted Island*. Five years before that he had produced a play called *The Law Against Lovers*, which (incredibly to us now) combines

Measure for Measure with *Much Ado About Nothing*. Even odder is Thomas Otway's *The History and Fall of Caius Marius*, grafting the story of the Roman general and statesman (which he took from Plutarch's *Parallel Lives*) on to *Romeo and Juliet*.

There is a line in the prologue to *The Enchanted Island* which could apply to my own aspirations for *Cardenio*:

> So from old Shakespeare's honoured dust, this day
> Springs up and buds a new reviving play.

Dryden's preface explains how he became involved in rewriting *The Tempest* with William Davenant, whom he praises as man 'of quick and piercing imagination'. He describes Davenant's 'excellent contrivance' of supplying a counterpart to Shakespeare's plot, and balancing the character of Miranda by creating Hippolito, a man who has never before set eyes on a woman. Miranda gets a sister, Dorinda, and so does Caliban. And in the busy pairing-off that happens in the final scene, even Ariel gets a mate – called Milcha:

> ARIEL. I have a gentle spirit for my love
>   Who twice seven years hath waited for my Freedom.
>   It shall appear and foot it featly with me.
>   Milcha, my love, thy Ariel calls to thee.
>
> *Enter* MILCHA.
>
> MILCHA: Here.
>
> *They dance a Saraband.*

When, in 1754, David Garrick produced his version of *The Winter's Tale* for the first time since its original performances, he called it *Florizel and Perdita*, and declared his purpose in a prologue:

> Lest then this precious Liquor run to waste,
> 'Tis now confin'd and bottled for your Taste.
> 'Tis my chief Wish, my Joy, my only Plan,
> To lose no Drop of that immortal Man!

He then proceeded to cut Acts One, Two and Three. So any sense of regard for the sanctity of Shakespeare's text at this period needs to be seen in that light. But before we condemn these Restoration and early eighteenth-century adaptations too readily, isn't it worth considering that every production of a Shakespeare play is in some sense an adaptation? In the *Macbeth* directed by Michael Boyd, which is playing in Stratford as I write this, the witches are played by Macduff's children, and the blasted heath is a post-Reformation church. Meanwhile, *The Merchant of Venice*, which Rupert Goold is currently rehearsing, is set in Las Vegas, with Portia's casket scenes played as a TV game show. In a way these interventions are surely as radical as anything Davenant envisaged.

So if Davenant did indeed take the text of *Cardenio* and adapt it for Thomas Betterton with the same freedom that he adapted *The Tempest*, then his play may have moved a considerably long way from what Shakespeare and Fletcher originally wrote. If it was that version that Lewis Theobald then adapted, and we consider how little relation his adaptation of *Richard II* bears to the Shakespeare original, then we would have to admit that *Double Falshood*, at not one but two removes from the original, may have very little to do with our lost play.

23

Stationers' Hall

One bright September morning, I decided to visit the Library and Archives of the Worshipful Company of Stationers and Newspaper Makers, at Stationers' Hall, at Amen Corner on Ave Maria Lane in the City of London, to view the Register for 1653.

As it was such a beautiful morning, I walked from my home in Islington, strolling downhill from Angel to Smithfield. Halfway down St John's Street before crossing the Goshawk road, the dome of St Paul's comes into view. Then I passed through the central Grand Avenue of the Smithfield Market, which divides the Poulterers from the Butchers, and across to St Barts, and down Giltspur Street. It struck me that if *Double Falshood* bears the sketchy evidence of previous versions of *Cardenio*, then the map of London is similar. It too is a palimpsest: although the old city may have been scraped away, its history is still present in its very street names. I pass Pie Corner and Cock Lane to the corner of Newgate where the church of St Sepulchre-without-Newgate stands, then down past the Old Bailey, and the end of Limeburner Lane, to Ludgate Hill.

I turned right into the ward of Farringdon Within, and into an alleyway. There across the yard in front of me stood Stationers' Hall.

The Stationers' Guild was set up to represent the interests of the booksellers who had their stalls (or stations) in nearby St Paul's Churchyard. St Peter's College, the Stationers' first premises, was one of the many pieces of church property being sold off after the Reformation. They then moved into Abergavenny Hall, on this site, which was largely destroyed by the Great Fire of London in 1666. The Stationers immediately built this grand edifice before me, and the company dined in their new Hall for the first time on Lord Mayor's Day 1673.

I wonder if it was here, outside the Hall, that the bonfire of books took place on 4 June 1599. Archbishop Whitgift and Richard Bancroft, Bishop of London, ordered all unlicensed plays and unapproved histories to be burnt alongside a number of satires and elegies. So into the flames went John Marston's *The Scourge of Villainy*, Thomas Middleton's *Six Snarling Satires*, Kit Marlowe's raunchy translations of Ovid's *Elegies*, and all the books of poor Thomas Nashe, whose work was forthwith banned from publication.

I followed signs for the offices and made my way inside to be greeted by the clerk, a city gent straight from central casting, with a pinstripe suit, and loud pink tie, who greeted me cheerily and showed me through to an office where I was welcomed by Deborah Rea, the recently appointed Head of Communications. Deborah showed me the backstage route upstairs to the library through the magnificent livery Hall where they were putting out tables for a banquet that evening.

It occurred to me that it must have been in a room on this site four hundred years ago, that the representatives of the twelve companies charged by King James to produce a new translation of the Bible had met together to review the whole book. Apparently they tested the efficacy of the translations by reading the text out loud, to hear what it sounded like, and therefore how it would land on the ear of their congregations.

There was a smoky smell in the air. 'We had a fire over the summer,' said Deborah, when I asked what it was. It happened during an event when the Hall had been hired out. The oak screen was badly damaged. Part of it had to be replaced. Much of the renovation had already been carried out but I could still smell scorched timber. The odd-job man who was setting out the tables said, 'It's still all charred at the back. We haven't had time to clean that yet.' When I checked the details on the Stationers' Hall website later, I read a note from the clerk, William Alden:

> At one point the flames were floor-to-ceiling high. It looked as though the whole Hall might be lost. The accident is obviously a tragedy and it is so sad that the 350-year-old screen, which survived the Blitz, should have fallen foul of twenty-first-century electrics.

It strikes me that fire flickers around this whole story. If the midsummer blaze had got out of hand, one of the prime pieces of evidence for the existence of *Cardenio* might have gone up with it.

Deborah showed me up a short flight of stairs into an attic room, where the Librarian, Sue Hurley, politely greeted me. There on the table in the middle of the room was a large calf-bound book on grey foam bookrests. It was open at the page I wanted to see.

At the top of the page I read 'September 9th 1653', then next to the name of the publisher, Humphrey Moseley, in the first column it says Entered for his copies a play called Alphonso Emperor of Germany by John Peele 6d' and then further down the page, under 'Die Eadem' ('the same day'), 'Entered also for his copies the several plays following' – and the sum of twenty shillings and sixpence. Sue explained that it cost sixpence per entry to register a work for publication, which effectively secured the publisher's copyright in that work. The Stationers had a monopoly on book production. So if anyone tried to publish something already registered by another publisher, the Stationers were legally empowered to seize the offending books.

So Humphrey Moseley was making a considerable investment. Twenty shillings and sixpence gave him the copyright of forty-one items. And they are listed below. Most are plays whose titles I am unfamiliar with: two plays by Ben Jonson's apprentice Richard Brome, *Wit in Madness* and *The Lovesick Maid*; *Osman the Great Turk*, *The Jew of Venice* by Thomas Dekker; Davenant's *The Siege* (presumably *The Siege of Rhodes*)... I detect a theme emerging in some of the titles: *The Puritan Maid, Modest Wife and Wanton Widow, The Widow's Prize* by Mr Wm. Samson; *The Woman's Mistaken* by Drew Davenport. And then there it is...

The History of Cardenio by Mr Fletcher. & Shakespeare.

The secretary hand is light and efficient. I wondered if Moseley himself was dictating his list, while the clerk copied down the titles.

It struck me that paying over a pound to secure the right to publish these plays was quite an investment. It also makes me wonder if the reason Moseley wanted to make sure that he had the right to publish *The History of Cardenio* was that there were other copies around and someone else might decide to publish theirs.

Sue and Deborah began pulling tomes from the shelves to see what else is to be found out about Humphrey Moseley. He was bound to the Company as an apprentice in 1620, and freed from his apprenticeship in 1627; he married Anne, and had four children, the last of whom would be still-born within a month of the day he was here, registering his list of plays.

He set up his first independent shop at the sign of The Three Kings, against the north-eastern wall of St Paul's Cathedral, in 1634, but four years later he had acquired premises at the sign of the Prince's Arms, across the churchyard, which he occupied for the rest of his life. When he published Milton's poems he started to become really successful and over the next fifteen years until his death, the list of poets and dramatists whose works appeared under his imprint included Beaumont and Fletcher, Middleton, Massinger, Shirley, Brome, Davenant, and poets such as Cowley, Crashaw, Suckling and Vaughan.

By the time of this entry, Moseley was a member of the governing body of the Stationers' Guild, and attended meetings at the Hall.

The surge of excitement I felt at seeing the actual written proof that a play called *The History of Cardenio* by Mr Fletcher and Shakespeare did actually exist in the possession of Humphrey Moseley is somewhat tempered when I follow the list down and turn over the page.

At the bottom, some plays by Thomas Middleton are listed, including *Women Beware Women*, and over the page there are ten by Philip Massinger. But then there is an item which reads: *The Merry Devil of Edmonton by William Shakespeare*, and under that *Henry I & Henry II by Shakespeare and Robert Davenport*.

Now the first is perhaps a simple misattribution of a title to Shakespeare. *The Merry Devil of Edmonton* is regarded as an apocryphal play which was very popular in its day, and went through a number of anonymous quarto editions since its first appearance in 1608. Does Moseley genuinely think it is by Shakespeare, or does the entry suggest that he is just hoping to cash in on his name by attributing the play to him once he publishes it?

Sue also got out another register to show me. It was the entry for the First Folio of Shakespeare's works in 1623. The date is 8 November. The ink is noticeably faded on this spread. It had been put on display too often, she said, and had deteriorated. 'We'll only get it out now for particular requests.'

The entry does not include all the thirty-six plays in the first complete works: nineteen had by then been published in quarto editions. The only plays listed here are those which have not hitherto been registered for publication:

> *Mr. William Shakspeers Comedyes Histories &*
> *Tragedyes soe manie of the said Copies as are not*
> *formerly entered to other men.*

It is sobering to think that if the Globe fire had burnt all the plays which Shakespeare had not already published, half of his plays would have perished. We would not just be mourning the loss of *Cardenio*, but all these plays on the Stationers' Register list. They appear in the following groupings:

> *Comedyes: The Tempest, The two gentlemen of Verona, Measure for Measure, The Comedy of Errors, As You Like It, All's well that ends well, Twelfe Night, The winters tale*

> *Histories: The thirde parte of Henry ye sixt, Henry the eight*

> *Tragedies: Coriolanus, Timon of Athens, Julius Caesar, Mackbeth, Anthonie & Cleopatra, Cymbeline*

(And in fact this list does not include *The Taming of the Shrew*, or *King John*.)

Imagine no *As You Like It*, no *Tempest*, no *Macbeth* or *Twelfth Night*. None of these plays might have survived, had Hemings and Condell not brought them to Messrs Jaggard and Blount to publish in the First Folio. And yet even without these plays, I suspect, we would still regard Shakespeare as the greatest writer in the world.

I dragged myself away from the Stationers' Hall, pondering about how vital to our heritage the work of the Stationers is.

Humphrey Moseley died in 1660, before, it would seem, he had a chance to publish *Cardenio*. Six years later the Great Fire of London destroyed the Stationers' Hall, along with forty thousand pounds' worth of books, and razed Moseley's city to the ground.

24

Faith under Paul's

Humphrey Moseley was buried in St Gregory-by-Paul's on 4 February 1661. Of the eighty-six churches that burned in the Great Fire, Wren decided to rebuild fifty-one, but St Gregory's was not among them, so I couldn't go and pay my respects that morning. I went instead to St Paul's to see if I could find St Faith under St Paul's, where the Stationers used to worship.

I headed for the crypt. I wandered past Nelson's great monument placed directly under the dome, and a bust of Lawrence of Arabia, and a model of the Old Cathedral. Eventually I discovered, with the help of one of the guides, a line on the floor, at the back of the crypt, to the north side of the OBE Chapel. The line is made up of white mosaic tesserae, and an inscription runs along it, indicating that this is the line of the wall of the old church of St Faith's Virgin and Martyr, which became 'under Paul's' when the cathedral was built over its ruins.

I crossed over the mosaic line and stepped into St Faith under St Paul's, while Paulina's line from *The Winter's Tale* ran in my head:

> It is required
> You do awake your faith.

The flagstones beneath my feet were the floor of the crypt. It was into this crypt with its stone-vaulted ceiling, that the booksellers, the stationers, ran with their stock, piling their books against the walls, trying to save them from the fire that had broken out in Pudding Lane about ten o'clock on the fatal night of Sunday 2 September 1666.

John Evelyn records in his diary his journey on foot from Whitehall as far as London Bridge the following Friday morning. He describes 'clambering over heaps of yet smoking rubbish' with extraordinary difficulty, frequently mistaking where he was. The ground underneath him was still so hot it burned the soles of his shoes. He finds 'that goodly church St Paul's now a sad ruin'. The portico is 'split asunder', and the immense stones had been 'calcin'd', or turned white by the heat,

> so that all the ornaments, columns, friezes, capitals and projectures of Portland stone flew off, even to the very roof, where a sheet of lead covering a great space (no less than six acres by measure) was totally melted.

He then reveals a telling detail:

> The ruins of the vaulted roof falling, broke into St Faith's which being filled with the magazines of books belonging to the stationers, and carried thither for safety, they were all consumed, burning for a week following.

St Faith, the patron saint of the ghost church (or Saint Foy, or Santa Fe), was a French girl from Aquitaine, who was tortured for her faith under the Emperor Diocletian. Miracles associated with St Faith are called '*joca*', the Latin for tricks or jokes. Ironically considering the fate of the vast quantity of books, brought as it were for her protection, St Faith was burnt to death on a red-hot brazier. No miracle but a sad, sick joke. Perhaps, after all, the booksellers should not have put so much faith in their patron saint.

I couldn't help wondering: was the manuscript of *Cardenio* destroyed in the fire in St Faith's?

Above: A statue of *El Príncipe de los Ingenios* – or 'The Prince of Wits' – Miguel de Cervantes in Alcalá de Henares, where he was born in 1547 (see page 11).

Left: Greg Doran, with his sister Ruth and the 'Bella Artes' gold medal, at the mosque in Cordoba, La Mezquita, 2006 (see page xvi).

The Burial of the Count of Orgaz by El Greco (c. 1586) in the Church of San Tomé (see page 130).

Left: *Henry, Prince of Wales* by Robert Peake the Elder (c. 1610). *Cardenio* may have been written by Shakespeare and Fletcher to celebrate a prospective marriage between Prince Henry and the Savoyard Infanta in 1613.

Right: *John Fletcher*, artist unknown (c. 1620), Shakespeare's collaborator on *Cardenio* (see page 203).

CARDENIO

NUNS

DOROTEA

PENITENTS

DON FERNANDO

Model box and costume designs for
Cardenio (RSC, 2011) by Niki Turner.

25

Betsy Baker's Pie Dishes

Humphrey Moseley left his business to his wife Anne, and a daughter (also called Anne), and they carried on his business after his death. But, of course, if he did have a copy of the manuscript of *Cardenio*, and his wife still possessed it after the restoration of the monarchy in 1660, there was then a very good reason that such a manuscript could have disappeared: the Great Fire of London.

However, much of Humphrey Moseley's collection of old play manuscripts and his copyrights came into the possession of a man called Henry Herringman (the first man to publish Dryden's works), and he had a reputation as a bookseller who actually profited from the Great Fire in which so many of his colleagues lost their stock. So perhaps *Cardenio* in his hands survived where so much else was destroyed. And if so what happened to it then?

Well, there is good news and bad news.

Many of Moseley's dramatic manuscripts were sold, some to Herringman, and some eventually came into the possession of one John Warburton.

Warburton was the Somerset Herald of Arms in Ordinary at the College of Arms. He was also a collector of old plays.

One day, he left a pile of fifty or so of these manuscript copies in his kitchen. A year later he came looking for them, only to discover that Betsy Baker, his cook, had used them all as either firelighters or as linings to the pie dishes. All of them had disappeared. One has to wonder why Warburton had left such a valuable pile of treasures in his kitchen.

Mortified, Warburton did at least have the grace to list the plays he thought the star-crossed pile contained. There are thirteen by Philip Massinger, as well as plays by Cyril Tourneur, John Ford, Robert Greene and Thomas Dekker. There's even one attributed to Marlowe, although the title, *The Maiden's Holiday*, sounds rather an unlikely subject for its author, a well-known hellraiser, atheist and spy.

As an act of vandalism it can scarcely be believed. And it clearly demonstrates just how easily these plays could become 'lost'. However, Warburton does also make mention of 'A Play by William Shakespeare' but does not elaborate. So if it survived the Globe Playhouse Fire in 1613, and the Great Fire of London, did *Cardenio* also survive Betsy Baker's pie dishes?

26

Filching from Fletcher

I need to fortify the script of *Cardenio*, but I must set myself some strict parameters. Antonio Álamo and I have gone as far as we can in extracting missing text from Cervantes. Now I will look for missing beats in Fletcher. Cervantes influenced many other plays in the Globe repertoire besides *Cardenio*. *The Exemplary Stories*, his collection of short stories, inspired a number of dramatised versions. John Fletcher himself seems to have been involved in writing several: *The Chances* is based in part on 'La señora Cornelia'; *Love's Pilgrimage* on 'Las dos doncellas'; *The Fair Maid of the Inn* might be from 'La ilustre fregona'. Then 'El amante liberal' emerges as *A Very Woman* by Fletcher and Massinger, and their bawdy *The Custom of the Country* seems to be derived from Cervantes' captivating romance *Persiles y Sigismunda*.

I have been re-reading these plays and decide I will allow myself to choose lines or phrases, or even whole speeches from any play that Fletcher wrote based on Cervantes. Or at least that will be my aim. That way, perhaps, I can retain a sense of linguistic integrity.

I find myself devouring Fletcher's plays. As they are not very readily available in Waterstone's, I have acquired most of them over the years in fairly tatty separate volumes of an edition published in 1812 in Edinburgh by Henry Weber, Esq. So I sit on the Tube, flicking through these wonderful old tomes, which smell of damp cellars, with their flaky spines, and torn marbled end-papers, their pages foxed and blotched and wavy, and am transported.

While I hugely enjoy reading these old plays, I realise that we are frankly unlikely to perform many of them at Stratford. But they still have marvellous passages. It may be cheating, but I feel no hesitation in plundering them for good lines. I feel a bit like a character in Act Three of *The Fair Maid of the Inn*, who is described as a 'pedant run almost mad with study' whose conversation is full of phrases 'out of old play ends'.

The Queen of Corinth has some dodgy sexual politics to our modern minds, and challenging gender issues, but it articulates the mental torment of a woman who, like Dorotea, has endured a rape. In one simple potent line she sums up her sense of being used: 'O, O, bitten, and flung away.'

In Act Two of this play the 'newly ravished' Merione cries:

> To whom now shall I cry? What power thus kneel to?
> And beg my ravished honour back to me?
> Deaf, deaf you gods of goodness, deaf to me?
> Deaf, Heaven, to all my cries; deaf hope, deaf justice,
> I am abused. And you that see all, saw it;
> Saw it and smiled upon the villain that did it:
> Saw it and gave him strength; why have I prayed to thee?

This seems to me to express perfectly Luscinda's frustration. Immured in a convent, she begins to doubt her faith. I borrow the lines virtually wholesale. And there is a reference in Act Four to a fool having a 'skull as empty as a sucked egg', and I pinch it straight away for one of the shepherds in the second half.

The Coxcomb, which derives its plot from 'The Curious Impertinent', the tale interwoven with Cardenio's story in *Don Quixote*, expresses close friendship between two young men, in a way which proves helpful in beefing up that element of our play.

Occasionally, I discover a line that fits so perfectly, it is as if it has been written for our play. In *Double Falshood*, we have had to invent a scene where Cardenio shows his friend, the treacherous Fernando, his beloved Luscinda. In the Cervantes story there is a rather complicated scene in which Luscinda throws a letter down to Cardenio concealed in a book. But I want Fernando's first sight of Don Bernardo's beautiful daughter to be more direct, and we have devised a piece of action where Luscinda and her father return in procession from benediction, with the duenna, and her ladies. Luscinda stumbles and drops her prayer book. As Fernando stoops to pick it up, her veil drops from her face.

Imagine my delight when, in a completely different context, I discovered this passage in *The Chances* (Act One, Scene Eleven), where Don Frederick, a Spanish gentleman, meets the Duke's mistress, Constantia, who removes her veil:

> Defend me
> Honest thoughts, I shall grow wild else.
> What eyes are there? What little heavens
> To stir men's contemplations! What a paradise
> Runs through each part she has. Good blood be
>   temperate.
> I must look off: too excellent an object
> Confounds the sense that sees it.

With no need to change a word, I drop it straight into the text.

Laurence Olivier chose to open Chichester Festival Theatre in 1962 with *The Chances*. Back then it may have been a disastrous choice, from a critical point of view, but it still contains some lively lines. One character in the play hushes his companion saying, 'Mum, there be bats abroad.' And another, when told by a doctor:

> I can cure you
> In forty days, if you shall not transgress me

replies:

> I have a dog shall lick me whole in twenty.
> Good man-mender, stop me with some parsley
> Like stuffed beef and let me walk abroad.

The Prologue to *The Chances*, added by another writer after his death, includes an interesting insight into our friend John Fletcher. It suggests that Fletcher's forte was not politics, or satire, and therefore we should not expect

> Objects of State, and now and then a rhyme,
> To gall particular persons with the time.

But it commends the play to the audience with a nice assessment of genial John, as himself 'a perfect comedy':

> Ingenious Fletcher made it, he
> Being in himself a perfect comedy.
> And some sit here, I doubt not, dare aver
> Living he made that house a Theatre
> Which he pleased to frequent.

I can picture Fletcher, a generous, big-hearted, sweet-natured, funny man, who could 'set the table on a roar'. I'm sure he wouldn't mind me filching some of his best lines.

So this is the fortified script, which I present somewhat nervously to my boss, Michael Boyd, artistic director of the company. 'It's a real page-turner,' Mike enthused, 'Shakespeare it ain't: but with a little more tweaking... it could be a runner.'

And then I get an unexpected opportunity to do a bit of tweaking, to have one more workshop on the script, when an invitation comes from Michigan University to participate in a creative residency.

27

The Michigan Residency

Spring comes late to Ann Arbor. A downy grey mist seems to hang over the clapboard houses on East Huron Street, as we make our way downtown to begin our next workshop on *Cardenio*. The University of Michigan has invited the RSC to conduct a residency on campus. This means that we get the opportunity to try out projects we have been working on and they get to have us around for a few days, popping into class, running workshops and talks, and so forth.

Michigan has been a vital supporter of the RSC over the years. Michael Boyd developed his first History cycle of *Henry VI* and *Richard III* here in 2001, generously supported by the university. We have brought a number of productions to the campus over three separate residencies including my own production of *Antony and Cleopatra* with Harriet Walter and Patrick Stewart in 2006.

This 'creative residency', as it has been termed, has been made possible by the extraordinary Professor Ralph Williams, who greets us now with his customary excitement. He has the brain of a Socrates, and the generosity of a Maecenas. He is as tall as an aspen tree and has the hands of a baseball player. A passionate humanist, with the manners of another age, his wit is as sparkling as his breadth of reference is legendary. In one short car journey between the airport and the university his conversation has ranged effortlessly from Petrarch's love for Beatrice, to the writings of Primo Levi in Auschwitz. He relishes language, and chooses his words with the precision of Henry James. A humble, kind and most delightful man.

We are concentrating on developing three scripts during the residency: a new play by Helen Edmundson about Sor Juana, the Mexican playwriting nun, whose play *The House of Desires* formed part of the RSC's Spanish Golden Age Season in 2004; a play I have been working on with David Edgar about the translation of the King James Bible, for the quatercentenary next year; and another look at *Cardenio*.

We are joined by actors from LAByrinth, a 'Latin-American Based' company in New York. For the *Cardenio* workshop I have a mixed cast. Cardenio is played by Raoul Castillo, a handsome dark-eyed actor from the Mexican border, with a wide smile and a rough rasp in his voice, which lends the role an earnest peasant quality, vulnerable to the sophisticated manipulation of Don Fernando (played by RSC actor Jamie Ballard). Luscinda is played by feisty Spanish speaker Emily Best, from New York. In one rehearsal they try the opening row between the lovers in Spanish, and the swift changes of direction and the volatility of their temperaments suddenly seems perfectly expressed.

Jason Olazabal, from Los Angeles, brings to Don Camillo a fiery Latin temper, which suggests why Cardenio is so intimidated by his father, and establishes a class difference between the two fathers. Don Bernardo is played with dripping disdain by our own Michael Hadley. LAB actors Trevor Long and Eric Cook are suddenly inspired in the public reading to make the shepherds Kentucky Hillbillies, which gives the scene a dark humour and a sense of menace worthy of the film *Deliverance*.

We've inserted a speech for Dorotea into the final scene, where she faces her abuser Fernando, as herself for the first time. It is taken directly from Cervantes, and gives extra weight (and complexity) to Dorotea's demand for the restitution of her rights as his spouse. It also negates the need for the absurd contrivance in *Double Falshood* that Dorotea is deemed worthy to be the wife of the Duke's son, simply because her father once saved his life when he was attacked by a wild boar.

Pippa Nixon, one of our English team, delivers the new speech with such integrity and honesty that it makes me catch my breath, and I determine two things on the spot; first that the speech solves something missing in the final scene, and secondly that Pippa has to play Dorotea if we finally get to a production.

But it is a long speech, longer than Shakespeare would be likely to use. Will it hold in performance?

The Michigan residency coincides with a lecture being given by Valerie Wayne of Hawaii University, under the somewhat daunting title of 'Metatextualities in the romance tradition of Shakespeare and Fletcher'. But it turns out to be a fascinating account of the influence of Cervantes on the drama of Shakespeare's period. I have already spotted that Beaumont's *The Knight of the Burning Pestle* has Quixotic borrowings, but am intrigued to hear just how influential the book was, even before Thomas Shelton's translation was published in 1612. Ben Jonson refers to *Don Quixote* in *Epicoene* and *The Alchemist*.

Professor Wayne talks with light erudition and wit about the eighteen-day visit of the Spanish delegation to London for a peace conference at Somerset House in August 1604, attended by the recently retitled 'King's Men' in their new livery. And of the subsequent embassy to Valladolid the following May, during which the Earl of Southampton, Shakespeare's patron (attending the Earl of Nottingham), bought some fifty books to send home, forty-nine of which were in Spanish. The Bodleian Library in Oxford acquired a copy of *Don Quixote* in the year of its publication in Madrid in 1605.

England apparently was a major importer of books in those days, but the trade did not go the other way as Europe was completely indifferent to English literature at this period.

Professor Wayne's conjecture that Fletcher himself may have spoken Spanish makes me prick up my ears. When I was directing his *The Island Princess* in the Swan in 2002, I had wondered how Fletcher might have read of the specific history of a spice island in the Moluccas colonised by the Portuguese, as there seemed to be no contemporary English account of that particular culture clash.

Apparently the drive among the English to speak Spanish at this time was similar to British business folk taking courses in Mandarin Chinese today. If Fletcher did speak Spanish then perhaps he could have read *Don Quixote* in the original, and would not have needed Thomas Shelton.

My partner Tony Sher, who has come over late to be part of the residency, and who was present at this afternoon's reading of the play, admits to me that evening that he feels it is still not firing on all cylinders. Something is wrong, and he can't quite put his finger on what it is. Perhaps the whole thing is nonsense, a sort of quixotic folly, and I should abandon it before I make a fool of myself.

28

Opening Programme

There is much debate about the programme to mark the opening in 2011 of the redeveloped Royal Shakespeare Theatre. The theatre was to have what was referred to as a soft opening from November 2010. Mike Boyd charged me with heading up the programming of that period. We needed some test events, for instance a licensing event, some preview performances, a 'Builders' Night', and, for one year only, we would move the annual carol concert into the theatre.

Then in early 2011 we would try out both the new RST and the refurbished Swan with productions from the previous year's ensemble company, followed by the new season opening productions. What would those be?

Everyone seemed to be in accord that a production directed by Michael Boyd himself should open the Main House, and that I should direct the opening production in the Swan. We have made further strides with the *Cardenio* script since Michigan, and I'm hoping to complete another draft during the summer. As the Swan had opened twenty-five years before, in 1986, with Shakespeare and Fletcher's *The Two Noble Kinsmen*, it would certainly be appropriate to reopen the theatre with our retelling of *Cardenio*.

But 2011 not only saw the twenty-fifth anniversary of the Swan, it would mark the fiftieth birthday of the company being awarded its Royal charter, and becoming the Royal Shakespeare Company under Peter Hall.

Moves were afoot to present a whole season in the new theatre representing a wide variety of new writing which the RSC had premiered over those fifty: from Pinter's *The Homecoming* to Peter Weiss's seminal *Marat/Sade*. And a whole range of other plays, from Peter Flannery's *Singer* to David Edgar's *Destiny*, were being discussed.

I was busy waving the flag for the repertoire for which the Swan was originally intended, works from 1570 to 1750, or 'the plays which influenced Shakespeare and which Shakespeare influenced'. I argued fiercely that we had neglected that audience now for some considerable time, and we should present a season of 'Swan plays'. Although we had managed in the years the Swan was open to mount most of the comedies of Ben Jonson, and all the major works of Christopher Marlowe and John Webster, we had hardly touched Kyd, Middleton or Ford, and only just begun to look at Fletcher, Massinger and Marston. The RSC have never yet done a play by Thomas Dekker or George Chapman, and at this rate, poor old Peele, Greene or Lyly were never going to make it.

I even tried suggesting a season of the kind of plays which reopened the theatres at the Restoration; Killigrew's *The Parson's Wedding*, or Shadwell's *Bury Fair*, or another Aphra Behn. Or what about the host of plays which followed: from Dryden's *All for Love*, to Rowe's *The Fair Penitent*, or Lillo's *The London Merchant*? Or a season relating to *Cardenio* such as Beaumont's anarchic *The Knight of the Burning Pestle*, and Middleton's *The Second Maiden's Tragedy* (with a little retitling), Fletcher's *The Custom of the Country*, or an adaptation of *Don Quixote* perhaps (I had found one by Bulgakov).

At one planning meeting, someone asked if I couldn't hold off *Cardenio* and do it the following year. At which point my head sank into my hands and I moaned that I had been trying to do this play for *eight years.* In the end a thoroughly British compromise was reached, and we decided to present a mixture of fiftieth-anniversary plays and an Elizabethan/Jacobean or Caroline piece. And yes, *Cardenio* would reopen the Swan.

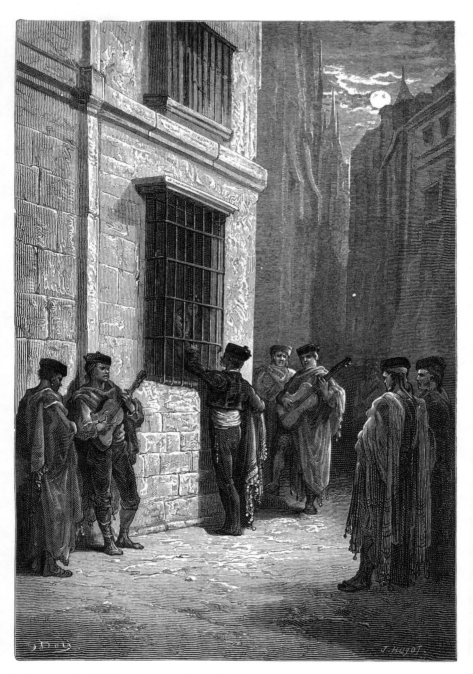

'A Seranata at Cordoba', from Gustave Doré's *Spain* (1876)

Part Three
Researching and Designing the Production

29

Preparing a Research Trip

Tuesday 13 July 2010

'Spain has been dancing for a month,' says Ann Bateson when I ring her in Madrid to congratulate her on her adopted country winning the World Cup last night. 'And I have some news too,' I say '*Cardenio* will open the Swan next April.' Ann is delighted, and promises to line up the mojitos for the next time we are over there. I tell her we have been invited to do a short research trip in the autumn, and ask her to help organise the visit.

Now the production is scheduled, I can assemble my creative team at last. I always start with the designer: in this case, Niki Turner, and, with their input, find a Lighting Designer (Tim Mitchell).

The composer is a crucial decision, and I am delighted Paul Englishby is free. I discovered, after having done two shows with Paul, that not only had he been brought up in Preston, like me, but that we went to the same school; he lived in the next village, and we even attended the same parish church. 'You know,' Paul said, 'we are listed on an internet site called *Famous People from Preston*.' I checked.

And there we both are, and in prestigious company, along-side Peter Purves from *Blue Peter*, Roy Barraclough from *Coronation Street*, and Nick Park, the inventor of the sublime *Wallace and Gromit*.

We start making arrangements for our research trip. Niki Turner is free to come, but we can't make the dates work for Paul Englishby.

So to compensate for missing the trip, I send Paul a double CD of music, which I was given when we were in Spain with *Coriolanus*. It is by the musical genius Jordi Savall and his ensemble, La Capella Reial de Catalunya. It is a recording of a concert they gave to celebrate the four hundredth anniversary of the publication of *Don Quixote* in 2005. There are readings from the novel, interspersed with music from the period. Some are settings of poems by Cervantes himself. One in particular catches my attention. It is a song about Palinurus, the navigator of Aeneas's ship, who fell overboard in a storm and was lost. The song, sung on the CD by Savall's son Ferran, is called *Love's Mariner*. It is achingly beautiful and it fits our story perfectly. It could be *Cardenio*'s theme tune. I hope Paul will feel inspired by it.

In preparation for the trip, I have also been looking at Gustave Doré's illustrations for *Don Quixote*. I have always been fascinated by Doré's engravings. My Auntie Mary and Uncle Bob in Slaithwaite had a huge old Victorian tome of Dante's *Inferno* with illustrations by Doré. Whenever we went over to Huddersfield for Christmas or Easter, I would ask to see it, and sit absorbed for hours staring at Doré's terrifying illustrations of the circles of Hell and their tortured inhabitants.

Doré's illustrations for *Don Quixote* hold a similar fascination for me now. Before he began his work on Cervantes, Doré travelled throughout Spain in the 1860s. He was accompanied by his friend, the Baron Jean Charles Davillier, who wrote a book about their travels, which Doré illustrated. He sketches bull fights in Seville, and gypsies dancing flamenco in the grottoes of Sacromonte. Here is the mournful magnificence of the Escorial, the great Alcazar of Toledo, the horseshoe arches of the Mezquita mosque in Cordoba, and shifty-looking tourists in Granada chipping azulejos tiles out of the Alhambra. He draws everything, from a shepherd in Extremadura to a procession of penitents in their white pointed hoods.

Serenatas in Spain

As I read Davillier's account of their journey through Andalucía, several interesting descriptions leap out. They might be very useful in trying to deepen our understanding of the story of *Cardenio*. For example, Davillier describes the serenata of Cordoba, and Doré illuminates the scene.

> If Cordoba is silent and dreary during the daytime, it seems to awake partially from its repose to listen to the serenades at night. This serenading appeared to us nothing more than a sort of amusing pleasantry... not so with the Andalucíans; to them the guitar is a noble instrument, and its jerking notes are listened to with melodramatic seriousness. A Spanish poet touchingly enquires 'what would an Englishman, Dane or Swede do to convince a lady of his adoration? Would he willingly deprive himself of a night's rest? But with us behold the difference! A majo [young dandy], guitar in hand, his mantle tossed negligently over his shoulder, sings and sighs his love patiently beneath a balcony, regardless of weather; he waits until daybreak, dreading the frown of his lady-love should he quit his post a moment too soon.

Apparently Andalucíans have another expression for characterising ardent lovers with their heads bent to the bars of the grille of their beloved's window: '*mascar hierro*' [to chew iron]. Davillier goes on to include a number of the classic serenatas, or *coplas de ventas* [window couplets] which are sung on these occasions:

> *Cuerpo bueno! Alma divina!*
> *Que de fatigas me cuestas!*
> *Despierta, si estás dormida,*
> *Y alivia por Dios, mi pena!*

[Rare beauty! Divine one! What trouble is mine! Wake,
if thou sleepest, and for God's sake my sorrows allay!]

Or:

La paloma está en la cama
Arropadita y caliente
Y el palomo está en la esquina
Dándose diente con diente.

[The dove is in bed, snugly wrapped up, while the
pigeon waits in the street, cold and gnashing his teeth.]

I'll send these verses to Paul Englishby. They may be useful
in developing the kind of music that Fernando brings with
him to serenade Dorotea in Act One of *Cardenio*.

In his book about his travels through Spain with Gustave
Doré, Baron Davillier describes his journey north by train
from Cordoba through the Sierra Morena mountains. This
is the journey I did back in 2006 in reverse, heading to pick
up a gold medal from the King of Spain.

> The railway runs through frightful gorges and along the
> verge of high precipices. A celebrated spot, where these
> gorges are contracted so as to darken the route, is called
> Despeñaperros.

Doré's illustration, *The Defile of Despeñaperros*, gives a
giddy sense of the epic scale of the rugged terrain, which he
was to draw upon later when illustrating Don Quixote's
trek through the Sierra Morena, where he encounters
Cardenio.

The Baron then quotes an earlier French compatriot, who
had travelled in these parts. His name was Voiture (an
uncommonly appropriate name for a French traveller), and
he was a great letter writer. In one such letter he writes:

> Three days ago I saw in the Sierra Morena the place
> where Cardenio and Don Quixote met, and the same
> evening I supped at the venta [inn] where the
> adventures of Dorotea ended.

'The Defile of Despeñaperros in the Sierra Morena', from Gustave Doré's *Spain* (1876)

Davillier comments: 'These lines, written seventeen years after the death of Cervantes, show how his immortal fiction was already accounted a genuine history.'

Later Davillier continues:

> A quarter of an hour after we had left the Despeñaperros, we passed the Venta de Cardenas. In spite of its sonorous name, the place only consists of two common buildings, used as granary, inn and stable. After interrogating the people as to any traditions belonging to it, all we could discover was that the venta was also known as the Melancotones – Melons – a name given to the proprietor of the estate. As to Cardenio and Luscinda, Cervantes' heroes, they said they knew nothing about such people; they had not been there lately.

I tracked Davillier and Doré's journey through the Sierra Morena on Google Earth. Off the main road through the Sierra Morena, there was a sort of lay-by, which the map indicated was Venta de Cardenas. I pondered whether we had time in our brief research trip to travel down there and check out whether it still existed. I decided that if Doré and Davillier found no trace of Cervantes' characters there one hundred and fifty years ago, we would be unlikely to find anything very useful after the lapse of further one hundred and fifty.

30

El Greco in Toledo

The Vincci Hotel, Gran Via, Madrid

Niki Turner was probably a Victorian lady adventuress in another life, trekking up mountains in her bustle, collecting rhododendrons. Since we first worked together (on an adaptation by Biyi Bandele of Aphra Behn's *Oroonoko* which Niki designed at The Other Place theatre in Stratford in 1999), I have received postcards from Niki from all corners of the globe, from Jordan to Belize. And I haven't seen her for a few years. When the lift door at the Vincci open I am reminded of what a beauty she is, with bags of individuality and flare. There are a few more laugh lines than when I last saw her, but fewer than the grey hairs that have sprouted in my beard in the intervening years.

Now she and her partner have settled down in Wiltshire, and had kids, and live in what I imagine is a big rambling house with a messy garden. She is determined to find a good manchego cheese during her brief Spanish visit, to send as Christmas presents, with her home-made quince jelly.

If Niki Turner is posh, Ann Bateson is common as brass tacks. She's from Northallerton, and has the good sense and love for life that characterises her county. Being with Ann is like breathing lungfuls of Yorkshire Dales air. A good laugh is never far away. I first met Ann when a production of *Titus Andronicus* I directed with Tony, at the Market Theatre in Johannesburg, toured to the Almagro Festival in La Mancha in 1995. Ann was then working for the British Council in Spain and it was her job to keep a rowdy South African company sober until the show started at eleven o'clock at night.

Since then Ann has worked freelance, and has set up her own English-speaking radio station in Madrid. She has been the fixer for our research trip to Spain.

Toledo

Toledo is to Spain what Kyoto is to Japan: it is a national treasure-house of history and culture.

I feel as if I already know Toledo, from the famous painting by El Greco, with its violent menace of sky, painted at exactly the time that Cervantes published *Don Quixote*. In the cathedral we buy iPod tours (partly because I want to know how they work, as I have recorded just such a tour for the new RST in Stratford), but I get bored with it, and set off at my own pace. I can't quite put my finger on why the cathedral fails to ignite a sense of the majestic antiquity of Old Spain that I was expecting, but Niki puts her finger on it. As she peers at one of the forest of pillars which soar to Gothic heights, she says, 'It's been painted.' The whole cathedral has been decorated, with the worn stone given a make-over in dove grey, which for me robs the place of its character.

But it is El Greco's painting of *The Burial of the Count of Orgaz*, in the church of San Tomé, which I most want to see. I can immediately understand why he called it 'my sublime work'. Its subject matter is gloriously absurd: the deceased Count in gilded armour is being lifted by the mitred St Augustine and the youthful St Stephen towards a crowded Heaven, where Christ and his mother wait to receive him. An angel with the wings of a great herring gull gently ushers the wispy spirit of the Count towards the celestial light, which reminds me of one of my favourite lines from the play:

> When lovers swear true faith, the listening angels
> Stand on the golden battlements of Heaven
> And waft their vows to the eternal throne.

El Greco was reproached by the Spanish Inquisition for contravening the canon law in the way he painted angels' wings.

King Philip II, although not actually dead at this point, is featured among the hordes of saints awaiting the pious young Count's ascension, while, below, a rank of be-ruffled faces look on. One splays his long white fingers in a gesture of ironic revelation, while another raises limpid brown eyes to the clouds. Only two of the faces stare out of frame right at you. One is probably El Greco himself; the other, a little boy downstage-right pointing at the corpse, is thought to be the painter's son, Jorge Manuel.

This child appears in another painting, which I saw in the Museo Provincial de Bellas Artes while in Seville. But there he's a handsome young man in his early twenties and carries a small palette in one hand and a brush in the other, poised to apply the final flourish. He followed his father into the profession. He wears an enormous ruff and a bright twinkle in his eye.

All the men in their jet-black doublets and organza ruffs look so awfully noble and so awfully Spanish, that Niki and I agree we must try and replicate their proud perpendicularity in the costumes for *Cardenio*.

Shakespeare knew of Toledo for its reputation for making the best swords in Europe. It is probably a blade from Toledo that Othello has concealed in his chamber:

> I have another weapon in this chamber;
> It is a sword of Spain, the ice-brook's temper.

Mercutio mentions the swords of Spain in the Queen Mab speech:

> Sometime she driveth o'er a soldier's neck,
> And then dreams he of cutting foreign throats,
> Of breaches, ambuscados, Spanish blades!

Oddly enough, when Baron Davillier refers to Mercutio's speech, in his travel diary, he quotes from what is presumably a French translation of the time: 'Toledo's trusty, of which a soldier dreams.'

The Escorial

Today, Niki, Ann and I visit the grim grey granite palace. The grid-like monastery-fortress was built by Philip II in the hills to the north-west of Madrid. As we walk up from the bus station through avenues of horse-chestnuts, burnished golden in the autumn sunlight, I find a little jingle running in my head:

> Love-light of Spain – hurrah!
> Death-light of Africa!
> Don John of Austria
> Is riding to the sea.

I don't know when these lines first seeped into my brain. I don't think it was a poem I had to learn at school. But I am sure I was caught in its thrilling rhythm before I ever realised what the piece was actually about. Lines like 'Dim drums throbbing, in the hills half-heard' create such a sense of tension and excitement and held breath. I have since remembered that they come from G.K. Chesterton's poem 'Lepanto' celebrating Don John of Austria's triumphal naval victory over the Ottoman Turks in 1571: a poem that demands to be spoken out loud.

One verse in *Lepanto* contrasts action-man hero Don John with the fungal pallor of King Philip II shut up in the Escorial:

> King Philip's in his closet with the Fleece about his neck
> (Don John of Austria is armed upon the deck.)
> The walls are hung with velvet that is black and soft as sin,
> And little dwarfs creep out of it and little dwarfs creep in.

It's baroque in its depiction of the decaying Spanish King, and it's almost comic book in its thrill at the fury of the sea battle:

> Don John pounding from the slaughter-painted poop,
> Purpling all the ocean like a bloody pirate's sloop...

I went back to the poem last week to see how much of it I remembered, and came across a line which obviously had not registered on my young brain. In the last verse Chesterton says:

> Cervantes on his galley sets his sword back in the sheath
> (Don John of Austria rides homeward with a wreath.)
> And he sees across a weary land a straggling road in Spain,
> Up which a lean and foolish knight for ever rides in vain,
> And he smiles, but not as sultans smile, and settles
> back the blade...
> (But Don John of Austria rides home from the Crusade.)

Yes, Miguel Cervantes fought at the battle of Lepanto. In fact, as he was suffering from malaria, he should not have been fighting at all: he had been told by his captain to stay below. Instead, he positioned himself at the head of twelve men in a fighting skiff, alongside the galley ship, *La Marquesa*, in a sea tinged red with blood. He was shot three times in the chest, and lost the use of his left arm. His valour was later recognised by Don John, who visited him in the army hospital, and wrote letters of recommendation on his behalf. He was twenty-three.

As we purchase our tickets to enter the Escorial, Chesterton's poem keeps ringing in my ears.

Wandering through this cheerless palace, we arrive at Philip's bedroom; the sombre little cell where he died in agony, his ulcerating body unable to bear the weight of even a single sheet. It isn't hung with velvet now, 'black and soft as sin', and the dwarves that Velázquez painted so frequently and whose portraits now hang on the walls of the Prado, no longer creep out and in. And I am disappointed to find that the crowned skull he kept by his bedside is no longer there.

At the far end of the room is a small window from where the sickly monarch could watch the services being conducted on the high altar of the echoing marble basilica below. Philip died early in the morning of 13 September 1598, as the seminary boys were singing the dawn mass, 'the last service held for his health, and the first for his salvation'.

The Pudridero is a rotting chamber, where the corpses of nearly every Spanish monarch since Philip have been left to decompose before being deposited in the Kings' pantheon. Unsurprisingly it is not open to visitors. Ann tells us that the present King Juan Carlos's father is still in there. We descend past it, into the sepulchral gloom of a circular vault. It houses the bodies of the kings and queens of Spain, Hapsburg or Bourbon, racked on shelves, in bronze and blue marble coffins.

At the end of several chilly chambers in this necropolis-palace there is a white marble tomb like an iced cake, carved with the image of the hero of Lepanto, the young Don John of Austria himself. Here he is, handsome in death, surprisingly slight, gripping the Toledo sword with which perhaps he signalled his ships to plunge into the smoke of the Turkish lines at Lepanto.

In fact Don John died tragically young: not in the roar of battle, but, like the young Prince Henry of England after him, of typhoid. He was just thirty. His legend is enhanced by miraculous events, such as the crucifix he had with him at Lepanto, which he later presented to Barcelona Cathedral. Christ's body is contorted, it is said, from twisting to escape a cannon ball during the famous battle.

As we wander round this humourless mausoleum of a palace, I get a profound sense of death as a central theme in Spanish life. This persistent flavour of mortality gives me a strong sense of the opening of *Cardenio*, where the Duke Ricardo, contemplating his imminent death with a steady gaze, tells his son not to grieve.

We leave the pantheons of the dead infantas, and head back into the cloisters. The vast spectacular mural painted by Luca Giordano on the vault of the Main Staircase of the

Escorial, depicts the then King, Carlos II, at the end of the next century, pointing to the apotheosis of King Philip II as he is welcomed into Heaven, surrounded by vast hordes of saints and angels in a vortex of pink and golden clouds. Carlos looks for all the world as if he is commenting blithely on a particularly charming sunset, and indeed in a way he is, for the sun had set by then upon *The Glory of Spanish Monarchy* as this baroque masterpiece is known. For with Philip II, the Spanish empire died also, the empire he had ruled over for so long slipping into decadence and losing its influence and grip, as the Inca and Aztec gold from its South American empires was frittered away.

The high point of Don John's glorious victory over the Ottoman Empire at the Battle of Lepanto should have been matched by trouncing the upstart English with a magnificent Spanish Armada in 1588, but instead, their defeat at the hands of Queen Elizabeth's ships marked the start of a slow decline.

Alcalá de Henares

Around the town square, La Plaza de Cervantes, white storks nest on the rooftops, clattering their bills at each other. They are symbols of luck and prosperity in Spain.

Gustave Doré's travelling companion, Baron Davillier, calls Alcalá de Henares 'the learned city, the ancient rival of Salamanca'. Don Carlos (famously the subject of Schiller's play and Verdi's opera), the son of Philip II, was a student here. He fell down a staircase and received injuries which dogged him for the rest of his life. His father, the King, rushed to Alcalá bringing with him the corpse of a Franciscan monk, the blessed Diego, which was reputed to effect miraculous cures. The dead body was then laid on top of poor ailing Don Carlos, who, says Davillier, 'happily escaped death'. But how did he escape the trauma of being nearly smothered by a dead Franciscan, I wonder?

Davillier and Doré visited the church of Santa Maria la Mayor, where he was baptised. And they were also shown the house where Cervantes was born. Today we visit it too.

Cervantes' birthplace is just about as authentic as Shakespeare's in Henley Street. It stands on the corner of a pleasant little street in Alcalá. The convent his sister entered as a nun is just around the corner. On a bench in the pedestrianised street outside the house sits the ubiquitous figure of Don Quixote in bronze with Sancho Pança sitting next to him, carving a slice of ham.

Juan Sanz Ballesteros, a theatre designer, who has helped to give Cervantes' House a sense of atmosphere, is our guide as we walk around it. Fired up by the idea of producing *Cardenio*, I make notes about the shady courtyard with its linen canopy drawn against the sunlight; about the rather stiff little parlour with its upright chairs, and leather hangings, stamped to make them look as if they are woven; the fascinating low wooden braziers which would have warmed every room; the women's room on the first floor, with its carpeted dais, spread with cushions, its spinning wheel, mandolin, marquetry chests and escritoires; and the child's room with its little altar to the Virgin Mary; all very useful material in trying to stage *Cardenio*.

Across the courtyard landing, in the exhibition room, there are copies of Cervantes' famous novel, from every intervening century, and in many different languages. Ann calls me over to one display case.

'Look!' she hisses. Thomas Shelton's 1612 *Don Quixote* is open at the very start of the Cardenio episode. Ann grins. 'It's a good omen.'

But the most special visit we made in Alcalá de Henares was to the theatre. When our guide Juan, a native of the town, was a young man in his twenties, he and a friend were poking around the dusty old building which they had known as a cinema since they were boys and discovered that behind the eighteenth-century galleries lay the remains of a courtyard corral theatre from the Golden Age of Spanish drama, from the time of Cervantes himself.

With the pride of a parent, Juan showed us round the now restored space, from the pebbles of the original courtyard, to the trap doors, wind machines, and thunder rolls still intact under the boards of the seventeenth-century stage. What a find. It was in a corral theatre such as this that Cervantes would have seen his early plays performed, and which must have staged the works of his contemporaries, Calderón de la Barca, Tirso de Molina and the prolific Lope de Vega.

The men sat or stood in one area of the theatre and the women crowded together in the galleries above. I wonder how this affected the audience reaction to the plays presented. Of course *Cardenio* was not devised as a play by Cervantes. But if it had been, I wonder how the audience would have divided in their reaction to Fernando's seduction of Dorotea. His question (as it appears in *Double Falshood*) 'Was it rape then?' would carry a potent charge in a segregated theatre like the corral at Alcalá.

Back in Madrid, that night, and at the end of our research trip, we make our way out to find something to eat. In a huge open market, Niki finds her manchego cheese, a great satisfying roundel, yellow and humming of La Mancha, which she triumphantly carries off. As we cross the Plaza Mayor, we are accosted by a street performer dressed in what looks like a dwarf Christmas tree with a goat's skull which snaps at us. It is weirdly modern and ancient at the same time.

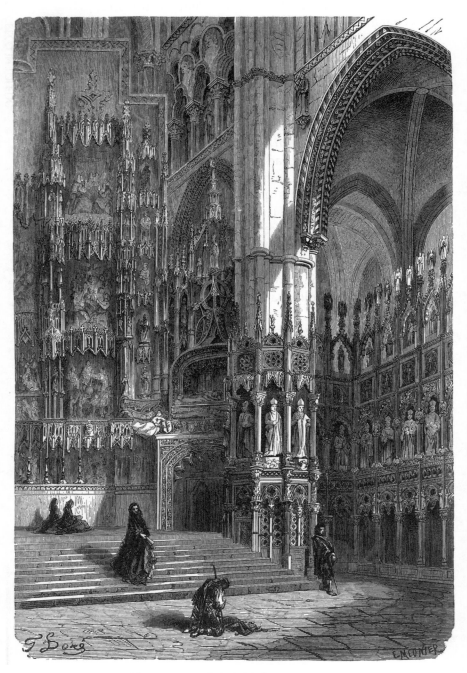

'Interior of Toledo Cathedral', from Gustave Doré's *Spain* (1876)

31

Bonfire Night

Friday 5 November 2010

It's an important weekend for the RSC. On Sunday we are having the first sneak preview of the new theatre. We have invited anyone within the company to come and fill the auditoria in both the Swan and the newly redeveloped RST, so that we can practise a full emergency evacuation of the theatres, and hopefully be granted our licence. I have devised what happens onstage, but I suspect the evacuation itself will upstage anything we do.

This morning I am meeting Niki Turner to discuss the design of *Cardenio*.

I haven't seen Niki since we returned from our research trip to Spain in October. She has brought me some medlars from her garden near Bath. They are the most Shakespearian of fruit. Mercutio refers to them by their expressive country name 'open-arses'. And looking at them in their cardboard punnet, all rude and russet, and full of mellow fruitfulness, we decide they look like a Spanish still-life painting by Zurburán.

There is a large model box on the table surrounded by little cardboard cut-outs and pieces of Perspex and bubble wrap. The model box represents the Swan Theatre, in 1:25 scale. It gives me a huge lift to see it. The Swan has been closed since 2007 when the redevelopment began. It is my favourite theatre. I did my first Shakespeare for the company in this space, and have since been lucky enough to direct some dozen plays here, from *All's Well That Ends Well* to Ben Jonson's *Sejanus*.

There is always a nerve-wracking moment when you first look at what the designer has placed in the box for you to see. What if they've got it completely wrong or you hate it? Generally I am surprised, and often relieved, but today I'm positively thrilled. Niki understands the space. She knows that the theatre itself resists too much set, that it won't be ignored for itself. We did a production of Fletcher's *The Island Princess* in the Swan as part of the Jacobethan season in 2002. Because of the quick change-overs from one play to the next, necessitated by a rapidly changing repertoire, the sets were minimal, but Niki managed to evoke the rich aroma of the Spice Islands with a few fretwork arches, and diaphanous drapes.

We settle in front of the model box. I love this bit of my job. We have the whole morning to sit and play. Perhaps it excites something of our childhood fascination for dolls' houses and train sets. For me it recalls the Pollock's Theatre I used to play with for hours as a child.

There are lots of references to things we saw in Spain: the great altar screen in Toledo Cathedral; the faces from the magnificent El Greco painting *The Burial of the Count of Orgaz*; the capering characters from Goya's haunting picture *The Burial of the Sardine*; or the brooding menace of his black paintings in the Prado. The window grilles in Alcalá de Henares and the household brazier from Cervantes' birthplace.

Niki and her RSC design assistant (Lily Arnold) have modelled up various elements, sometimes quite roughly, and sometimes with wonderful ingenuity: the base of one of the little chairs is a small coin; the crown on the tiny statue of the Virgin Mary is a bead; and the water jug on the table is cut from a length of plastic piping.

We push things around the box, throw things out, and introduce new elements. Her design allows me a lot of flexibility, while at the same time creating the social stratification of the society so particularly described in Cervantes' novel.

After a couple of hours, we give our production manager Mark Graham a call. I first worked with Mark as far back as 1992 when I directed Homer's *The Odyssey* in Derek Walcott's adaptation in The Other Place. He is endlessly resourceful, and tireless in his pursuit of clever ways to make the impossible possible. We chat him through the story, and how we think the set might be used. There are lots of things to solve: how to string up something in mid-air over the audience's head; how to create at least the illusion of candles or firecrackers; how maybe to have a metal floor, without the edges curling up and slicing people's toes, as he knows can happen from past experience.

Then we head over to the Swan, which like the rest of the building is being hastily prepared for Sunday's event. I can't help grinning. It's like recognising an old friend. Niki is grinning too. And I can really begin to see the production now. I can imagine just how the play will work in this space. It is going to be a real thrill to kick off our fiftieth-birthday season with the extraordinary tale of Cervantes' madman, the crazy Cardenio.

32

A Letter to Bouncy, in Madrid

I've worked with movement director and choreographer Mike Ashcroft many times. I can't remember who first called him 'Bouncy' but the nickname captures something of his indefatigable energy and irrepressible spirit. He choreographed Fletcher's *The Tamer Tamed* for me in the Swan in 2003, and created a real showstopper of a dance number, as all the women of London Town join with Petruchio's second wife Maria to assert their rights, in a song called 'The women must wear the breeches'.

Because Mike was in Madrid, choreographing a new production of *Los Miserables*, I had to write him a letter to give him some idea of the kinds of things I was looking for in our production of *Cardenio*:

Dear Mike,

I am enclosing a draft of *Cardenio* for you to read. As I said, the original play was based on an episode in Cervantes' great novel *Don Quixote*. *Double Falshood*, the eighteenth-century adaptation, has lost its Spanish guts. I want to put the Iberian 'cojones' back into the play!

There is a scene (which we've had to invent) where the heroine, Dorotea, is seduced by the villain Don Fernando. He gets into her room, and effectively rapes her. Meanwhile, the fiesta (which he has paid for, to bribe the villagers and win them over) is taking place in the street below. I want this to get faster and faster, and begin to express or parody the sex act that is taking place upstairs.

I have been reading Gerald Brenan's book, *South from Granada*, where he describes his life in Spain after the First World War. He is very good at detailing the rituals, dances and small village life of Spain.

He also describes the use of peleles, 'or dummies that have been stuffed with straw and which often had a sexual or bacchic significance. Phalluses made of sausages would be placed in appropriate positions; female bodies would be bellied out with pumpkins and calabashes and decorated with strings of figs... Other dummies would be hung up on ropes stretched across the street, and in the evening would all be set on fire and burned with great cackling of homemade fireworks and loudly shouted insults and obscenities.'

I can imagine a great carnival where we string up some rude dummies in the middle air of the Swan and make them jig about obscenely, as people dance beneath them. And Niki Turner (who is designing) has notions of creating crackers, and fireworks and candles and lanterns to illuminate this scene.

But if you have any time in Madrid go and see the 'Black' Goyas in the Prado, which express this sense of superstition and darkness, and if you can find it, look for his fiesta painting *The Burial of the Sardine* in the Real Academia de Bellas Artes de San Fernando. It's full of men dressed as women, masked devils and demonic dancing. Inspirational.

Perhaps we should start off the fiesta with a wonderful singer who can really belt out the *cante jondo*, or 'flamenco' singing, and then maybe a couple start to dance and then it all gets really wild. I have some great descriptions in Jan Morris's *Spain* (the best book I know about Spain), in which she talks of the dancing and singing of the Sacromonte gypsies from Granada, and their zing, their flare and their unutterable nerve. And she describes a fantastic night when a singer she had got to know 'soon led us from the sad cante jondo into the most raucous kind of flamenco, and before long the whole room was an uproar of violent clapping, clicked fingers, wild laughs, and cries, stamped feet, ear-splitting songs and side-splitting witticisms'. That's the kind of energy I want to release onto the stage, but darker perhaps.

Anyway, I am buzzing with thoughts about how to create an authentic sense of the Iberian world of seventeenth-century Andalucía, from the stiff formality of the Court, to the restricted courtship of Luscinda and Cardenio's world (constantly conducted through an iron grille), to the farmer's daughter's world that Dorotea inhabits with its beehives, lace-making, olive and almond trees and rustic simplicity; to finally the world of the shepherds, with their own traditions, songs and instruments.

And I would love to finish the show with a great company dance too.

Sorry for all the random thoughts, but hope that's a start to get you going!

Love Greg.

PS. I am still haunted by the weird goat man Niki and I saw one night in the Plaza Mayor in Madrid, snapping his jaws in a frenetic jabber. I'm sure it could be part of our frightening black fiesta!

'The Aragonese Jota', from Gustave Doré's *Spain* (1876)

33

Opening the New RST

Tuesday 9 November 2010

This Sunday we opened the new Royal Shakespeare Theatre in Stratford-upon-Avon. We held an event, a sort of sneak preview, in order to obtain our licence.

I had been given the job of organising the onstage entertainment. We had closed the theatre in 2007 with a single special performance in which a line or a speech from every Shakespeare play was each performed by an actor who had graced that stage over the years. So I decided that the first words of Shakespeare in the new theatre should be spoken by the next generation of actors who will inherit this great new Globe. I invited students from the Conference of Drama Schools, hosted by their president, Janet Suzman, to open the show with 'O for a muse of fire'.

We reopened the Swan simultaneously with Jaques's 'Seven Ages of Man' speech from *As You Like It*. Cis Berry, our Head of Voice, spoke the opening words, 'All the world's a stage...', followed by actress Rebecca Johnson holding her infant son, Robbie, who represented the first age. He luckily refrained from mewling or puking and ultimately stole the show. One of the young actors playing Mamillius in our current production of *The Winter's Tale* was the whining school boy; an ex-Prince in the Tower from Mike Boyd's recent History Cycle was the lover, and so on until Clifford Rose (who was an actor in the original RSC company fifty years ago, and still often appears with us) represented the 'lean and slippered pantaloon', and finally John Barton, the distinguished RSC advisory director, rose and delivered the lines about the last age 'in this strange eventful history'. Now approaching his eighty-second birthday, John has no trace of second-childishness about him.

Later on, one of the CDS students, Alex Cobb, invited me to see him in one of his final shows at RADA. They are doing a production of *The Second Maiden's Tragedy*.

This morning, as I was lying in my bath, Tony called up from the kitchen. 'There's a review for *Cardenio* in the *Guardian*.'

'What!' I splutter, my hair and eyes full of shampoo.

He brings it up for me to read. Michael Billington is reviewing a production of the very same play that Alex is doing at RADA, at the Croydon Warehouse. But whereas RADA have called it *The Tyrant*, Croydon Warehouse are calling it *Cardenio*.

I had heard that they were doing the play, and guess I am not all that surprised at their decision to retitle it. It's not the first time that this play has been presented as *Cardenio*, following the spurious claims by an American called Charles Hamilton, who decided that this was Shakespeare's lost play, and in 1994 published it under this title. It is not, of course. It has practically nothing to do with *Cardenio*, although it is based on a tale which occurs within the history of Cardenio in *Don Quixote*, the story of 'The Curious Impertinent'.

The manuscript of this play (in the British Library) is missing its title page but someone has scribbled a title on the cover by which it has always since been known: *The Second Maiden's Tragedy*. This is possibly because they thought it was a second part of Beaumont and Fletcher's *The Maid's Tragedy*. It is now thought to be by Middleton, and has been retitled *The Lady's Tragedy*, after the lead character who is called simply 'the Lady'.

We are about to put next season's brochure to bed. The print deadline is tomorrow. Have we got the title right? And what about the all-important byline?

Jeanie O'Hare, the RSC's dramaturg, Jeremy Adams, our producer, and I have been struggling with this. I don't want to call the production *Double Falshood* because although Theobald's play is the backbone of the production, it is not the whole story. We can't call it *The History of Cardenio* by Mr Fletcher and Shakespeare, the title Humphrey Moseley registered for publication in 1653, because we know it isn't. We have, however, included what we are sure are the missing scenes, by adapting them from Shelton's 1612 translation of Cervantes' novel, but if we include all those names it will look like the credit sequence for a Hollywood blockbuster. Surely we should just call it *Cardenio*, and include the subtitle 'Shakespeare's Lost Play Reconstructed'; that way we acknowledge the initial instigation for the project, and declare precisely what it is: not the lost play, but a reconstruction of it. But that sounds too pompous, and frankly too authoritative. This debate is going to run and run.

Michael Boyd then proposes that we put inverted commas around the words lost play, and then the scrupulous Jeanie, at the last minute, has a stroke of genius, and suggests that we call it 'Shakespeare's "Lost Play" Re-imagined'. It's the perfect word to describe what we are doing and allows the creative process to be acknowledged. And that's what we decide to print.

Now all I've got to do is cast and rehearse this play. But I am still anxious to know if the script is working properly. As we have a long rehearsal period, perhaps there is time to get it right.

'A Shepherd of Extremadura', from Gustave Doré's *Spain* (1876)

Part Four

Re-imagining *Cardenio*

34

'Spoiled for an Actor': John Downes

In 1728, in the preface to the first edition of *Double Falshood*, Lewis Theobald clarified how he came to have discovered what he calls 'this dear relic'. 'One of the manuscripts which I have,' he writes, 'is of above sixty years standing, in the handwriting of Mr Downes, the old famous prompter.' Who was this Mr Downes?

Imagine the scene. It is Tuesday 2 July 1661. An indoor tennis court in Lincoln's Inn Fields has been converted into a theatre, and Sir William Davenant's *The Siege of Rhodes* (*Part Two*) is being staged. It has just opened. Young Thomas Betterton is playing the great Ottoman Sultan, Suleyman the Magnificent, and Betterton's wife appears as the heroine Ianthe. Everyone is here. Samuel Pepys has ridden over in his coach from his singing lesson, and records the scene. There is tremendous excitement because the King himself, recently returned from exile in France, restored to the throne and crowned Charles II, is about to arrive. It is the first time he has ever attended a public playhouse.

While the audience is waiting, just above Pepys, a board breaks in the ceiling over their heads: 'we had a great deal of dust fell into the ladies' necks and the men's hair, which made good sport.' Amidst this laughter the Royal party arrives.

Pepys continues: 'The king being come, the scene opened; which indeed is very fine and magnificent.' It is also a great novelty – for the theatre, unlike the open-air playhouses such as the Globe, has painted scenery. A backdrop reveals the whole harbour of the Mediterranean island of Rhodes. This is something splendid.

The action proceeds and the character of the eunuch, Haly, appears onstage. The music finishes, and he stands there ready to speak. His mouth opens but nothing comes out. He can see the King, and the Duke of York, and the whole assembly of London's finest and best. The lamps flicker and the house goes silent expecting him to begin. His mouth dries, his brain swims and panic seizes his chest and throat. The full house puts him into a sweat, a tremendous agony of nerves. The King, the Duke of York, all the nobility. The august presence simply drives his lines from his head, and he can do nothing but gape. Davenant in the wings must have been clenching his fists in fury. And then the hissing starts.

Every actor can relate to the heart-stopping terror of forgetting your lines. It's like drowning. I recall playing Octavius, in Terry Hands's production of *Julius Caesar*, when I first joined the RSC as an actor in 1987. One midweek matinee, in the parley before the battle of Philippi, I completely dried. Roger Allam, playing Brutus, gave me a wan smile of such abject pity that I determined there and then that acting was not for me.

The poor soul playing the Eunuch in 1661 was that same John Downes, who, ironically, went on to be what Theobald calls 'a famous prompter'.* Writing nearly fifty years later,

---

* There is a strange little footnote to this story. In the Royal party, witnessing poor John Downes's humiliation that afternoon at the Lincoln's Inn Theatre, was the King's aunt, the Queen of Bohemia, the Winter Queen herself. Now sixty-five, Elizabeth Stuart had been the young Princess at Whitehall, in that Christmas season of 1612 when *Cardenio* was first performed. Her marriage to Frederick Elector Palatine had made her briefly the Queen of Bohemia, until his death nearly thirty years before. She had come to London to visit her nephew the new King, and she would die there the following February.

he said of his nightmare that it 'spoil'd me for an actor'. He went into stage management. I concentrated on directing.

Later in his retirement, Downes wrote *Roscius Anglicanus*, his pithy account of the theatre of his day. Our knowledge of much of late seventeenth-century British theatre is largely due to his book.

Roscius Anglicanus rambles with dry lists and play titles, but here and there are some charming anecdotes, peppered with the odd rather racy one. When writing about a production of *Romeo and Juliet*, he tells the following story:

> There being a fight and scuffle in this play, between the House of Capulet and the House of Paris: Mrs Holden acting his wife, entered in a hurry, crying 'O my dear Count!' She inadvertently left out, O, in the pronunciation of the word Count! Giving it a vehement accent put the house into such a laughter, that London Bridge at low water was silence to it.

It was John Downes's job to look after the scripts, to write out all the parts for the actors, to call and attend morning rehearsals and afternoon performances, and indeed to prompt the actors, a responsibility which I suspect he took rather seriously in the light of his own near catastrophe. And it was John Downes, so it would seem, who wrote out a copy of a manuscript of an old play called *The History of Cardenio*.

It is feasible that the manuscript Theobald refers to had been written out by Mr Downes, as a clean copy after the original had been adapted by someone else, perhaps Davenant himself. As Theobald makes no mention in his preface of the name Cardenio, it is also likely that whoever adapted the play for Betterton also changed the names from the Shakespeare/Fletcher original.

The part of Cardenio could have been a very good part for Betterton, whose madness as Hamlet had been so commended. For some reason, however, it seems the play did not go ahead. But we still don't know how the manuscript copy in John Downes's handwriting came into Theobald's hands, and how he acquired his other copies.

35

Casting *Cardenio*

The great theatre director Tyrone Guthrie is supposed to have said that good directing is eighty per cent good casting. I agree with him, and spend a great deal of time trying to see as many actors as I can for the plays I am directing. If you are doing a Shakespeare play it is a good idea to know which actors have played each part before. Apart from anything else, it can be useful in persuading actors to play a small role: 'Well, you know of course that Helen Mirren played Hero.'

With this play there is no such precedent; unless you include Barton Booth and Robert Wilks in the original production of *Double Falshood* in 1727. That particular casting may indicate that Cardenio is the tragic lead, and Fernando has to be able to play comedy, but that's about all. However, I know for sure that casting the central quartet is going to be vital to the success or otherwise of this production.

I have been seeing actors for a couple of months now. Many have been sent scenes from the rehearsal draft of our play. Listening to their first responses is fascinating. Most seem to think it is a real thriller, and have no idea what is going to happen next. Some are unable to predict the tone of the piece, or are shocked that characters they thought were good guys suddenly turn into bad guys. All of which is very encouraging.

Casting takes place in a variety of different venues: sometimes in the RSC's rather cramped offices in Earlham Street, with the tables pushed back; or the Actors Centre opposite in Tower Street; or sometimes at the Spotlight Offices off Leicester Square. Today we are in the basement hall at the American Church on Tottenham Court Road. There are some tatty Christmas decorations on the stage, and the heating has failed so the staff here have wheeled in some paraffin stoves. In a few days the snow which is beginning to flurry outside will close airports.

Hannah Miller, the RSC casting director, has lined up another whole day of actors to meet. I have auditioned a brilliant, charismatic young actor called Alex Hassell for Fernando. He played Cassio in an RSC touring production of *Othello* directed by Kathryn Hunter a couple of years ago. He was at the Globe with Mark Rylance in a three-man *Tempest*, and has recently been running a company called The Factory with Tim Carroll. They do mad improvisatory flash performances of *Hamlet*, playing different parts each night, in different venues, with whatever props the audience provide them with. I think that is very courageous. He has a wild, dangerous edge, reminiscent of Oliver Reed, but an enormous smile and wide bright eyes. Dorotea recalls Fernando having the eyes of a lynx. If I can land Alex in the role, I may have to put that line into the text.

But today we have called back a young actor I interviewed a few weeks ago. His name is Oliver Rix and at his first audition he did a speech of York's from *Henry VI, Part Three*, where he hears of the death of his son Rutland: 'These tears are my sweet Rutland's obsequies.' It was carefully chosen and despite the cramped office, he did it with stillness and feeling, a lone tear rolling down his cheek as he spoke.

Hannah had seen him at LAMDA a year ago and was impressed, though she was not convinced by the tear. Too easy? Oliver has a broody, almost Mediterranean look with piercing eyes and a flashing white smile, and I suspected TV and film agents would have already snaffled him up. But when I asked him what he has been doing since he left drama school a year ago, the answer gave me rather a shock. He's been working on a building site in Southampton.

I got him to read a bit of *Cardenio*. This was the first time I was going to hear one of the speeches which I have constructed. It's the moment Cardenio emerges from behind the arras at Luscinda's wedding. Oliver did it quietly with great sensitivity. I thanked him and suggested he might have to come back to meet the other directors. I think he might have just the right balance of strength and vulnerability that Cardenio needs. But this would be his very first job and Cardenio is a big role to carry. So Hannah and I decided to see some other candidates, just in case.

A week later, I got a letter from Oliver. It was a plea to consider him as Cardenio. He had taken the script away to read and was now sure he could play the part; he understands it, both his ineptitude at the beginning and his madness in Act Four. I think he might just be right. But it's a gamble.

So today he has come back in to meet Dominic Hill the director of Massinger's *The City Madam*, Nancy Meckler for the *Dream*, and finally Anthony Neilson who is directing *Marat/Sade* later in the season. Anthony doesn't start rehearsals for over eight months, and is in the middle of opening another show at the Royal Court. How on earth he can concentrate his mind on casting at all is a miracle.

As Oliver does the speech, a brass band starts blaring Christmas carols outside, and we can hardly hear him over the noise. In the table chat, he reveals he was a gymnast as a teenager, and a trained boxer. Maybe there is something a bit too pugnacious about him. Anthony gives him quite a hard time. He asks Oliver what makes him angry. 'Rude people,' he replies.

I'm not sure this audition has gone down well or not. I don't know whether I can find a line for him through the season: Lysander and Demetrius have already gone in the *Dream*; there are only officers and servants left in *The City Madam*; and if Anthony doesn't think he's right for *Marat/Sade*, I will have to find another actor to play Cardenio. But I am now determined on him. He is the missing corner to the quartet of lovers which make up this play, with Pippa Nixon from the Michigan workshop, as Dorotea, a deliciously sparky actress called Lucy Briggs-Owen as Luscinda, and Alex Hassell as Fernando.

I catch Oliver as he is walking out looking very dejected. He has been waiting weeks with no news. That is how it so often is with the RSC. I tell him not to lose heart; hopefully he should hear one way or another in the next few days.

Three days later, having twisted my fellow directors' arms a little, we make him an offer for the 2011 Stratford season. I get another letter. He describes it as the best Christmas present he has ever received.

36

Pantomime at the Garrick Club

Since giving up a career in the law, Lewis Theobald had tried everything: classical translation, poetry, opera libretto; he even tried publishing a magazine (which folded), and a novel (which flopped). He was so desperate to make it on the literary scene, he had even tried adapting Shakespeare, attempting to apply the classical unities to *Richard II*, and cutting about one thousand lines. It was not a success. He eventually found a lucrative niche writing pantomimes.

I need to understand how writing pantomimes might qualify Theobald to adapt the treasured manuscript of a lost Shakespeare play. What were those pantomimes actually like? They are the precursors to our modern Christmas pantos, certainly, but do they bear any resemblance? In search of an answer, I visited the famous Garrick Club, in Covent Garden, to see a Harlequin called 'Lun'.

On my arrival the porter invites me to go up and wait in the drawing room on the first floor. But as I climb the stairs there are so many extraordinary things to see that I don't get very far. There is a portrait of Thomas Betterton, looking dignified and rather sad, in his heavy, dark, curly periwig. On the landing is a display case full of Garrick memorabilia, including a medal with its rainbow ribbon commemorating the 1769 Stratford Jubilee, and Garrick's own powder puffer. And in the writing room ahead is one of the Club's best pictures, the diminutive Colley Cibber in his greatest role, as Lord Foppington in Vanbrugh's *The Relapse*. He looks as if he is just about to deliver a scintillating punchline, while flourishing a pinch of snuff. Cibber was one of the triumvirate of managers of Drury Lane Theatre when Lewis Theobald presented *Double Falshood* in 1727.

In the drawing room I meet the theatre consultant, Iain Mackintosh, who is to be my guide as to the kind of pantomime Theobald was writing. But it is easy to get distracted, and we have to tear ourselves away from all the treasures: Henry Irving's death mask, or Zoffany's glowing painting of David Garrick, in *Venice Preserved*. Tucked away on the back stairs going up to the library is a faded portrait of one of Cibber's less famous partners at Drury Lane, Barton Booth, the original Cardenio in *Double Falshood*, but I have no time to examine it.

In 1723, pantomime made a spectacular arrival on the scene in England. There had been interludes featuring Harlequin and Columbine before, and several burlesques on classical themes, but the autumn of that year marks the moment when the success of pantomime was assured.

At the end of November, the Drury Lane Theatre seems to have stolen a march on their rivals by producing *Harlequin, Dr Faustus* as an afterpiece to Fletcher's *Rule a Wife and Have a Wife*. Then just before Christmas, the Lincoln's Inn Theatre produced its own version, *The Necromancer, or Harlequin Doctor Faustus*. Both were so successful that they ignited a boom in pantomimes which held the stage for decades, and seems to have changed the face of British theatre.

In the Drury Lane version, Harlequin (the Faustus figure), having signed his pact with the Devil performs several spectacular tricks. He cuts his own leg off, and then replaces it with a shapely female leg, which flies in from the wings, then he attaches donkey's ears to his fellow scholars, Pierrot, Punch and Scaramouche, and is carried away by devils at the end. At which point a troop of classical deities express their joy in a dance.

But at Lincoln's Inn, they had a star turn. Their Harlequin was John Rich. Playing under the stage name 'Lun' (as in 'Lunatic'), Rich became the most famous Harlequin of the day – indeed it's a role he would play until his retirement thirty years later. Rich employed Lewis Theobald.

Harlequin Dr Fauftus in the Necromancer.

RICH, THE HARLEQUIN.

Thank you Genteels. Thefe ftunning Claps declare,
How Wit corporeal is yr darling Care.
See what it is the crouding Audience draws
While Wilks no more but Fauftus gains Applaufe.

John Rich as Lun, artist unknown (c. 18th century)

In the library at the top of the Garrick Club, Librarian Marcus Risdell gets out their engraving of Rich as Lun. He is wearing a costume of close-fitting trousers and short jacket with long sleeves and strikes an almost balletic, mock-chivalric pose, as he swings back, doffing his hat and drawing his panto slapstick in his left hand. Lun wears a beetle-browed black commedia half-mask. This leaves his mouth free, although Lun never spoke, as David Garrick's own verse about Lun suggests:

When Lun appeared, with matchless art and whim,
He gave the power of speech to every limb:
Tho' masked and mute, conveyed his quick intent,
And told in frolic gesture what he meant.

Marcus reminds me of one of Lun's most spectacular entrances. In a show called *Harlequin a Sorcerer* performed in January 1725, he used to hatch from an egg. This description (recalled at the end of the century by John Jackson), suggests what an expert mime Lun was:

A masterpiece of dumb show from the first chipping of
the egg, his receiving of motion, his feeling of the
ground, his standing upright, to his quick harlequin
trip round the empty shell.

In the climax of the Lincoln's Inn *Faustus* panto, Harlequin is dragged away not by devils but in even more spectacular style. Here is a brief description of the scene:

Doctor (Harlequin) waves his Wand, and the Scene is
converted to a Wood; a monstrous Dragon appears, and
from each Claw drops a Daemon, representing divers
grotesque Figures; several Female Spirits rise in
character to each figure and join in an Antick Dance.
As they are performing, a Clock strikes, the Doctor is
hurried away by spirits, and devour'd by the Monster,
which immediately takes flight; and while it is
disappearing, Spirits vanish, and other daemons rejoice
in the following words:

'Now triumph Hell, and Fiends be gay
The Sorc'rer is become our Prey.'

But an attack on pantomime, by none other than Alexander Pope, is perhaps one of the best accounts we have of the sort of effects in the new rage:

> He look'd, and saw a sable Sorc'rer rise,
> Swift to whose hand a winged volume flies:
> All sudden, Gorgons hiss and Dragons glare,
> And ten-horn'd fiends and Giants rush to war.
> Hell rises, Heav'n descends, and dance on Earth,
> Gods, imps and monsters, music, rage and mirth,
> A fire, a jig, a battle and a ball,
> Till one wide Conflagration swallows all.

The 'He' referred to by Pope at the start of that extract is none other than our Lewis Theobald. In 1727 (the year *Double Falshood* was presented), Theobald composed the libretto for a pantomime called, rather surprisingly to our ears, *The Rape of Proserpine*. It was advertised as 'partly grotesque, partly vocal but far exceeds all ever yet shown in the magnificence and beauty of the scenes'.

The pantomime opened on 13 February 1727, and it ran for an astonishing 462 performances. Although Lewis Theobald enjoyed several benefit performances of the show, by May he was writing begging letters to friends asking for help from his dire financial straits.

However, that same month a notice appeared in the *London Journal* announcing the news of a miracle: a new Shakespeare play had been found; and was to be presented by Lewis Theobald. How did this panto writer come to have such a thing in his possession?

37

Rehearsals Start

Monday 24 January 2011

So finally, after weeks of meeting actors and negotiating with my fellow directors, I have a cast. There are seventeen actors in *Cardenio* (twelve men and five women). All of them are cross-cast in Massinger's *The City Madam*, which has another five actors making a company of twenty-two altogether. These two plays will rehearse opposite one another. And we all started on Monday, at the rehearsal rooms on Clapham High Street, alongside the parallel company which is rehearsing *Macbeth* and *The Merchant of Venice* to open the new Main House.

Why is it that every time a new company assembles to start rehearsals (no matter how many times we do this job), it feels just like the first day at school? The morning spins by in a whirl of new faces, and welcome speeches and parish notices. In the afternoon the *Cardenio* company assemble in the upstairs room, which is going to be our home for the next several weeks, and I begin to chart the history of the project. Chris Godwin, playing Cardenio's father, Don Camillo, was in the first workshop we did on Theobald's

Double Falshood back in 2003 in Stratford, when he was in *The Taming of the Shrew/Tamer Tamed* company. And Pippa Nixon, playing Dorotea, participated in the workshop we did as part of an RSC residency in Michigan last April. On the other hand, Olly Rix, our Cardenio, who is grinning all over his face today, has never been part of the RSC. So there is an interesting combination of people I know well, and don't know at all.

We will mostly be sitting around a table, for the next couple of weeks, examining the text in microscopic detail. Simon Callow, in his book *Being an Actor*, describes this process beautifully, as we try to feel the play's aura, 'almost its force field'. It is a bit like sitting round a Ouija board. The research we do is like lobbing a pebble into the collective pool of our unconscious and watching the ripples. Some research will be useful, some not so.

In my pocket I am clutching a piece of amber. It's not a lucky charm, it's something I spotted on my mantelpiece in the morning, and thought I'd bring along. It's from the Baltic, and I bought it from a stall in the cloth market in Krakow some years ago. When you hold it up to the light you start to see within its rich, golden, globby glow a number of specks of grit floating inside, and if you look very carefully there is a tiny fly trapped in one corner, suspended in the resin. Who knows how long it has been there? Perhaps millions of years. Perhaps it's the kind of fly from which scientists might extract the DNA of dinosaurs, who knows?

The great Shakespeare scholar Stanley Wells said he thought that there may well be some Shakespeare DNA in *Double Falshood:* it's intriguing, but trying to spot it is like trying to spot the fly in the corner of this piece of amber. Now the question of how much Shakespeare is or is not present in our *Cardenio* script is irrelevant. Now our script must take on its own identity, establish its own integrity, if it is going to work onstage.

38

'Bard-dei Defensor'

The great poet of the Augustan age, Alexander Pope, used the image of a piece of amber to describe his exact contemporary, Lewis Theobald. He wrote:

> Yet e'en this Creature may some Notice claim,
> Wrapt round and sanctified with *Shakespear*'s Name;
> Pretty, in Amber to observe the forms
> Of Hairs, or Straws, or Dirt, or Grubs, or Worms:
> The Thing, we know, is neither rich nor rare,
> But wonder how the Devil it got there.

His accusation was that Theobald was an upstart trying to gain attention by associating himself with the name of Shakespeare. Theobald had aroused the poet's fury by daring to challenge the edition of Shakespeare's plays Pope had produced in 1725. Not only did Theobald regard it as sloppy and inaccurate, he disliked Pope's tendency to correct Shakespeare's rhyme and improve his metre. So he published his response, *Shakespeare Restored*, in 1726.

Theobald combed through the plays, focusing particularly on *Hamlet* in Pope's edition and criticising his emendations and corrections. Theobald felt that Pope's job should have been to reveal what Shakespeare had written, not what he ought to have written.

Though *Shakespeare Restored* maintains a polite tone throughout, apparently courteous to his 'fellow scholar', I suspect Theobald knew just how devastating its effect would be on Pope, and the insult is made explicit in the quotation from Virgil which he places on the frontispiece. It is from Book Six in *The Aeneid*, the story of Aeneas's journey from Troy to found Rome: the moment when the hero goes down into the underworld and sees the mangled corpse of the Trojan Prince, Deiphobus:

> *... laniatum corpore toto*
> *Deiphobum vidi et lacerum crudeliter ora,*
> *Ora manusque ambas.*

In Dryden's translation the passage is rendered as follows:

> Here Priam's son, Deiphobus, he found,
> Whose face and limbs were one continued wound:
> Dishonest, with lopp'd arms, the youth appears,
> Spoil'd of his nose, and shorten'd of his ears.

And the passage continues:

> He scarcely knew him, striving to disown
> His blotted form, and blushing to be known;
> And therefore first began: 'O Teucer's race,
> Who durst thy faultless figure thus deface?
> What heart could wish, what hand inflict, this dire
>   disgrace?

It must have been clear to any of those readers who recognised the quotation that Theobald regarded Pope's editing of Shakespeare as a dire disgrace: a mutilation of the text. No wonder Pope was furious.

Pope had a vicious wit, and satire was the rage of the age, so Theobald must have known what an audacious step this was. But I believe that attacking Pope was just Step One of Theobald's master plan. It put him on the map as a *'Bard-dei defensor*'. Step Two: to secure his place in the pantheon of Shakespeare idolaters, Theobald's *coup de théâtre* was to produce a lost Shakespeare play.

39

Horsemanship in *Cardenio*

Friday 25 February 2011

A visit to the Household Cavalry Mounted Regiment this morning. While Mike Ashcroft, our choreographer, drills the rest of the company in a bit of movement work, and Paul Englishby teaches the motet which opens the play, I take Olly Rix and Alex Hassell to the Hyde Park Barracks. Much is made in *Cardenio* of the eponymous hero's horsemanship. It is for his skill that Cardenio has been called to Court as companion to the Duke's son, Fernando.

Don Camillo says of his son, in Theobald's text:

> Horsemanship? What horsemanship has Cardenio? I think he can no more but gallop a hackney, unless he practised riding in France. It may be he did so, for he was there a good continuance.

Neither Olly (Cardenio) nor Alex (Fernando) have had much experience of horses, and we want to explore ways of expressing onstage the close familiarity of working with horses that both men are assumed to possess. How better than to talk to the elite horsemen of the Life Guards and the Blues and Royals?

We are met at the Barracks' ceremonial gate by our host for the morning, Captain Lukas. He has just come from inspecting the guard who are about to set out for Horse Guards Parade. Ahead of us is a group of young girls from a local pony club. We stand on the veranda and watch while the soldiers line up their splendid black mounts. They look immaculate in their plumed helmets and shiny cuirasses. These are the men who in a few weeks' time will undertake all the ceremonial duties required at the Royal wedding, a far cry from their last posting, on the front line in Afghanistan.

We ask if each man has his breastplate specially fitted, and are greeted with polite laughter. The uniforms look spectacular, but can be incredibly uncomfortable. Apparently there is a saying in the Barracks: 'If it hurts, it fits!' I must remember to tell that to our armourer in Stratford, Julian Gilbert, who takes great care to ensure that every piece of armour he makes fits precisely.

We meet up with one of the mounted soldiers in Captain Lukas's troop. His boots have the gleam of patent leather, and we are surprised to learn that in fact they take up to sixty hours of beeswax, polish and elbow grease to make them sparkle like that. I suddenly feel very scruffy indeed.

Our tour includes a visit to the forge, where one trooper, a Geordie lad with the word 'Danger' tattooed on his arm, is shoeing a grey stallion. The ease with which he leans in to the horse and lifts its hoof is remarkable. An acrid stench, like burnt hair, fills the place. On the wall, there is a chart of all the horses in the barracks. There are over 140 animals here. Like car registration numbers, the horses are named with an initial letter according to the year. This year it's K. So there are young horses called Krypton and Kalashnikov. Olly notices one of the oldest: Yorick.

In the stable block, another soldier is grooming Spartacus, one of the heavy horses which carry the great silver kettle drums on parade. Again his ease with the horse and the gentle manner in which the two work together is impressive. But horses, Captain Lukas tells us, can be very sensitive to anyone around them who is anxious, and can pick up fear, or indecisiveness in their rider. At that moment as if to prove his point, Cedric is led past us. Cedric is renowned in the barracks for his temperament. He has bucked many a nervous new recruit off his back.

In the Full Dress Store we see some of the extraordinary and highly valuable uniforms the regiment possesses. Here are dress coats, and drum banners laden with heavy gold thread; and I learn a great new word: 'Shabraque' (it's a saddle cloth). Alex tries on one of the regimental plumed helmets adorned with gilded oak and bay leaves. The red plume on one of the helmets of the Blues and Royals is made of yak hair. The ivory plumes of the Life Guards used to be horsehair, but now (rather disappointingly) are made of nylon.

As Corporal Beaumont shows off some choice pieces, I spot a dangerous-looking weapon, a sort of large steel axe on a wooden haft with a sharp spike on the butt end. It's a poleaxe. They were at one time used for chopping off your horse's hoof if it fell in battle to prove it had been killed rather than stolen by the enemy. So is this what Hamlet's father used when he smote the ice with his poleaxe?

In the saddler's workshop, Corporal Worsley gives us a rundown on the kit. The room hums with the tangy smell of the leather. There is an impressive range of snaffles and bits, of military whips and crops, of reins, stirrups, and swan neck spurs; all of which gives us a sense of just how much clobber is involved in working with horses. Jenny Grand, our Deputy Stage Manager, who has come along on the trip, is making a lot of mental notes.

As we come to the end of our visit, it is difficult to know precisely how we will use any of the information we have learned. It is likely that some little moment will have its effect; some sense memory of the symbiosis these soldiers evolve with the horses they work with may inform an element of Olly and Alex's performances, and give a deeper understanding of Cardenio's horsemanship. We'll see.

Cardenio in rehearsal
(RSC, 2011).

Photographs of the 2011 RSC production of *Cardenio*.

Left: Luscinda (Lucy Briggs-Owen) and her father Don Bernardo (Nicholas Day).

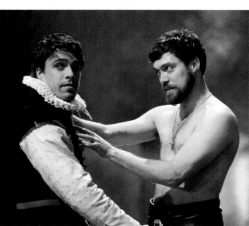

Right: Cardenio (Oliver Rix) is called to court to be companion to the Duke's son Fernando (Alex Hassell).

Below: Fernando (Alex Hassell) serenades Dorotea beneath her window.

Above: The seduction scene, Dorotea (Pippa Nixon) and Fernando (Alex Hassell).

Left and below: The Fiesta.

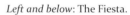

Above: Dorotea (Pippa Nixon), disguised as the shepherd boy Florio, meets the mad Cardenio (Oliver Rix) in the Sierra Morena Mountains.

Below: Fernando (Alex Hassell) seizes Luscinda (Lucy Briggs-Owen) in the final scene.

40

As You Find It

Lewis Theobald had a patron. He was Charles Boyle, the 4th Earl of Orrery, who gave his name to a mechanical device that illustrates the relative positions and motions of the planets and moons in the solar system in a heliocentric model. There's a wonderful painting of an orrery in Derby Museum, by the city's favourite son, Joseph Wright.

It may have been the 4th Earl of Orrery who was 'the noble person, who supply'd me with One of my copies', as Theobald writes in his preface to *Double Falshood*. Professor Peter Seary (who wrote *Lewis Theobald and the Editing of Shakespeare*) thinks so. He quotes a contemporaneous story which illustrates Orrery's generosity to Theobald:

> My Lord asked Mr Theobald if he took snuff: which he
> answering in the affirmative, his patron made him a
> present of a very handsome box made of Egyptian
> pebble, the top and bottom the rims and hinges being
> of gold all together, perhaps of about twenty-four
> pounds value which Mr Theobald could not but think a
> very genteel acknowledgment of the compliment he
> had made his Lordship; but how agreeable was his

surprise when he came home and found a bank bill of a hundred pounds enclosed in it.

And if Orrery was indeed the noble person who supplied Theobald with the manuscript of *Cardenio*, how did his lordship come to have it in his possession? Now here we get into the realms of 'Perhaps, perhaps, perhaps...' and I'm going to sound like Doris Day but follow me on this one. It's about to get complicated.

Charles Boyle's grandfather, Roger Boyle (1621–79) was a soldier and a statesman. He was made the 1st Earl of Orrery by King Charles II, at his restoration, although he had in fact fought for Cromwell in Ireland during the Commonwealth.

Roger Boyle was as an expert in seventeenth-century warfare, and a friend and patron of writers of his day. But he also wrote plays himself. Not unsurprisingly, considering his love of military history, he wrote one about Henry V, and another about the Black Prince. He also wrote a heroic tragedy called *Mustapha*, in 1668, in which Thomas Betterton had appeared as Suleyman the Magnificent, reprising the role he had played for Davenant in *The Siege of Rhodes* a few years earlier. Thomas Otway turned one of Boyle's books, *English Adventures by a Person of Honour* (1676), into his tragedy *The Orphan*. So Boyle was very familiar with Davenant's company at the theatre in Dorset Garden.

Roger Boyle's publisher was Humphrey Moseley. So is it possible that Moseley showed Boyle his *History of Cardenio by Mr Fletcher. & Shakespeare*? Interestingly enough, Roger Boyle was married to Margaret, the daughter of Theophilus Howard, the 2nd Earl of Suffolk (remember him?). Thomas Shelton had dedicated his translation of *Don Quixote* to Theophilus. Even more reason then that Moseley should show Boyle the play Shakespeare had adapted from a book dedicated to his father-in-law?

Perhaps Roger Boyle obtained the Moseley copy in some way. Perhaps he kept it in his library, which was eventually inherited by his grandson, the 4th Earl of Orrery. Perhaps the 4th Earl showed the manuscript to his ambitious but struggling protégé, Lewis Theobald, who was clearly a Shakespeare fanatic if nothing else.

Perhaps when he had finished with it, Theobald returned that manuscript to the Earl. After all, Lewis apparently already had one copy in the handwriting of John Downes. In which case might not a manuscript of *Cardenio* still be uncovered in the library of the Earls of Orrery and their descendants?

Lewis Theobald's patron, Charles Boyle, the 4th Earl of Orrery, also wrote a play, which might one day prove prophetic, if *Cardenio* were ever to be discovered in the Orrery libraries. It was called *As You Find It*.

'Dorotea's secret engagement', from Gustave Doré's *Illustrations for Don Quixote* (1863)

41

'A Thousand Perjured Vows': Rehearsing the Seduction Scene

Every morning on my way to work at the rehearsal rooms, I pass a series of posters on the escalators at Clapham Tube station. '*Flirt/Harass*' reads one. '*Back to mine/Back off*' reads another. Yet another reads '*Get it on/Get off me*', and at the top of the escalator, a final version cautions: '*Harmless Fun/Sexual Assault*'. The byline reads '*Real men know the difference*'. The posters are part of a campaign by the Metropolitan Police to alert men to the gap between flirting and sexual harassment, between seduction and rape. That is a distinction which engaged us a lot in rehearsals for *Cardenio*.

In the story, the Duke's son, Fernando is obsessed with the wealthy farmer's daughter, Dorotea. He pays for parties in her village; 'every day was a holy day, and a day of sports in the streets where I dwelled,' she later says (*Don Quixote*, Part Four, Chapter One) and he hires musicians to serenade her under her balcony.

She repulses his advances, although she admits in the novel that she was flattered by his attention. 'Nor was I anything offended to see his papers written in my praise; for if

I be not deceived in this point, be we women ever so foul, we love to hear men call us beautiful.' In the end Don Fernando bribes Dorotea's maid to let him into her room one night.

What precisely happens in this room is key to interpreting the story.

Fernando emerges later and shares his thoughts with us, protesting: 'Was it rape then? No, her shrieks, her exclamations then had drove me from her. True, she did consent, as true she did resist, but still in silence all.' Dorotea has resisted him forcibly, and volubly, but he has tried a number of tactics and arguments to impel her to yield to him. It is not, however, until he promises her marriage and takes her hand in front of the statue of the Virgin Mary, and in the presence of the treacherous maid, that Dorotea gives in.

This hasty ceremony constitutes a troth-plight, or handfast. This means not only that they are engaged, or betrothed, but that they are plighted to each other, and all that remains is the solemnisation of the wedding service. As far as Dorotea is concerned she is now married to Fernando.

Such troth-plights were recognised as legally binding in Shakespeare's day. Indeed in Renaissance Spain according to Professor Felipe Fernández-Armesto (in his essay, *The Improbable Empire*) one saintly lobbyist in 1551 proposed invalidating all such marriages

> because an infinite number of maidens have been
> deceived and undone, sinning with men and trusting
> in the promise of marriage made to them; and some
> left their parents' house and are gone to perdition.

This is what happens to Dorotea. Once Fernando has possessed her, he no longer wants her. It is a classic situation brilliantly summed up by Shakespeare's Sonnet 129.

> The expense of spirit in a waste of shame
> Is lust in action.

In fact Fernando has enough self-awareness to realise that he has an addiction, which he describes as 'a disease in me that fancied graces in her'.

Dorotea had protested to Fernando that were she married, no matter how she felt about her husband, she would subject herself utterly to his will:

> I would subject my will
> To his, nor shall it vary not one jot,
> So that if I remain with honour there
> Although I rested void of more delights,
> Yet would I willingly bestow on him,
> That which you labour so much to obtain.

(Cardenio: Act One, Scene Six)

A woman, by biblical injunction, was her husband's property, as Petruchio reminds the assembled congregation when he marries Kate in *The Taming of the Shrew:*

> She is my goods, my chattels, she is my house,
> My household stuff, my field, my barn,
> My horse, my ox, my ass, my anything...

(The Taming of the Shrew: Act Three, Scene Two)

Dorotea believes Fernando is her husband, and she therefore acquiesces to his demands. After the seduction, she feels guilty about what has happened:

> Whom shall I look upon without a blush?
> There's not a maid whose eye with virgin gaze
> Pierces not to my guilt.

(Double Falshood: Act Two, Scene Two)

But she soon realises that her own 'belief and childish love' has been misplaced. Fernando dumps Dorotea by letter. This changes her status profoundly. Was it rape then? Dorotea knows immediately that she has been abandoned. Nevertheless, she still regards herself as legally bound to him, and realises that her position in society will be impossible if she cannot get him to honour his oaths to her.

The question then remains: did Fernando rape her? Ironically, in the epilogue, published in the text of Theobald's *Double Falshood* and spoken by a woman, the celebrated actress Anne Oldfield, the morals of eighteenth-century London are satirised, as she provocatively declares of the Dorotea figure (called here Violante):

> And Violante grieves, or we're mistaken,
> Not because ravished, but because – forsaken!

And later Mrs Oldfield continues:

> Then as for rapes, those dangerous days are past:
> Our dapper sparks are seldom in such haste.

We no longer treat the issues of rape so dismissively, as the Metropolitan Police adverts testify.

One of the most challenging elements of the *Cardenio* story for a modern audience will (I suspect) be the decision by Dorotea, even though she has been raped by him, to pursue Don Fernando when she discovers that his marriage to Luscinda has not occurred. Cervantes makes her appearance before her attacker one of the highlights of the narrative, for she not only insists upon her status as his wife, but confesses the 'matchless affections' that she still holds for him; a climax that may be dangerously provocative for modern sensibilities, but which is also theatrically riveting, and psychologically profoundly complex.

42

The Triumvirate at Drury Lane

When Lewis Theobald brought his lost Shakespeare play *Double Falshood* to the house in 1727, Drury Lane Theatre was run by a triumvirate of big personalities: Robert Wilks, Colley Cibber and Barton Booth.

Three years earlier, in 1724, William Hogarth had produced a satirical engraving called *A Just View of the British Stage: or Three Heads are better than One*, showing this management team on the stage of Drury Lane Theatre. On the left, Robert Wilks sits manipulating a puppet of Mr Punch, and crying 'Poor Rich, faith I pity him.' In the middle the diminutive Colley Cibber gazes above looking for inspiration from the Muses painted on a cloth above him, crying 'Assist, you sacred nine', and on the right, a rather hefty Barton Booth holds a puppet which is disappearing down the privy, next to which hang pages of *Hamlet*, *Macbeth* and *Julius Caesar* as toilet paper. Booth huffs 'Ha, this will do God Damn me!' They are preparing to mount the escapades of a flash convict called Jack Shepherd, while the ghost of Ben Jonson rises from a trap at the side of the stage, and howls.

The impresarios are being lampooned for attempting to rival John Rich at Lincoln's Inn Fields, and succumbing to the popularity of pantomime, and the profits it could reap – and in so doing, dumbing down the theatre. And these are the men Lewis had to impress.

Much of what we know about the in-fighting between this threesome comes from Cibber's bitchy autobiography, *An Apology for his Life*, written over a decade after these events, and after the deaths of his fellow triumvirs. There emerges a picture of bitter rivalries, touchy personalities, and inflated egos; and these may have impacted upon the way Theobald adapted his version of *Cardenio*.

Cibber blames an earlier walk-out by eight actors, who abandoned Drury Lane for Lincoln's Inn, on 'the shocking temper of Wilks, who upon every occasion, let loose the unlimited language of passion upon them in such a manner as their patience was no longer able to support'. People gave way to Wilks merely 'in order to avoid a disagreeable dispute with him'. Worse is Cibber's accusation that Wilks would prefer a bad play over a good one, if it offered him a better part:

> He would take as much, or more passion in forwarding to the stage, the water-gruel work of some insipid author, that happened rightly to make his court to him, than he would for the best play, wherein it was not his fortune to be chosen for the best character.

> So great was his impatience to be employed, that I scarce remember, in twenty years, above one profitable play, we could get to be revived wherein he found he was to make no considerable figure, independent of him.

John Dennis, himself a rejected playwright, cried, 'The Theatre is now in the hands of players; illiterate, unthinking, unjust, ungrateful and sordid.'

Wilks was to play the glittering villain character, Henriquez (Fernando). And there is a clue perhaps as to why Lewis Theobald chose the name *Double Falshood or the Distressed Lovers* (if indeed he did so) over the single name of the eponymous hero of Mr Fletcher and Shakespeare's play, as Humphrey Moseley had registered it. If it had been called after *Cardenio*, Wilks may not have sanctioned it for performance.

To illustrate Wilks's ego, Cibber tells the story of how Wilks had tried to get out of playing Macduff, in *Macbeth*, by passing it on to 'one Williams, as yet no extraordinary, though a promising actor'. It was Wilks's custom, according to Cibber, to give up a part to 'some raw actor who he was sure would disgrace it, and consequently put the audience in mind of his superior performance'.

However, Lewis Theobald did manage to get his play accepted by this tetchy triumvirate and prepared for his big break.

At sixty-two, Robert Wilks might now be thought a little old to be cast as Henriquez (Fernando). Barton Booth as Julio (Cardenio) was a mere forty-seven. Booth's wife Hester (the beautiful former dancer, Miss Santlow) would play the Dorotea character, Violante; and Leonora (Luscinda) would be played by the charming tragic actress, Mary Porter.

But though a date was set for rehearsals to begin, Lewis Theobald's troubles were not over yet.

A Just View of the British Stage, William Hogarth (1724)

43

Pancake Tuesday

As this is Shrove Tuesday, we are rehearsing the fiesta scene today.

Cervantes says that in order to win Dorotea's affection, Fernando bribed the servants and paid for music and dancing in the village every night, so we are staging this in the production. We pored over all the research material we had collected for inspiration: the amazing photographs by Cristina García Rodero of Spanish festivals and rituals; Goya's dark carnival painting *The Burial of the Sardine*; and read a lively diatribe against the festivities enjoyed at Shrovetide in 'popish countries' in the sixteenth century. This last is by Thomas Kirchmaier, 'englyshed' by Barnabe Googe in 1570. We note how certain factors are common to all. The dressing up, the presence of devils, and masks, and a love of cross-dressing!

> But some again the dreadful shape of devils on them take,
> And chase such as they meet, and make poor boys to
> fear and quake.
> Some naked run about the streets, their faces hid alone,
> With visors close, that so disguised, they might be
> known of none.

Both men and women change their weed, the men in
    maid's array,
And wanton wenches, dressed like men, do travel by
    the way.

Some like wild beasts do run abroad in skins that divers
    be
Arrayed and eke with loathsome shapes that dreadful
    are to see:
They counterfeit both bears and wolves, and lions
    fierce to fight,
And raging bulls. Some play the cranes with wings and
    stilts upright.
Some like the filthy form of apes, and some like fools
    are dressed,
Which best beseem these papists all, that thus keep
    Bacchus' feast.

It's an amazing description, and it goes on… and on: this is
just a fraction of it. I like the idea of cranes or storks (like the
ones we saw on the rooftops of Alcalá de Henares). And the
use of stilts could be very effective. But one aromatic detail
in Barnabe Googe's apoplectic puritan howl catches the eye
of Michael Grady-Hall, one of our young actors, who suggests this might be a potent addition to our invented scene:

But others bear a *turd*, that on a cushion soft they lay,
And one there is that with a flap doth keep the flies
    away,
I would there might another be, an officer of those,
Whose room might serve to take away the scent from
    every nose.

Next we peer closely at the intriguing engravings by de
Gheyn of masquerade costumes from 1599. Here are strange
back-to-front people, a man with a turkey wattle mask, and
a haunting character doing something with a stick. The
V&A, who hold this collection of masquerade costumes,
suggest that the man pictured is stirring a pot, but we think
he's playing a zambomba, an instrument which still featured
in Andalucían festivities in the 1950s when Brenan described
it as consisting

183

of a piece of rabbit or goat skin drawn tightly across the mouth of a broken flowerpot or drainpipe; a stick is inserted through the skin, and after the hand has been wetted, is pushed up and down, so that it gives out a half squeaking, half moaning sound. The sexual significance is obvious, and no doubt it was originally intended as a magical rite to give strength to the declining sun.

This sounds like a great noise for our fiesta.

Engraving, Jacques de Gheyn II (1599)

In common with other accounts, Gerald Brenan also mentions the straw dummies or peleles, with vegetable genitalia, which were regularly used as part of midsummer mayhem in Andalucía. Kirchmaier, too, describes dummies stuffed with straw and dressed as winter and summer and made to fight each other. Goya has a painting of a straw dummy being tossed in a blanket: that's another way of filling that middle air of the Swan. These peleles could be very useful. Our resourceful Assistant Stage Manager, Mark McGowan, mocks up a pair of peleles for our rehearsal, by stuffing pairs of pyjamas with scrunched up newspaper. His addition of a stuffed sock raises a great guffaw in the company.

I have decided to separate the fiesta into two parts. First a rather well-behaved version which allows us to introduce the different elements: in particular the male and female peleles, paraded on poles. (While they process around the perimeter of the stage, we can set up Dorotea's room in the centre.) And then, after the seduction scene, a more dangerous chaotic riot, during which the masked revellers echo what is happening in Dorotea's room, by making the peleles simulate a violent sex act. This is a straight pinch from Strindberg's play *Miss Julie*, where the peasants enter to perform a wild midsummer dance, as Miss Julie and the valet, Jean, disappear to have sex.

Once the company don a few masks, and try on some of the trashy frippery and glistering apparel from a costume rack we have had brought up from the store, they are transformed, and all inhibitions fly out the window. What unspeakable acts Chris Ettridge (playing the dignified Duke) and now dressed as a green devil performs upon the dragged-up Nick Day (Don Bernardo) would earn the show an X-certificate. Maybe I had better contact Chris Hill, our head of marketing, about a parental guidance warning.

44

'Never Acted Before'

My indefatigable stage manager, Alix Harvey-Thompson, has spent her Saturday up at Colindale in North London, at the British Library Newspaper Museum, looking through back copies of the *London Daily Post* and the *Evening Journal* for 1727 on microfiche. She has brought back photocopies of the relevant pages. She has tracked down the *London Journal* announcing the first performance of *Double Falshood*, on Wednesday 13 December 1727.

> Never acted before
>
> By His Majesty's Company of Comedians
>
> At the Theatre in Drury Lane, this present Wednesday, a play called Double Falshood; Or, The Distrest Lovers. Written originally by Shakespear. The principal parts to be performed by Mr Wilks, Mr Mills, Mr Williams, Mr Corey, Mr Harper, Mr Griffin, Mr Norris, Mrs Porter, and Mrs Booth. With proper decorations.

The rest of the page conjures a brief snapshot of the Georgian era. There's a notice of an item lost on the Woodford Stagecoach: 'a wicker basket containing a small bandbox tied with packthread', with the appeal 'If the said box be brought and delivered at the Bar at the Dolphin Tavern in Tower Street, the person who delivers the same shall have four guineas and no question asked.' It sounds like the start of a novel by Henry Fielding.

Meanwhile on that same Wednesday, at the recently opened theatre in the Haymarket, there is competition from a group of French acrobats:

> The famous Mr Francisco will dance on the stiff rope
> with fetters at his feet. Mr La Fevre will perform
> equilibres, and Signor Guilmarine will perform several
> surprising things the like never yet seen in England.

But Alix has also found a copy of the first-night review of Theobald's play in the *Daily Post*. This makes the whole thing seem so real and immediate, I can imagine Theobald rushing out to buy his copy of the paper, or reading it in his local ordinary in Great Russell Street.

Scanning the page, among the Port-News we read that the *King George* packet boat had arrived in Falmouth from Lisbon; Mrs Vanderbank, the King's tapestry-maker, had died, while Mr Cheesdon, on being appointed Her Majesty's surgeon, 'had the honour to kiss the Queen's hand'. And then the following:

> Last Night was acted an original play of William
> Shakespeare's in Drury-lane, where the audience was
> very numerous and the most remarkable attention
> through the whole... Mr Wilks shone with his usual
> spirit in the Prologue; and Mrs Oldfield even exceeded
> herself with the highest gracefulness in the epilogue.

No mention of Theobald again, but Wilks (who played the villain, Henriquez) had clearly charmed the house, shining 'with his usual spirit' in the prologue. It's a jingoistic piece of verse, in heroic couplets, all about Shakespeare's genius.

> O, could the Bard, revisiting our light,
> Receive these honours done his shade tonight...
> How would he joy to see fair merit's claim
> Thus answered in his own reviving fame!

Finally the prologue imagines Shakespeare crying out with gratitude and pride:

> Oblivion I forgive,
> This my last child to latest times shall live:
> Lost to the world, well for the birth it stayed;
> To this auspicious era well delayed.

It's quite a clever tactic to present *Double Falshood* as a child lost to the world, like Perdita, and only now recovered, to the gratitude of Shakespeare himself.

45

Creating a New Scene

On 15 March 2011, the *International Herald Tribune* carries a review of a production of *Double Falshood* in New York, by the Classic Stage Company. Brian Kulick, the company's artistic director, having stated his belief that the text is derived from Shakespeare, has invited several scholars to debate the issue. Shakespeare scholar Harold Bloom declares the play is a 'palpable forgery' but commends Kulick's courage and 'his marvellous foolhardiness' in staging it. The journalist Alexis Soloski argues that even if textual analysis proves Shakespeare's participation, 'it does not mean that *Double Falshood* in its present form is particularly fine or playable'. I think she's right.

One of the major problems with *Double Falshood* as it stands is that Cardenio and Fernando do not actually meet until Act Five. It was one of our dramaturg Jeanie O'Hare's main notes on the script to come out of the workshops: the need to establish a relationship between Fernando and Cardenio early on in the play. If the audience see no evidence of that friendship they can hardly be expected to be shocked when Fernando betrays it.

But this demands a new approach to the script. Instead of dramatising a scene which already exists in narrative form in Shelton's prose, and simply rendering it in iambic pentameters, I have to invent an entirely new scene. The challenge is how to avoid it sounding like mock-Tudorbethan pastiche.

I shape out the bare bones of a scene (the essential structure), derive what elements I can from the original text, and then plunder the six or seven Fletcher/Cervantes plays I've identified for coincidental passages, suitable phrases or expressions, or 'liftable' imagery, and then start piecing together a linguistic jigsaw puzzle. And if that sounds absurdly painstaking or pedantic, it probably is.

Today we try out my invented scene: Act One, Scene Five. Cardenio is welcomed to Court by Pedro (the Duke's older son). He has been called to be companion to Pedro's brother Fernando, on the grounds that they share a love of horsemanship, a skill in which Cardenio apparently excels. During the opening conversation, Cardenio also realises that he is being asked to spy on Fernando, which presents him with a conflict he must later resolve.

This is surely the scene to explore and fortify the theme of horsemanship, and our trip to the Household Cavalry has given us a few ideas.

So Fernando arrives from riding. He has been breaking-in horses. As this scene follows his serenading of Dorotea, it allows Fernando to sublimate his frustration in the horse-riding imagery he adopts. Alex Hassell (Fernando) makes very effective use of a rather whippy riding crop.

As we can't bring a horse onto the stage, we introduce a Spanish saddle and wooden saddle-stand, which Fernando can mount during the scene. Our stage manager Alix Harvey-Thompson, who has her own horse, brings a saddle in to rehearsal. The pungent scent of the leather, and the jangle of the brass stirrups, and the weight of the whole saddle make a fine impression.

But for any imagery or language about horses, I have to look further afield than the Fletcher/Cervantes texts. I've derived some of the training language from a book called

The Compleat Horseman, published in 1614 (a year after the original *Cardenio* was played at Greenwich). This delightful volume is full of practical instruction and advice on the management of horses. It is by the prolific Gervase Markham, who was a horse breeder himself, and is said to have imported the first Arabian horse to England. It prompts Fernando's speech:

> The English with their slothful industry
> Aim for the most part for no greater skill
> Than riding of a ridden perfect horse.
> But a true rider breaks the horse himself,
> And brings his mare from utter ignorance
> To the bravest skill can ever be desired.

We've learnt from Don Camillo that his son learnt his horsemanship skills in France, which reminds me of a passage in *Hamlet*. In Act Four, Scene Seven, King Claudius spends an inordinately long time telling Laertes about a particular Frenchman:

> Here was a gentleman of Normandy –
> I've seen myself and served against the French,
> And they ran well on horseback, but this gallant
> Had witchcraft in't; he grew into his seat
> And to such wondrous doing brought his horse
> As he had been incorpsed and demi-natured
> With the brave beast.

Laertes recognises him as Lamord: 'the brooch and gem of all our nation'.

It's one of those bits of Shakespeare plotting which arouse suspicion in me. Lamord has apparently so praised Laertes's pre-eminence with the rapier that Hamlet cannot wait to challenge his skill. Why does Shakespeare invent and name a whole new character, so late in the play, to back up this piece of conspiracy? Perhaps there was someone in the original audience with a similar name, famous for his skill in horsemanship. These single references to characters always make me frown a little; none more so than Orsino's young nephew Titus, who, we are told out of the blue, in Act Five of *Twelfth Night*, lost his leg in a naval battle off Illyria.

The Lamord section is almost always cut in production, so I decide to borrow the details of his horsemanship, for Fernando to describe Cardenio now:

> Why, you may see him grow into his seat,
> And to such wondrous doings bring his horse
> As he had been incorpsed with the beast.

But it's a bit risky. Surely the critics will recognise a line stolen from *Hamlet*?

The scene continues. Once Pedro leaves, Fernando encourages Cardenio to talk about his beloved Luscinda. This is merely a pretext for Fernando to be able to discuss his own obsession with Dorotea.

I have drawn much of the text from Shelton's translation, which yields some rather modern lines such as Cardenio's 'How love delights to chatter of its self'. This is an opportunity to include some of the detailed backstory to Cardenio and Luscinda's relationship. They have known each other since childhood, and when they reached puberty, her father denied him access to the house 'as Thisbe's father did to Pyramus'.

At a later rehearsal, we realise that having now established the men's friendship, it can now be tested if Cardenio comes across Fernando in the night-time fiesta. Fernando is raging about in the dark, in a trauma of guilt and shame precipitated by his treatment of Dorotea in the seduction scene. In *Double Falshood*, this scene is witnessed by two characters called Fabian and Lopez, comedy townsfolk who comment on the action, and then never appear again. This gives us the idea of substituting them for Cardenio instead.

Fernando spots his friend approaching, and concludes 'my guilt conjures him hither'. He cannot tell Cardenio what has happened, but the presence of his virtuous mate seems to exacerbate his self-loathing. Cardenio steadies the nerves of his jittery friend (as he would calm a frisky horse):

In adversity, true school of friendship,
We learn those principles which do confirm
Us friends, never to be forgotten, sir.

(*Cardenio*: Act Two, Scene One)

Some of the passages we have identified in 'The Curious Impertinent' (the tale interwoven with the Cardenio episode in *Don Quixote*) prove be very useful here to deepen their relationship. With a little alteration, they re-emerge as:

You seem to me, Cardenio, like the sun,
And from my dark and ill-perturbed streams,
You rise, like morning after darkling dreams.

Fernando realises he needs to find an escape route, and get away from Dorotea's village. He suggests that they make a trip to Almodovar, Cardenio's home town, to buy horses. According to Cervantes the best horses in the world are to be found in Andalucía.*

This provides Cardenio with a dilemma: should he encourage Fernando to return to Court, and inform his father of his son's business, or should he take the advantage of the offer to return home, and the prospect of seeing his sweetheart, Luscinda?

By the time the two men arrive in Almodovar (as they do in Cervantes, but not in *Double Falshood*) their friendship is sealed. Cardenio has shown his loyalty and trustworthiness during Fernando's crisis, and they are now confirmed soulmates.

And inevitably the insatiable Fernando, upon seeing Luscinda, forgets Dorotea, and is smitten by his friend's intended bride.

---

* In the aftermath of the Gunpowder Plot a year later, the Spanish Ambassador delivered 'six jennets of Andalucía' to King James. One of them was snow white, with a mane so long it reached the ground.

46

The First Night of *Double Falshood*, 1727

There's a more sinister note in the first-night review of *Double Falshood* that Alix, our stage manager, has found. It says:

> Mr Williams supplied, not unsuccessfully, Mr Booth's part.

It must have been nerve-wracking night for Lewis Theobald: Barton Booth playing Julio, the Cardenio character, was off.

In *The Memoirs of the Life of Barton Booth, Esq.* published six years later 'by an intimate acquaintance of Mr Booth', we read that Booth was conducting a happy life with his wife Hester, 'in the full possession of all the felicities that human nature could enjoy till the fatal year of 1727; when he was seized with a violent fever'.

He returned to the stage that autumn season for the celebrations surrounding the coronation of the new monarch. King George II had been crowned at Westminster, two months before, with a new anthem composed by Handel. 'Zadock the Priest' has been played at every coronation since.

The theatre decided to revive their production of *Henry VIII*:

which was played a great number of nights successively on account of their present majesties' coronation, a pompous representation of which ceremony was introduced into that play.

The *Memoir* goes on to describe how Booth began rehearsing *Double Falshood* with his wife Hester as Violante:

> After this he rehearsed the part of Julio in a play called *The Distressed Lovers* [*Double Falshood*'s subtitle], which is said to have been written by the famous Shakespeare, and was completed from an old manuscript and brought to the stage by Mr Theobald. When the actors were all perfect in their several parts and the piece just in readiness to be given to the public, Mr Booth was unfortunately confined by a relapse, and this fever was so violent, that his part was supplied two or three nights by the late Mr Williams.*

Can you imagine Theobald's distress? His big break! His adaptation of *Cardenio* is about to open in one of the two major London theatres, with arguably one of the greatest actors of the day, and instead an understudy goes on: Williams, the unremarkable actor upon whom Wilks had tried to palm off the part of Macduff. The *Memoir* goes on:

> ... but being solicited by Mr Theobald to return, if possible, for the good of his play, his good nature made him disregard his indisposition, and prevailed on him to perform it himself from the fifth night to the twelfth, which was the last of his appearance on the stage.

So Lewis begged Booth to go back on, for the sake of his box-office takings. What did Hester think of that? She must have been very conflicted, anxious about her husband, ill at home, while she herself had to continue playing the lover with the

---

* Booth's *Memoir* claims that *Double Falshood* 'was completed from an old manuscript'. Is there a clue here which has been overlooked? Perhaps any manuscript that Theobald obtained was only a fragment of *Cardenio* to begin with.

understudy. The effort of returning to finish the role, clearly wiped out the poor man, for he never returned to the stage.

Three doctors were sent for, and all concluded that Booth had an 'inveterate jaundice'. Poor Booth travelled to Bath to take the waters, but returned after eleven weeks none the better. Then 'fancying the sea-sickness might prove a cure for his jaundice', he and Hester embarked for Ostend in a packet boat. When that didn't work he moved to Hampstead, and began chewing rhubarb every day which made him 'purge eighteen, sometimes twenty times, in every twenty-four hours'. Barton Booth spent the next four years in varying states of agony, until May 1731, when he suffered 'the last violent torture in his bowels' and expired. The writer of Booth's memoir goes to great lengths to portray the agony Booth must have suffered including in his account the autopsy by Mr Small 'who opened the body'. It makes grisly reading, for on the advice of his doctors, Booth had consumed huge quantities of crude mercury: 'the inside of the intestines... were as black as your hat'.

Nearly forty years later in 1772, Hester had a plaque to her husband placed in Westminster Abbey.

Booth was only fifty-two when he died. Later that year, Wilks followed him to the grave, and was buried in the actors' church, St Paul's Covent Garden, in September 1731. It was a tragic period for Drury Lane Theatre, as Mrs Oldfield had also passed away the previous year, and even Mary Porter, the Luscinda (Leonora) 'then in her highest reputation for tragedy' (according to Cibber), was lost to the company 'by the misfortune of a dislocated limb, from the falling from a chaise'. The rest of the acting company then forced Cibber out, by buying his share of the company.

In his *Annals of the English Stage*, the Victorian theatre historian Dr John Doran (my namesake but no relation), suggests that Booth's 'retirement from the stage may be laid to the importunity of Mr Theobald'. But if the first night of *Double Falshood* was a nightmare for Lewis Theobald, worse was to follow.

47

Week Four Already

In Clapham, it's hard to believe we are starting our fourth week of rehearsals already.

Last week we were joined by Antonio Álamo, our Spanish dramaturg. To see just what a bit of Spanish flare and passion could produce, he recommended a visit to the Flamenco Festival at Sadler's Wells, where some friends of his were performing. We watched the astonishing, iconoclastic Israel Galavan spin flamenco into the twenty-first century. With just the help of David Lagos, a *cante jondo* singer from Jerez, and his brother Alfredo, on guitar, he kept us on the edge of our seats for an hour and a half.

In *South from Granada*, Gerald Brenan writes about the singing of *cante jondo*. He talks of music that has 'black sounds' in it; and of dancers whose feet can summon up the spirit of 'Duende'. I had witnessed that before, but I was not expecting flamenco to make me laugh too, and that is part of Galavan's genius: clapping out intoxicating rhythms, even at one point upon his teeth.

The entire acting RSC company have been taking flamenco classes (even the *Macbeth* and *Merchant* company, for whom it is not directly relevant) with the inspiring Jaki

Wilby, so they are learning about how to concentrate and focus a passion that seems to rise from the ground. It is up to Mike Ashcroft, our choreographer, to translate that into a language that our actors can comprehend and master in the time we have. But even after one session last week, our company all seem taller. Perhaps, they are beginning to understand something about the Spanish people that Jan Morris describes beautifully in her book *Spain* when she says that the Spanish are more 'perpendicular' than any other nation.

Antonio Álamo spent his week in rehearsals, sitting and listening. Occasionally he would interrupt and explain precisely how important the code of honour is in Spanish culture, and at the same time, how Cervantes (in *Don Quixote*) deconstructed the nonsense that surrounded that code, and how his book was said to have destroyed a nation.

We discuss how the word 'honour' may have lost some of its currency with modern audiences. Honour, the esteem with which society regards you, has a particularly Spanish flavour, and Antonio alerts us to its significance: how the eternal nature of honour means that it transcends and outlasts this earthly life.

Antonio would argue passionately, for example, why for him, Dorotea is such a determined, strong woman, who has no life in society if she does not recover her rightful place as Fernando's wife. Unless Fernando honours his vows to her, she is a non-person in her world. Antonio also explained that what occasionally might seem black-and-white melodrama in *Double Falshood*, is complex and subtle in the novel, encouraging us to embrace those nuances.

Fernando, for example, is only too aware how he is damaging his reputation by his wild behaviour. He knows that by betraying his friend and attempting to marry Luscinda he is wilfully 'murdering' his honour, and without that he says 'my dog's a creature of the nobler kind'.

As we work through all the instances in our play where honour is mentioned, the word itself begins to gain weight and significance, and as Nick Day points out, nobody is eliding 'honour' with any word which precedes it any more. So no one says 'from-**m**onour', 'for-**r**onour' or 'and-**d**onour'.

One night Antonio visited the tiny Union Theatre in Southwark, near Tate Modern, to see Phil Wilmott's fringe production of *Double Falshood*, and was perplexed about how they have staged one of the scenes which does not appear in that play. They make Fernando/Henriquez's 'seduction' of Dorotea/Violante a violent rape, with the added insult of money being chucked at the victim as if she were no better than a prostitute. Antonio saw no textual evidence for this in either Theobald or Cervantes, and insisted that it diminishes the story.

Antonio has been invaluable in helping me to untie the convoluted and confusing plotting in *Double Falshood*, and to restore important story beats which render the characters' journeys more complex, more satisfying, more 'Cervantian', perhaps more Shakespearian too, and certainly more Fletcherian.

If the keynote of this entire project is the spirit of collaboration, then Antonio has been one of its shining lights.

Meanwhile my assistant director, Ben Brynmor, has been finding out about duennas. In an early scene between the lovers, Don Bernardo upbraids Cardenio for wooing his daughter in public. 'What, Cardenio, in public? This wooing is too urgent.' Then later, in the wedding scene, Luscinda tells Cardenio that they cannot run away as her 'steps are watched'. We have decided to fortify this aspect of Luscinda's segregation by inventing the character of her duenna.

Ben has been exploring one of the tales from Cervantes' *Exemplary Stories*. It is my favourite: 'The Jealous Old Man from Extremadura'. An old man hides away his young wife behind the walls of his impenetrable house, and keeps her under the guard of a fearsome duenna. Cervantes reveals his detestation of these women in the story:

> O ye smooth-filed tongues! O ye pleated veils! The
> honourable wear of grave matrons, chosen out of
> purpose for to authorise the rooms and the estrados of

your principal ladies, how contrary to your place and
duty do ye exercise this your powerful, nay rather in a
manner enforcing office.

This particular Exemplary Story was 'turned into English' in
1640 by Don Diego de Puede-Ser. The name is a pun. 'Puede-
Ser' means 'May-be' and James Mabbe was the real
translator.

Ben has directed Cervantes' own adaptation of the short
story. He has been working with a few of the *Cardenio* cast:
Liz Crowther (the duenna), Maya Barcot (the nun), Matti
Houghton (Dorotea's treacherous maid), Chiké Okonkwo
(Fernando's shady manservant Gerardo), Felix Hayes (the
shepherd who gets attacked by Cardenio); and Chris Godwin
(Don Camillo), who has taken on the role of the jealous old
man himself. The Interlude isn't quite as sharp or detailed as
the short story, and indeed cuts out the character of the
duenna, but nevertheless their research throws up some
fascinating material which we can use in the production.

Today we take a break from rehearsals to watch the Interlude. It is short, only twenty minutes or so, but very
entertaining.

On a playbill for the Drury Lane revival of *Double Falshood* in 1770, the play is paired with an afterpiece called *The
Padlock*. This two-act 'operetta' with music by Charles Dibdin, and text by Isaac Bickerstaffe, is based on 'The Jealous
Old Man from Extremadura'. I wonder if they were aware of
the Cervantes connection in the two pieces.

The company later revive their performance of the Spanish Interlude at a celebration of Cervantes organised by the
Shakespeare Birthplace Trust in Stratford.

Elsewhere rehearsals continue at a steady pace. In one of
the fitting rooms, Pippa Nixon (Dorotea), is being taught
lace-making by local expert, Marion Stubbings. In Cervantes' novel, Dorotea, the wealthy farmer's daughter,
spends her free time lace-making and playing on the harp. I
pop in to say hello. I've brought a copy of a painting by the
seventeenth-century artist Zurburán, known as the Spanish
Caravaggio for his use of chiaroscuro, the play of light and

dark. In this image, and several like them, the young girl is depicted making lace on a small cushion.

'Oh no,' says Marion, 'that's a Belgian cushion. This is a Spanish cushion,' and she reveals a large oblong block. Not the dainty prop I was looking for. I feel a little churlish, suggesting that the traditional Spanish cushion might be a little too large for our purposes as it requires propping up, and we have nowhere onstage to prop it. And that, Belgian or not, the cushion in Zurburán's painting might just be a little more convenient for us.

48

Pope's Revenge:
Piddling Tibbald Crucifies Shakespeare

When Alexander Pope was riled he could be vicious. Take, for example, the famous and devastating demolition job he did on one of his bitterest rival, the sexually ambiguous Lord Hervey whom he dismissed as 'Sporus' (the name of Nero's castrated lover):

> What? that Thing of silk,
> Sporus, that mere white Curd of Ass's milk?
> Satire or Shame alas! can Sporus feel?
> Who breaks a Butterfly upon a Wheel?

Who would not reel from the slap of such satire? So what on earth did Lewis Theobald expect when he attacked Alexander Pope for his sloppy edition of Shakespeare? Criticising this master satirist would have been the equivalent of taking on *Private Eye* today. Pope had harboured his grudge over *Shakespeare Restored* and used *Double Falshood* to further his revenge on Theobald.

In 1728, shortly after the run of *Double Falshood*, Pope anonymously published *The Dunciad*. The poem's very name echoes *The Aeneid*, or *The Iliad*, and suggests its mock-epic flavour. *The Dunciad* satirises all the dunces in London, the 'sons of Dullness' as he calls them. And whom does Pope make the King of the Dunces? Poor Lewis Theobald.

Here's how he gets his own back for the criticism over his Shakespeare edition (and note: this is the evidence that Theobald's name must have been pronounced as Pope renders it here: 'Tibbald'):

> In future Ages how their Fame will spread,
> For routing Triplets and restoring 'ed'.
> Yet ne'er one Sprig of Laurel graces these Ribbalds
> From sanguine *Sewell* down to piddling *Tibbalds*,
> Who thinks he reads when he but scans and spells,
> A Word-catcher that lives on Syllables.

(Sewell is another editor who had incurred Pope's wrath.) Pope imagines the 'word-catcher' Theobald, obsessively and pedantically working to revive Shakespeare's worst jokes:

> Old puns restore, lost blunders nicely seek
> And crucify poor Shakespeare once a week.

At one point in the third book of *The Dunciad,* Pope gets himself into such a pickle that he has to attack Shakespeare as a bad writer. He quotes Cardenio's line about Fernando's treachery:

> None but itself can be its parallel.*

In fact he rather lazily misquotes it as:

> None but thyself can be thy parallel.

---

* There is some argument for thinking this disputed line of Cardenio's could be a genuine Fletcher line. I popped into the National Portrait Gallery one afternoon after rehearsals to check the beautiful portrait of John Fletcher, newly acquired for the nation (see the first colour plate section). There he stands, left hand on hip, right hand resting on a table by inkstand and quills. There is a piece of paper under the heel of his palm, on which is written:

> Non but thy owne penn could
> Thy witt express.

John has a twinkle in his eye, and seems almost to be suppressing a playful smirk, as if he knows something I will never know.

And then he includes a note:

> A marvellous line of Theobald, unless the play called
> *Double Falshood* be (as he would have it believed)
> Shakespeare's. But whether this line be his or not, he
> proves Shakespeare to have written as bad.

In a poem called *The Battle of the Poets*, Thomas Cooke describes the controversy which followed. He tries to defend Theobald ('great Shakespeare's friend') from the abuse adopted by Pope, more worthy of the foul-mouthed porters of Covent Garden Market:

> Pope and his forces disappointed bend
> Their fury doubled on great Shakespeare's friend.
> The style of porters he would bring in use
> As if all wit consisted in abuse.

Nevertheless, Pope's satirical attack landed, and the name stuck. Lewis Theobald would gain his immortality, but not the fame he sought. He was consigned to history as 'piddling Tibbald', a risible literary footnote, denoting at once both word-splitting pedantry and dribbling incontinence.

The Yale professor Thomas Lounsbury, writing in 1906, began to try to defend poor Lewis Theobald's posthumous reputation, saying 'Theobald in fact had a curious confidence in the ultimate triumph of truth, which has about it... something almost pathetic.' And later, 'modern impressions about Theobald have been derived almost wholly from the assertions of the poet... succeeding generations have derived their knowledge from the notes to *The Dunciad*.'

49

Stage Shepherds Can Be Hard to Do!

The shepherds in the Sierra Morena mountains in Act Four of our play live a hard life.

Baron Davillier, and Gustave Doré, encountered immense flocks of travelling sheep on their trip around Spain in 1863, and provide us with some useful information about shepherds, which may help us to locate and root these sketchily drawn characters as real working folk. The Baron describes an old tradition known as the *Mesta*, the name given to a 'very ancient gathering' in Spain, where shepherds bring their sheep, in huge numbers, down to warmer pastures to escape the cold. Presumably these were the same sorts of flocks that Don Quixote mistakes for a battalion of marching soldiers and attacks. Davillier calls them 'armies of peace'.

In the *Mesta*, each flock of up to 10,000 sheep is called a *cabaña*. It is directed by a master shepherd, or *mayoral*, who has fifty shepherds under him, accompanied by an equal number of dogs. The shepherds don't get paid much, but are allowed two pounds of bread a day, and can own a number of sheep. The wool belongs to the owner of the flock, but the shepherd can dispose of the meat, the lambs and the milk. Doré sketches one of these shepherds sitting among his flock.

This mass movement of sheep still happens in Spain on the Sunday nearest to the 20th of November, when shepherds move their stock from the higher mountains in Leon, north of Madrid, to the winter pasture in the warmer, flatter Extremadura.

In rehearsal, we try and imagine what these shepherds might look and sound like. I can hear the sheep bells, I can imagine the dogs barking, and what of the echo, mentioned in Dorotea's song?

The scene starts with a song among them. I have searched the archives of Alan Lomax, the American folksong archivist. He gathered and recorded many European folk songs, which could date back many centuries. Lomax travelled Spain in the fifties, recording songs all over Spain. In Extremadura, which borders Andalucía, he spent a night in a *chozo*, a shepherd's hut, listening to an old man chant his song. He describes the place in his notes:

> A hut of straw... an oil lamp, a three-legged frying pan
> in a little square hearth in the centre of the hut, forks
> and spoons stuck in a wall of rushes, rush beds of
> aromatic branches around the room... no windows, airy
> and clean... low stools of cork and knotted branches.

The recording is an archaic chant-like melody about a murdered shepherd whispering his last words to his sheep with his dying breath.

In Gerald Brenan's *South from Granada*, he describes shepherds who have lived so much of the year in solitude that they have almost forgotten the power of speech. But they can sing songs which would cross the huge distances between the mountains, and which would be understood, he says, by other shepherds from Albania to Switzerland.

Other than recreating the sound of the sheep, their bells and the dogs, we ponder how to create a sense of the mountainous terrain in which the shepherds live. Martin Slavin, our sound designer, today comes up with a fascinating contribution. We had discussed how shepherds might communicate from valley to valley. Having rejected yodelling, Martin has done some research into whistling.

There is a language called Silbo, which is a Spanish form of whistling from La Gomera in the Canary Islands. It was a language invented by the original inhabitants of the islands, the Guanches, and adopted by the Spanish settlers in the sixteenth century. Martin has discovered a film on YouTube. It demonstrates the extraordinary tonal whistling language, and sends the actors who are playing shepherds off on a spree of tonal whistling.

Like the mystery play at Elche, 'El Silbo' was declared as a Masterpiece of the Oral and Intangible Heritage of Humanity by UNESCO in 2009.

Today we bring all this sporadic research together. Paul Englishby teaches the shepherds the song he has composed. It incorporates an antiphonal call and response, suggesting the cries of shepherds across the valleys.*

---

* There is an alternative to the 'Fond Echo' song that Dorotea sings in a later scene.

Back in 2001 I was asked by historian and television documentarist Michael Wood to help him work on his BBC series *In Search of Shakespeare*. In researching the programme, Michael had uncovered, in the British Library, an anonymous set of music and lyrics among the papers of Robert Johnson (1583–1633), the King's lutenist, and composer for some of Shakespeare's late plays.

The lyrics of one of these songs (which begins 'Woods, rocks and mountains') has distinct verbal parallels with Shelton's translation of the scene in *Don Quixote*. Excitingly, Wood concludes that the music may well be a setting of Dorotea's song from the original production of *Cardenio*.

In the end, in our production, composer Paul Englishby and I chose to set the words in Theobald's adaptation, *Double Falshood*, instead ('Fond Echo'), as Johnson's Jacobean musical setting – although very beautiful – did not chime with our heightened Spanish setting.

A facsimile of the music score is available in Brean Hammond's edition of *Double Falshood* for the Arden Shakespeare. The lyrics read:

Woods, rocks and mountains, and you desert places,
Where nought but bitter cold and hunger dwells,
Hear a poor maid's last words, killed with disgraces,
Slide softly while I sing you silver fountains
And let your hollow waters like sad bells
Ring, ring to my woes while miserable I
Cursing my fortunes, drop a tear and die.

The Distrest Poet, William Hogarth (1736–7)

50

Distressed Poets and
Half-a-Crown Tale-Turners

In Birmingham Art Gallery there is a painting by William Hogarth. It is called *The Distrest Poet* and was painted around 1736. It shows a man scratching his head under his wig and staring out of the window of a dreary garret, trying to write. The sparsely furnished room is a mess, the plaster is cracked, and the cupboard stands bare. A baby squeals in the shabby bed in the corner. A forlorn wife attempts to patch ragged breeches. At the door, a sturdy milkmaid demands payment of her bill. Unseen, a dog steals a mutton chop from a plate.

This is a picture of the destitute Lewis Theobald. The title is a jibe at his great folly, *Double Falshood*, the subtitle of which was *The **Distrest** Lovers*. The picture may also allude to the poem Theobald wrote in his youth, in imitation of Shakespeare, 'The Cave of Poverty'.

William Warburton left a description of Theobald's reduced circumstances. He addresses Lewis in print saying that Alexander Pope

> knew you at the first to be of the beggarly brotherhood
> of half-a-crown tale-turners; that you was monstrously

in debt, your lumber of a library almost all pawned;
your tailor unpaid; and that you have an ugly trick of
going supperless to bed.

Despite the effects of Pope's devastating satirical attack on
'piddling Tibbald', Lewis did get to publish his own edition
of Shakespeare in the end (in 1733), and indeed is now
widely recognised as one of the greatest editors of the eighteenth century. For one brilliant deduction in particular he
deserves our lasting thanks. Mrs Quickly has a baffling line
in the Folio about the death of Falstaff in *Henry V*. It reads:
'for his Nose was as sharpe as a Pen, and a Table of greene
fields'. Nick de Somogyi calls this 'the most knotty locked-
room mystery in all Shakespeare studies'. Pope suggested
this was a stage direction; that a table was brought onstage,
belonging to a man called Greenfields, who must have been
the prompter at the Globe. But instead, Lewis had the happy
felicity to realise that Falstaff might in his last moments have
'babbled o' green fields': ineffably beautiful. Shakespeare
Restored indeed. Thank you, Lewis.

Theobald had been granted the King's 'royal privilege and
licence for the sole printing and publishing [of *Double Falshood*], for the term of fourteen years', and he proclaimed
that privilege on the front page of the first edition of the
play. However, he sold those rights within a year, and did not
include the play when he came to publish his own Shakespeare edition. Had he lost confidence in his assertion of
Shakespeare's authorship?

Brean Hammond suggests that the whole affair may have
been an embarrassment to Theobald. If the manuscript with
which he had been entrusted had nothing to do with Shakespeare, or indeed was in reality based on a play by Fletcher,
then it would not reflect well on his fiercely acquired reputation as a Shakespeare scholar. As Hammond puts it: 'If
confessed, it would have been a humiliation on the scale of
Lord Dacre's, when he failed to recognise the Hitler diaries
as an obvious fraud.'

Now, I have to admit, as this story has unfolded, that I have
been rather prejudiced against Alexander Pope, preferring

instead to champion the underdog, Lewis Theobald. Pope had done a frankly slapdash job on his edition of Shakespeare, and he'd been found out. He didn't like that. And he especially did not like being used as a stepping stone by an ambitious writer of pantomimes.

I felt sorry for poor Theobald, and found myself leaping to his defence. Did he deserve to be condemned for all time as 'piddling Tibbald'? It would have been bad enough to have been included in *The Dunciad* at all, but to have been singled out so vindictively, as the Chief of all the Dunces, must have been intolerable.

It is possible that Pope's revenge on Theobald and his kin was suggested to him by a house guest he had with him at the time, the Dean of St Patrick's Cathedral, in Dublin: Jonathan Swift. In 1726 Swift had published his great satire, *Gulliver's Travels*. He was staying with Pope in Twickenham, and must have witnessed the humiliation that his friend endured from Theobald's condemnation of his slack scholarship in *Shakespeare Restored*.

But what made me begin to review my prejudice against Pope was reading a letter he wrote to Swift on his departure for Ireland. It is full of such tender regard for his friend and such surprising vulnerability that I began to see the torment that Pope endured, particularly given his physical deformities (he never grew above four foot six, and was hunchbacked) and the lack of more intimate friendships in his life. Dated 22 August 1726, his letter to Swift reads:

> Many a short sigh you cost me the day I left you, and many more you will cost me, till the day you return. I really walk'd about like a man banish'd, and when I came home, found it no home. 'Tis a sensation like that of a limb lopp'd off, one is trying every minute unawares to use it, and finds it not. I may say you have used me more cruelly than you have done any other man; you have made it more impossible for me to live at ease without you: Habitude itself would have done that, if I had less friendship in my nature than I have. Besides my natural memory of you, I have a local one, which presents you to me in every place I frequent: I

shall never more think of Lord Cobham's, the woods of Ciceter, or the pleasing prospect of Byberry, but your Idea must be joined with 'em; nor see one seat in my own garden, or one room in my own house, without a Phantome of you, sitting or walking before me... In real truth, I have felt my soul peevish ever since with all about me, from a warm uneasy desire after you. I am gone out of myself to no purpose and cannot catch you.

Who would not warm to such an expression of devoted friendship?

Alexander Pope, William Hoare (c. 1739–43)

51

The Final Act

In the rehearsal room for *Cardenio*, we are still working on the script.

Our challenge this week is to crack the play's denouement. Lewis Theobald's *Double Falshood* wraps everything up rather too neatly. He has so many loose ends to tie up, so many revelations to juggle; far more than Cervantes, who only has the quartet of lovers to manage. *Double Falshood* introduces three different fathers into the action (Fletcher's influence, I suspect). Shakespeare's late plays manage these final scenes brilliantly, perhaps most astonishingly in *Cymbeline*.

George Bernard Shaw, however, had such a problem with the last act of *Cymbeline*, he unapologetically 're-finished' it. But he missed the point. In a good production managed well, the revelation piled upon revelation has a joyous cumulative effect. More characters have asides in that play than in any other in Shakespeare's canon. These asides are crucial to how the final scene works, because they demand that you, the audience, see the action from each character's perspective. So when the final impossible outcome is achieved, you are waiting eagerly for each of your new confidants to tell their side of the story.

It must be the same with *Cardenio*. It is vital that the audience have made sufficient investment in each character to allow them to await the final unravelling with eager anticipation. We have to make the audience experience, however unlikely the circumstances, a balance between the fantastic and the plausible; what Coleridge called 'the willing suspension of disbelief'. And we must do that by infusing these 'shadows of imagination' with genuine life-blood.

Olly Rix is worried that Cardenio has disappeared in the final scene, in which he says virtually nothing. He's right. In *Double Falshood*, he seems either still demented, or a bit of a sap, merely accepting Fernando's apology when he's forced into a corner. Antonio Álamo had suggested giving him some of Dorotea's long speech, but this seems to me to dilute her impact.

We try rejigging the scene.

The Duke's older son, Pedro, has contrived to bring his wayward brother, Fernando, face to face with his father; and to reunite Luscinda with her dad. He then provokes his brother even further by challenging him with the abuse of one of his pages (Dorotea, still in disguise as the herds-boy). The page swears he has a witness to Fernando's crimes, and leaves to fetch them. In fact the witness is herself, and she will return dressed as a woman again.

So far so good.

It is at this point in *Double Falshood* that Pedro introduces not only Cardenio, but also the Dorotea character *as a woman*. And within thirty lines or so has wrapped up all the confusion, and reconciled all the couples. It's too fast, and oddly unsatisfactory.

We are waiting for Fernando to come face to face with Cardenio, the friend he so violently betrayed. In the novel, Cervantes is constrained by the social etiquette of his day, and Cardenio, as a vassal of the Duke's son, must restrain any violent impulse he may feel towards his superior. The novel becomes extremely exciting, as Fernando cannot bear to see Cardenio and Luscinda reconciled and seizes Luscinda, keeping Cardenio at bay with his sword. It is Dorotea who then persuades him to release Luscinda, and to accept her as his true wife, in a long, passionate and moving speech.

This has got to be a better scheme, and we try adopting it.

So we separate the entry of Cardenio and Dorotea, holding up her return to a more crucial moment in the denouement. Cardenio enters and faces Fernando. As a company we discuss what should happen now. What do we want to happen next? The reaction is almost unanimous, and it is the same solution adopted by Pichou back in 1628. In *Les Folies de Cardenio*, when Cardenio and Fernando finally see each other again, a fight breaks out, and Dorotea intervenes. We take our cue from there.

Fernando is shocked to see Cardenio, and seems about to beg forgiveness from his old friend, but instead he suddenly punches him in the stomach and a fight breaks out. (Terry King, our fight director, can sort this out later, and we mark something in for now.) Fernando might be more accomplished with a rapier, but in a fist fight, Cardenio easily wins, and Fernando is dispatched into a pile of chairs.

This allows the group assembled in the inn to recognise the mad Cardenio in his rags and shaggy hair, and for the reconciliation between the boy and his father, Don Camillo, to take place. 'This almost melts me,' the crusty old man whimpers.

But then, after much discussion on the rehearsal floor, we decide to introduce the episode in the novel where Cervantes has the volatile Fernando impulsively seize back Luscinda in a fit of jealousy.

'It's like the moment in *Fatal Attraction*,' someone says. 'You know, when we think Glenn Close is dead, but she suddenly bursts out of the bath, wielding a knife.' And actually, that is rather like what happens. Just at the touching moment when Cardenio opens his arms to receive Luscinda, Fernando leaps through the crowd of onlookers to grab her, throws Cardenio to the floor and seizes someone's sword. And at that instant, Dorotea suddenly appears.

Fernando is shocked into dumbness by the appearance of the girl he had once been so obsessed by and had once professed to love.

After all the noisy hurly-burly there is silence.

I once did a workshop with some actors in the Noh Theatre in Tokyo. They told me that there is a fundamental difference between music in the West and the music used in the Noh Theatre. The function of the former is to create sound, but the function of the latter is to create silence. In other words, the furious drumming that occasionally punctuates the action in Noh is used to create the emptiness which follows it. It is into that silence, that vacuum, that something important will drop. They call that silence 'ma'.

This is our 'ma' moment.

Dorotea claims her silence to speak. The long appeal she makes, which I had worried about in Michigan, now earns its place.

The last scene, which is so feeble in *Double Falshood* and so exciting in *Don Quixote*, now delivers. Its impact is powerful. The invention, suggested by Cervantes, in reaction to Theobald, borrowed in part from Pichou, and reinterpreted by us on the rehearsal floor, works. We run the scene, and as we reach the end, the assembled company burst into applause. Everyone has invested in the process, and feels a sense of ownership and pride in the outcome. Suddenly the play feels like ours.

'The reunion of Dorotea, Luscinda, Cardenio and Fernando in the inn', from Gustave Doré's *Illustrations for Don Quixote* (1863)

In the lunch break, I have to check the proof for the frontispiece to the printed script of the play which will go on sale alongside the production. It reads:

CARDENIO

Shakespeare's 'Lost Play' Re-imagined

After
Double Falshood; or The Distrest Lovers
by Lewis Theobald (1727)

Apparently revised
from a manuscript in the handwriting of John Downes
and conceivably adapted by Sir William Davenant for
Thomas Betterton from
The History of Cardenio
by Mr Fletcher and Shakespeare (1612)
performed at Court in 1612/13

Which may have been based on an episode in
Don Quixote
by Miguel de Cervantes
Which was translated into English
by Thomas Shelton
First published in 1612

And here adapted and directed by Gregory Doran
for the Royal Shakespeare Company
With additional Spanish material supplied
by Antonio Álamo
via a literal translation by DuncanWheeler

And I add an extra line:

And developed in rehearsal by the original cast.

52

Old St Pancras Church

One afternoon during rehearsals, I headed home from Clapham, and decided to make a detour at King's Cross. I wanted to visit St Pancras Old Church behind the railway station.

It was here on 20 September 1744 that Lewis Theobald was buried.

'He went off quietly,' said his old friend, John Stede, 'without agonies.' Stede, who like John Downes was a prompter in the theatre, had known Lewis for nearly thirty years. He was with him when he died, of jaundice, noting the remarkable fact that 'he was so composed as not to alter the disposition of his body, being in an indolent posture, one foot out of the bed, and his head gently supported on one hand'.

The old prompter left a gentle eulogy to his friend, saying, 'He was of a generous spirit, too generous for his circumstances, and none knew how to do a handsome thing, or confer a benefit, when in his power, with a better grace than himself.' The funeral took place at six o'clock in the evening, and Stede records rather sadly, 'I only attended him.' He was the sole mourner.

Theobald was fifty-six when he died. His nemesis, Alexander Pope, born in the same year, had died some three months before him at the end of May.

A benefit performance of *Double Falshood* for Theobald himself had been held some three years before in May 1741, and Lewis had written somewhat pathetically to the Duke of Newcastle:

> The situation of my affairs, upon a loss and disappointment, obliging me to embrace a benefit at this late and disadvantageous season, it lays me under a necessity of throwing myself on the favour of the public, and the kind assistance of my friends and well wishers.

There had been one late recognition of Lewis Theobald's knowledge and understanding of Shakespeare. He was asked (probably by John Rich), to contribute a prologue for a play mounted at Covent Garden to raise funds for a statue of Shakespeare to be erected in Poet's Corner in Westminster Abbey. Designed by William Kent, executed by Peter Scheemakers, and paid for in part by Alexander Pope among others, the life-size marble statue was finally unveiled in January 1741.

> Immortal Shakespeare, we thy fame admit
> Like thy Caesar, thou art mighty yet.
> Fast rise the marble, and long last the pile
> O'er which thy venerable bust shall smile.

It's not great poetry, but it attests to Theobald's adoration 'on this side idolatry' of his beloved bard.

St Pancras graveyard is still looking wintery, but here and there clumps of daffodils are beginning to break through. It was here that the Romantic poet Shelley met Mary Godwin, when she was visiting the grave of her mother, Mary Wollstonecraft, the advocate of women's rights. Among the other people buried here in Theobald's day are two of the celebrities featured in Gay's sensational hit show *The Beggar's Opera*, which opened within months of *Double Falshood*.

The model for Peachum, and the principal character in both Henry Fielding's satire and Daniel Defoe's eponymous novel, the notorious kingpin of London's underworld, Jonathan Wild, was buried here, in 1725. He was laid next to his wife, but his body was 'fished', or snatched by tomb robbers, and sold for dissection at a local medical school. His skeleton is still preserved in the Hunterian Museum of the Royal College of Surgeons. And the pickpocket Jenny Diver, hanged at Tyburn and also a character in *The Beggar's Opera*, is here too.

The majority of the gravestones were cleared when the railway at King's Cross was expanded in 1865, but in the south-east corner of the cemetery, overgrown with ivy, I spot a few old stones. A couple date back to the 1720s. You can tell by the style of the engraved calligraphy that they are much older than the rest. One headstone shows a death's head staring fiercely above crossed palm branches, and on another, a skull in profile cowers under thundery clouds. I think this is more like what Lewis might have had, had he been able to afford the carving. It sums up a life beset by storms and trials.

Surprisingly, St Pancras Old Church stands on one of Europe's most ancient sites of Christian worship, possibly dating back to the fourth century. The present small church has been here since the eleventh or twelfth century. Inside, an old man has come for a quiet afternoon nap, so I tiptoe around looking at the monuments. Here in the chancel is one to the man who, for twenty-nine years, was cook to both Queen Elizabeth and King James; and there's another to Samuel Cooper, the miniaturist who painted everyone from Oliver Cromwell to Mrs Pepys.

I light a candle for Lewis Theobald, and tiptoe back out, leaving the gent to his snooze.

53

Last Week of Rehearsals

The Circle of Ears

On Wednesday, we did a session which I call the circle of
ears. In Thomas Overbury's book of *Characters* (posthu-
mously published in 1616), he describes 'An Excellent Actor'.
In all probability, he is referring to Richard Burbage. He
writes, 'Sit in a full theatre and you will think you see so
many lines drawn from the circumference of so many ears,
while the actor is in the centre': the actor in the centre of a
circle of ears. It could be a description of the Swan Theatre.

So we sit in a circle. And work through the play. It can be
useful at this late stage of rehearsal to forget any blocking or
business and just get back to the text. The actors who speak
in each scene stand in the circle and just speak the lines to
each other. But their fellow actors sitting around can ask
them to repeat a line they have not heard, or which they
want to hear again. Initially the exercise produces laughter,
as people are thrown off their stride, or get irritated at being
challenged to supply an all-important final consonant. But
eventually the exercise starts to yield interesting stuff: adjec-
tives that have been taken for granted, antitheses that have

been ignored, or images that have grown stale are minted anew, coined afresh, and invested with a real need. And it puts an end to any mumbling, declaiming, or over-stressing.

Missing final consonants can lead to some pretty disastrous misunderstandings: when, for example, 'my honoured guest' turns into 'my honoured guess', or 'a friend in trust' becomes 'a friend in truss', or 'I could weep' becomes... Well, you get the point.

Jacquie Crago, who is entrusted with taking care of 'voice and text' on this show, rigorously pursues dropped consonants and urges greater muscularity. One of the most difficult of consonants to convey in the theatre is 'V'. And it is often vital. Love, live, grieve, grave, strive, swerve, heave, move. 'M' is another: dream, stream, etc.

I have a personal antipathy for stressed pronouns. It seems to me they are usually the least interesting word in the line to stress, but actors often love ponging them. In Hamlet's line 'What's Hecuba to **him** or **he** to Hecuba', it is valid. But not in 'Oh what a rogue and peasant slave am **I**', for example, where the things 'I am' are surely much more interesting. So in our play, for example, we avoid 'He takes our victuals from **us**', preferring the more informative 'He takes our **victuals** from us'.

And occasionally of course, over such a long rehearsal period, actors have investigated various shades of meaning, and stress, and the line can become laboured, or weighed down with significance – 'over-minted', if you like – in the search for an impression of spontaneity. So, for example, the breathtaking simplicity of Macbeth's cogitation on Duncan's murder:

> If it were done when 'tis done, then 'twere well
> It were done quickly

becomes:

> IF (*let's just say*) 'IT' (*you know what I'm talking about*)
> were DONE (*and when I say 'done', I mean over and
> done with*) when 'tis DONE (*I'm not actually going to*

say the word 'murder'), then 'twere well (*how can I put this...*) it were DONE (*I know you are following me...*) QUICKLY.

You can feel battered by nuance.

It is important too that the actor builds from word to word, from sentence to sentence, but also to the shape of a speech as a whole; otherwise, if the audience is presented with each sentence in isolation, they can fail to get the whole picture, to see the wood or the trees.

The circle of ears encourages a more direct approach, propelling the line to the full stop, and the speech to its conclusion.

Run-throughs

Thursday 31 March 2011. Our first run-through.

We managed to work through the entire play yesterday, slowly, scene by scene, in order. So, because I have to hand over priority rehearsal to *The City Madam* for the rest of the week, I decide that we should seize the opportunity of this morning's session to do our first run of the play. It's a real roller-coaster ride. The entire company pull out all the stops, and the story becomes urgent and felt.

Jacquie Crago has been making copious notes, while Kate Sagovsky, who is working as a placement in the movement department, and hasn't seen any of the play so far, is our first guinea pig audience member. She sits on the edge of her seat throughout. She voices what we all hope will be the audience's eventual reaction:

'It's like seeing a Shakespeare play, but one in which you don't know what is going to happen next.'

That has to be a good reaction.

Final Run-through

Friday 8 April 2011. One day a couple of weeks back, Bruce O'Neil, our music director, called me out of rehearsal. He wanted me to meet someone. We went upstairs to the Voice room where our composer Paul Englishby was auditioning a singer to be part of the band for the production.

Javier Macías is a flamenco singer. He comes from Cadiz, but now lives in Portsmouth. He seems quite shy and retiring. Paul asks him if he will just give me a little sample of his voice and as Javier opens his mouth a great gust of sound emerges, as warm and Spanish as the Leveche, the southwest wind of Andalucía.

Javier is keen to be a part of the show, but he is nervous. He openly admits he is unused to repeating himself. As a flamenco singer, no two performances are the same. He must be moved in the moment to express what he feels. So singing precise cues, to exactly the same length every night might be a challenge. But we all think it is worth the risk.

Our final run on Friday was given a big lift from the presence of Javier and our band. Paul Englishby, with the help of the RSC music department, has assembled an inspiring line-up of musical talents. There are two guitars, a percussionist – and Javier.

One of the guitarists, Nick Lee, is a regular RSC band member, the other, Luis Carro Barquero, is also Spanish and regularly plays with Javier. Nick sidles up to me before the run to inform me that the musicians have been discussing their different working practices, and he feels he should inform me that the Spanish musicians won't work through the afternoon, but expect to break for a siesta. Unfortunately I can see a grin breaking out at the side of his mouth and see through his ruse. April Fool's Day was last week.

As the run starts and Javier starts to sing, embroidering the notes with a cry that seems to come from some unfathomable part of his being, from his soul perhaps, I begin to understand why they say that *cante jondo* has black sounds in it. His singing lends the play an urgency, as if it comes from a deeper Spanish core.

At the end of the run Jeanie O'Hare, the RSC's dramaturg, admits she wept for most of the second half.

Then it is time to spend the money built up in the mobile-phone fund. I have a rule that if your mobile phone goes off in the rehearsal room you are charged £5, and £25 if it goes off in a run. Nobody's phone has ever gone off in a run. But there are inevitable lapses, so that by the time we reach the end of our eleventh week of shared rehearsal, the mobile-phone kitty is enough to pay for some refreshment to celebrate our transition from rehearsal room to the theatre. Alix and her team wheel in the bottles and the cake, and while everyone relaxes we contemplate the move into the Swan next week.

I remind the company that, however smoothly our final run may have gone, we are likely to lose that intensity and concentration over the next seven days, as we transfer into the theatre. There will be all the excitement of the move to Stratford, the thrill of walking into the Swan, the charge of seeing the set, and admiring everyone in wigs and costumes. Then, as we start the technical rehearsal, and we see the lighting, hear the full musical score, work with new props, and start to negotiate all these distractions, we will struggle to get back the simplicity and directness we had achieved in the rehearsal room. Then there are the gathering nerves, and the sheer terror of facing the audience for the first time. All these factors will combine to pull the play away from us. But we will get it back, and when it comes back, if we are lucky, it will be a more intense, a finer experience.

The proof of the programme has arrived today for me to check. Valerie Wayne, the professor from Hawaii University whom we met in Michigan, has provided one of the essays for it; wittily placing our endeavours in a wider context: 'In 1965,' she writes:

> *The Man of La Mancha* burst onto Broadway as a hit musical. Its signature song 'To dream the impossible dream' may be thought to characterise any attempt to recover the elusive *Cardenio*, but the RSC are working within a venerable dramatic tradition as they stage this tale of fractured friendship and impetuous desire.

54

Stratford Bound

It's a perky April morning as I drive up to Stratford to begin the technical week of *Cardenio*. The meadows are silly with lambs, the hedgerows all frothy with blossom, and even the motorway's central reservation is a-dazzle with dandelions.

Every time I come up to Stratford at this time of year I am reminded of a line from *The Merchant of Venice*:

> A day in April never came so sweet
> To show how costly summer was at hand.

This morning the weather is as full of promise as the bright green buds on the sycamore trees. And as the actors all arrive and settle into their new homes for the summer, there's a collective crossing of fingers that the new season's shows will live up to the huge level of expectation surrounding the new theatre building on the banks of the Avon.

The 'tech' (or technical rehearsal) is always exciting, as we start putting the bits of the production together. Niki Turner's set is in place, with its huge iron-grille gates, looking like the rood screen of Toledo Cathedral. There was a slight problem in the fit-up, when Mark Graham, our production manager, realised that over the twenty-five years since the Swan opened, the wood has twisted and buckled slightly, so the uprights are no longer quite as upright as they were, and the gates had to be adjusted to fit between them.

Luscinda's window ('the rigorous iron grate' through which the lovers 'were wont to parley night by night') works well, and the brass back wall with its stormy El Greco sky could suggest either a mountain terrain, or a smoky chamber. Tim Mitchell's kinetic lighting transforms the stage from interior to exterior, from cosy chambers with the chiaroscuro of a Zurburán still-life painting, to the wilderness of the Sierra Morena, to a quiet autumnal convent.

The costumes have been magnificently achieved by the wardrobe department, with particular applause for Luscinda's wedding dress, the inspiration for which Niki has taken from Frans Pourbus's wedding paintings of the Savoyard Infantas. And just like Elizabeth of Valois finding the Spanish bell-farthingale impossible to wear without kicking the front, Lucy, playing Luscinda, has to learn to glide when she is wearing it, as if she has no legs.

Original costume design by Niki Turner (2011)

Pippa Nixon as Dorotea looks exactly like the painting of St Margaret of Antioch in the National Gallery in London, but without her dragon.

Teething problems with the systems at the new Royal Shakespeare Theatre mean that we keep being interrupted by fire alarms. On our second morning of the technical rehearsal, as *Macbeth* began their tech in the Main House, the alarms went off. It transpires that the newly installed smoke detectors could not distinguish real smoke from 'haze', a smoke effect regularly used in the theatre. So both acting companies in varying states of costume and make-up trooped out into the theatre garden to await instructions. Passing Easter tourists delightedly took snapshots of bleeding sergeants bumming cigarettes off Spanish nuns, and Goya-esque grandees giggling with butch warriors in leather combat gear.

The rest of the tech went so smoothly that I gave the company the evening off on Wednesday night. We worked the fiesta for safety in the morning, and Luscinda's quick-change into the wedding dress, and then did our second dress rehearsal in the afternoon.

On Thursday evening (14 April 2011), we had the first preview. It was exciting to watch the story emerge in front of a full house, as actors realised how funny parts of the play were, and the audience (predictably and delightfully for a Stratford first preview audience) rose to the occasion. By the end everyone was feeling relieved and a little euphoric.

I wonder what Lewis Theobald would have made of tonight? Would he recognise his play, or the original play he adapted, within it? Would he be offended at the changes we have made, or simply amazed that his forgery is still fooling people over two centuries later?

Wandering through the town centre, on my way home, I see a banner stretched across Union Street. It reads: 'Think you have seen every Shakespeare play? Think again...: *Cardenio* at the Swan Theatre'. I suspect Lewis Theobald would have approved of the broader instincts of our marketing department.

55

Was *Double Falshood* a Forgery?

In 2005, when we were preparing the Gunpowder Season for the Swan Theatre in Stratford, I came across a reference to play called *The Fifth of November or the Gunpowder Plot* by William Shakespeare, in Tucker Brooke's *The Shakespeare Apocrypha*. In fact it was a forgery by George Ambrose Rhodes (a surgeon from Exeter) in the 1830s. It began, as I recall, with the plotters viewing the Houses of Parliament from a safe distance on Westminster Bridge. The bridge was not built until 1750. Not a very good forgery then.

But bardolatry is littered with forgeries. Perhaps the most famous is *Vortigern* by William Henry Ireland. And if Alexander Pope was responsible for trashing Lewis Theobald's work, he is unwittingly responsible for inspiring Ireland's.

William Ireland was six years old when *Double Falshood* hit the London stage. On a childhood visit to Alexander Pope's villa, his father, Ireland Senior, sighed to his son, and said, 'I fear you will never shine such a star in the hemisphere of literary fame.' William took this as a challenge. As a young man, Ireland worked as a clerk in a conveyancer's office. First he claimed to have found a Shakespeare signature, which his father was wont to say he would give half his library to possess; then he uncovered a courting poem to Ann Hathaway; and finally a lost play: *Vortigern*.

Now I can claim to have seen *Vortigern*, which concerns the fifth-century British King of the same name. It was presented at the Bridewell Theatre in 1998. Its discovery created a sensation with various London theatres vying to produce it, until Richard Sheridan actually read it and declared that 'Shakespeare must have been very young when he wrote it.' The opening night was scheduled for the first of April 1796, until someone pointed out that this was April Fool's Day, and it opened the following night. It was a disaster, and its run ended immediately.

I don't believe Theobald did forge a lost Shakespeare play. I don't think he would have risked being found out. As a few lines written 'by a young gentleman of Cambridge' and published in the *Grub Street Journal* suggest, Theobald had trained in law, so he would have known the consequences:

> See Theobald leaves the lawyer's gainful train,
> To wrack with poetry his tortured brain;
> Fired or not fired, to write resolves with rage,
> And constant pores o'er Shakespeare's sacred page;
> – Then starting cries, 'I something will be thought.
> I'll boldly write – then – boldly swear 'twas Shakespeare
>   wrote'.
> Strange! He in poetry no forgery fears,
> That knows so well in law he'd lose his ears.

Theobald had had his fingers burned once already. In 1716, a watchmaker called Mestayer attacked the twenty-eight-year-old Theobald for plagiarism, swearing he had stolen the plot for a play he had given him to review and palmed it off as his own, calling it *The Perfidious Brother*. Lewis did not deny the charge, but claimed that he had 'drawn it as from a chaos'. The affair doesn't reflect very well on poor hungry Theobald, but to forge Shakespeare was another thing altogether. He was certainly fiercely ambitious, but I think he also loved Shakespeare too much to foist a total fabrication on the world.

56

Previews to Press Night

I had to drive back to London after the first three previews of *Cardenio* in Stratford. Although I always try to avoid returning on a Monday morning, today I had no choice, and found myself inching along in the Westway's commuter traffic. As I approached the Edgware Road exit, I glanced to my left. There, shaded by the plane trees of Paddington Green sat the rather imposing marble statue of Sarah Siddons, enthroned as the Tragic Muse. In the early nineteenth century, this was a fashionable area for the celebrated queen of Drury Lane Theatre to live. But between her burial in St Mary's cemetery in 1831, and the unveiling of her statue by Sir Henry Irving in the churchyard in 1897, the neighbourhood had declined. Now, hemmed in by high-rises, and skirted by traffic lanes, she glowers dolefully at the flyover jammed with cars.

Sarah was spotted when she was just nineteen, and fast-tracked too speedily to Drury Lane Theatre, where she made a terrible hash of Portia, and spent the next few years touring the provinces. It was in Bath in 1781 at the Theatre Royal, as a tall, striking twenty-five-year-old, that Sarah played Leonora (the Luscinda role in *Double Falshood*). It was her

fourth appearance in the role. I can see her grandly flourishing the knife at her beloved, in the wedding scene, and
intoning:

> Nay hide thee straight or see I'm armed, and vow
> To fall a bleeding sacrifice before thee.

Just over a year later she would return in triumph to Drury
Lane, which she would then dominate for two decades,
redefining such roles as Lady Macbeth and Katherine of
Aragon in her brother John Kemble's production.

A subsequent performance of *Double Falshood* in Bath on
5 July 1793 was the last known professional performance of
the play for over two hundred years.

That Monday morning I was making my way to BBC
Broadcasting House to appear on *Start the Week* with the
formidable Andrew Marr. There has been a lot of media
interest in *Cardenio* from all around the world. The other
guests on today's programme are Nick Astley, head of Blood-
axe Books, who has brought out a new poetry anthology in
his *Staying Alive/Being Human* series; Nicola Shulman, who
has written a biography of Thomas Wyatt; and Claire Armitstead, who is books editor for the *Guardian*. Claire reminds
me of a rather neat definition to remember ahead of our
press night: 'Critics may be vultures,' she said, 'but they are
sacred birds who are a necessary part of the cultural ecol-
ogy.' Neil Astley neatly suggests that our production of
Cardenio is a 'Shakespeare remix'. I like that.

Nicola has brought along a doggie toy (a sort of heart-
shaped whoopee cushion) to demonstrate how Wyatt's
poems can really only be understood as performance
pieces. The poem might perhaps have been written, for
example, on a squeaky balloon, and Nicola demonstrates
'Why sighs thou heart (squeaky-squeaky) and will not
break.'

The idea that the written poem is only part of the story is
something that fascinates me. In the same way Shakespeare's plays were merely regarded as the raw material for
the performance. Perhaps the so-called 'Bad Quarto' of

Hamlet, for example, is a clearer idea of how that play was performed in the theatre. It is a mere two thousand lines as opposed to the text in the First Folio, which is nearly twice that length, and would have taken five hours if it was ever performed in its time, which is unlikely. Professor Andrew Gurr makes the point that we are habituated to the written word, and conditioned to conceive as fixity what was then really flux. We have regarded the *Double Falshood* text as the raw material for our re-imagining of *Cardenio*.

After *Start the Week* I dash back to Stratford for Channel 4 News, who are filming that afternoon. Matthew Cain and his team come in to record an extract of the wedding scene. He then asks me on camera whether I am not just doing exactly what Lewis Theobald did: exploiting the tentative Shakespeare connection in order to make money. I respond in fulsome manner that I have spent much of my career excavating every corner of Shakespeare hagiography, and how valid an exercise this actually is. But there is something wrong with the take and we have to go again. This time faced with the same question, I just nod and shrug: 'Probably.' And that's the take they broadcast. Of course.

The press photo-call on Thursday is attended by only three photographers, as there is an accident on the M40 and everyone is held up. But the three are the famous Donald Cooper for *The Times*, Tristram Kenton for the *Guardian* and Geraint Lewis for the *Telegraph*, so they have much more access to the action than they would normally enjoy, and instead of jostling with a whole phalanx of cameras, they can get closer shots of exactly what they want. We do both the wedding scene and the seduction of Dorotea.

A film crew arrives from Russian TV, and we run the seduction scene. The young Russian reporter seems to enjoy the extract and asks Alex and Pippa what it feels like to be the first to perform in a 'new Shakespeare play'.

Saturday Preview

My partner, Tony Sher, arrives back from South Africa. He has been performing in a production of Arthur Miller's *Broken Glass* at the new Fugard Theatre in his native Cape Town. With some trepidation, Tony accompanies me to see the Saturday preview of *Cardenio*. He knows how much time I have spent on this project, and how much it has meant to me. What if he doesn't like it? And I'll know if he doesn't. And he knows I'll know.

As the company line up at the back of the stage to sing the opening motet, echoing the mourners in El Greco's Toledo altar piece, their candles glinting in the brass wall behind them, I hear Tony take a deep breath. And as Javier opens his lungs and sings the final song, filling the air with the dark sounds of Duende, Tony's eyes are welling. I know he likes it. Phew!

57

The Dear Relic

So, if *Double Falshood* was not a forgery, whatever happened to the manuscripts of Shakespeare's lost play which Theobald claimed to have? What happened to the 'dear relic'?

Brean Hammond, the editor of the Arden edition of *Double Falshood*, told me that one of the pieces of research of which he was most proud was the discovery of a newspaper report in the *Gazetteer* for 31 March 1770. It reads 'the original manuscript of this play is now treasured up in the Museum of Covent-Garden Playhouse'. He concludes that this must have been the manuscript of *Cardenio*, as Theobald's own copy of *Double Falshood* would not have been worth treasuring up. But if it was the foul papers of Shakespeare and Fletcher's original play, or a Restoration version by Davenant, belonging to Betterton, or a copy of that version written out by John Downes, we will never know. For on the night of 19/20 September 1808, Covent Garden Theatre burned down.

Mrs Siddons, writing to a friend, described what happened. She mourned:

I lost everything, all my jewels and lace, which I have
been collecting these thirty years and which I could not
purchase again for they were really fine and curious. I
had a point veil which had been a toilette of the poor
Queen of France, near five yards long... I myself was in
the house till near twelve o'clock. Mr Brandon and the
watchman saw all safe at near one, and it is as true as it
is strange that not a fragment of the whole structure
was discoverable at six, at which time my brother first
heard of it, and he declared that at that time it was so
completely destroyed that you could not have known a
building had stood there.

Sarah's brother, poor John Kemble, was by then the theatre
manager at Covent Garden. An acquaintance visited him
that morning at his house in Great Russell Street, and found
'the great actor in his dressing room, standing before the
glass, totally absorbed, and yet at intervals attempting to
shave himself...' He presently burst into speech, in the
inflated language in which he was occasionally wont to
indulge.

'Yes, it has perished that magnificent theatre. It is gone
with all its treasures of every description,' which he proceeded to describe in their order of importance:

That library, which contained all those immortal
productions of our countrymen prepared for the
purpose of representation. That vast collection of
music composed by all the greatest geniuses in that
science, by Handel, Arne, and others. That wardrobe
stored with the costumes of all ages and nations,
accumulated by unwearied research, and at incredible
expense... Of all this vast treasure, nothing now
remains, but the arms of England over the entrance of
the theatre and the Roman eagle standing solitary in
the market-place.

Kemble echoes stuttering John Hemings before him, standing in the rubble of the Globe Theatre that fateful June day
in 1613. With diabolical symmetry, the fire at Covent Garden
had been caused it was thought by a piece of smouldering

wadding fired from a gun at that evening's performance of *Pizarro*; the fire at the Globe by wadding from a cannon. But also like the Globe, Covent Garden Theatre was open again a year later.

Fire has flickered around the history of *Cardenio*. As we approached press night, I hoped that particular curse had been laid to rest.

The Covent Garden Theatre fire, artist unknown (1808)

58

Press Night: Mucha Mierda!

In a recent move at the RSC we are experimenting with separating our press nights from our first night.

The first night is not the first performance (you may have had five or six preview performances by then), but is traditionally the night you have the company party to celebrate finishing rehearsal work on the production, which has continued through the previews.

Press night is when you invite the critics in to see the work.

When the first night and the press night are combined (as is usually the case) the audience is crammed not only with the critics, but also with nervous directors, designers, composers and choreographers, with all the company's friends, families, agents, partners and lovers, and the reaction is seldom spontaneous or representative. Half the audience is wondering what to write, and the other half are wondering what they are writing. Too many of the audience are seeing the play for the second time, having checked out a preview, and either don't laugh at the funny bits, or beat the actor to the punchline. We really don't give ourselves the best chance. And the smaller the house, the worse it gets.

So with *Cardenio* we decided to finish our rehearsal work on the Saturday, and have our party that night. The company was scheduled to resume rehearsals for *The City Madam* on Monday, and continue understudy work, so a clean finish to the work on *Cardenio* was in order. As that Saturday also happened to be Shakespeare's birthday, and the date upon which both Shakespeare and Cervantes died, it seemed like an appropriate day to choose.

The company had a matinee that afternoon, which went off without incident. Dorotea's hairpin fell out, and Luscinda couldn't light the candle, but otherwise a clean show, and a very appreciative house. I always like having a matinee before a first night, as it relaxes the actors, and stops them fretting about the evening performance. Nevertheless, before the show the usual dashing about occurred as cards and little presents were given and received, keys left for arriving family members, bribes offered to the inimitable Jondon (RSC company manager) for extra tickets for the party, and frocks titivated for the do in the Ashcroft Room later; all traditional biz on a first night, but a distraction from the focus required for that performance; and merely another reason to separate the event from the evening that the press will see the show.

The show went well: so well that, inevitably and despite all my determination that there would be no critics present, I had a little twinge of regret that they hadn't seen such a joyful, well-received show.

In the squash of the party afterwards some of the faces who have been part of this experience from its early days were there to celebrate with us. Emilio Hernandez from the Almagro Festival had arrived with his wife, the distinguished flame-haired actress, Magui. Professor José Manuel González from Alicante also seemed to have enjoyed the show, and our Spanish dramaturg, Antonio Álamo, was wreathed in smiles, and plans to bring the production to Spain.

The Fletcher expert, Gordon McMullan, arrived with Professor Tiffany Stern from University College, Oxford. Tiffany has been humouring me in my crazed notion that a script of *Cardenio* might actually still exist in the ducal libraries of Turin, deposited there by Ambassador Gabaleone on his return from the command performance in June 1613. She laughs that, in the manner of a *Da Vinci Code* thriller, the plot would play out like this: she would fly to Turin, secure entry to the libraries, discover the lost manuscript, smuggle it out in a brown-paper envelope, then phone me during rehearsal in Stratford. As I came to the phone, the line would suddenly go dead, and she would have been murdered in the most gruesome manner. The script would never be seen again.

Despite Tiffany's scepticism about the provenance of *Double Falshood*, or any genuine evidence that Shakespeare wrote *Cardenio*, she sweetly expressed her delight at the show.

I pulled the company together on the afternoon of the press performance to focus everybody's minds on the night ahead. We step into a hall of mirrors on press night, and it can be a bewildering experience: some reviews will reflect accurately what we think we've achieved, but others might horribly distort those perceptions. We run the fight sequences, sing through the motet, check the final dance, do a thorough vocal warm-up with Jacquie, and give each other a group hug. 'Mucha Mierda!' I say, a phrase I learnt from our Spanish fixer Ann Bateson. It is the Spanish version of 'Break a leg!' and with an understanding of the precise relationship between fear and the bowel that perhaps only an actor about to go onstage might appreciate, it means 'Big Shit!'

My only real anxiety that press night was the smoke alarms, which have been jinxing the Main House. I feared they would go off again tonight, and the evening would be interrupted. This had happened a week into our previews. On the Wednesday night, in the Swan, *Cardenio* was stopped when an alarm sounded sub-stage in the RST. The ensuing evacuation lasted a full twenty-seven minutes. The following day, the fire officer got stuck in the lift during the show, so the stage-management team kept an extra especially careful eye on the flambeaux, candles and torches used in the show.

When ten of the acting company were trapped in the lift during the technical rehearsals, they activated the emergency communication, only to be asked by a disembodied voice what country they were in.

The stage manager, Alix Harvey-Thompson's show report for one of the previews read:

> At 8.47 p.m. we were given a three-minute warning that the alarms would go off. At three minutes the standby was extended to four minutes. At 8.51 p.m. during Mr Rix's 'Lost' speech the alarms went off and the house lights came on. The alarms were immediately silenced and Mr Rix continued with the house lights up. When Mr Rix exited at the end of his speech we held the show whilst the system was reset.
>
> The FOH Manager made a short speech to the audience.
>
> For Part 2 I was advised by the Duty Fireman to limit the amount of haze for the remainder of the show even though the problem had come from the RST with smoke reaching an alarm in a toilet.

I really did not want to have to deal with fire alarms with the press in. We had already had a mysterious hammering in the auditorium, which turned out to be water pressure: when *Macbeth* reached its interval, and all the toilets were flushed, the pipes started to bang. Luckily that problem had been sorted out by the final preview.

The press night show was extremely well received, and the audience had reacted enthusiastically. It was a relief that the critics could watch the show in front of a crowd of ordinary punters for once. Michael Boyd, sitting along the row from me (even though he had had his own press night the night before), was glowing with compliments, and we stood and applauded Javier Macías singing his flamenco play-out, before slipping backstage to congratulate the cast.

In the prompt corner, I met Alix, our stage manager, ashen with the stress. With ten minutes of the show to go, in the very final scene, suddenly the gremlins had hit. Not only had Olly Rix (Cardenio) dislocated his shoulder (he had popped it back into place: Doctor Theatre is an amazing healer), but the haze in the RST had, after all, set off the fire alarm. The team, only too aware that there was no fire, and praying that the actors would hurry up and get through the protracted denouement, had managed to keep silencing the alarm panel to get us through to the end of the show. Alix sighed: 'That was the longest ten minutes of my life.'

Is this the curse of *Macbeth*? I pondered. Perhaps, after all, it was a little foolhardy to open the new theatre with that play and ignore its fearful malediction. Or perhaps it is just the fiery gremlins that have singed the history of *Cardenio* from the Globe fire to the Covent Garden conflagration which probably destroyed the manuscript. Whatever the reason, a phantom fire had very nearly spoiled *Cardenio*'s re-emergence from its phoenix ashes.

59

The Critical Reception

Did we get away with it? Well, to quote Cervantes himself, 'at least they didn't throw cucumbers'.

Paul Taylor writing in the *Independent* said: 'I could use up all my space detailing the complicatedness of this show's provenance.' Luckily he did not do so, and determined instead to 'judge from the evidence of seeing the show'; and most critics followed suit.

Mark Lawson writing in *The Tablet* gave perhaps the most imaginative description of the whole process: 'What we have in effect is the theatrical equivalent of the process in forensic archaeology by which computer projections and 3D-modelling imagine a face and character for a medieval or Egyptian skeleton.' He went on to say, 'The provenance, however, finally doesn't matter because the project results in such a viscerally exciting evening in the theatre.'

In an enthusiastic review by the recently appointed *Times* critic, Libby Purves detected some Shakespearian notes. 'There are vivid flashes and some late scenes that could be Shakespeare and the plot – cross-dressing, amusing rustics, and final reconciliation, are all within his idiom.' 'But,' she continued, 'mainly it is a rumbustious Gothic melodrama fit for Georgette Heyer: a striding, brawling, ranting, romancing riot.'

The language got an occasional light slap. The *Evening Standard* missed 'the condensed eloquence of Shakespeare's most skilfully wrought lines', while *The Times* allowed that 'the frequent banality of the language is treated nimbly, naturalistically and with magnificent humour'. Libby Purves picked out some of the lines which caught her ear: 'Expressions such as "Disasterous Dorotea" [a direct quote from Shelton's translation] are to be treasured, as is "Thou goat, whose lust is more insatiate than the grave" [which I pinched from a Fletcher play based on Cervantes].' She was less complimentary about 'Sure every swine must have his Martinmas', which she said 'comes straight out of *The Art of Coarse Acting*'. In fact, it is a rather colourful Spanish proverb provided by Antonio Álamo from elsewhere in *Don Quixote*.

I got a knuckle-rapping from Katherine Duncan-Jones in the *TLS* in iambic pentameter. And she's obviously had a great deal of fun doing so.

> Composing blank verse isn't hard at all
> Lots of us do it almost every day
> Like Sarah Siddons in the post-show pub:
> 'I asked for porter and you gave me beer.'
> Greg Doran's lines are far too regular
> Lacking great William's teasing twists and turns.
> To illustrate I'm going to quote a few:
> 'Please you, madam, I'm not so certain now'
> 'My rage has poured upon my reasoning
> Clouds of error.'

She has a point, but I can't forbear noting for the record that the second line she quotes (above) is not mine at all, but Fletcher via Cervantes and is plagiarised from *The Fair Maid of the Inn*.

In Charles Spencer's review for the *Daily Telegraph*, headlined 'Echoes of Greatness', he admits his fairly low expectation for the production. 'I feared this production...

would probably prove little more than a dry-as-dust exercise in theatrical archaeology. In fact it turns out to be one of those enjoyable discoveries in which the Swan has long specialised, though the jury must still be out on just how much of this play is Shakespeare's and how much by others' hands.'

In his Theatre Round-Up he calls me 'That great theatrical archaeologist', so now I'm determined to put that on my CV.

Spencer notices what is perhaps *Cardenio*'s most Shakespearian element. He writes that 'the recognition scenes and hard-won forgiveness of the last act recall the late romances'. I think he's right. Spencer concludes that, though the play may not be a lost masterpiece miraculously restored, 'it undoubtedly offers a spirited, entertaining and at times remarkably touching night in the theatre'.

Michael Billington in the *Guardian* echoes that reaction, calling the play 'a theatrically powerful piece', and adds wryly, 'one that should both please audiences and keep academic scholars in work for years'. This prompts the thought that I should perhaps produce an addendum listing all the various sources used, to save any interested academics the trouble of trying to spot the quotations. But I am relieved by Billington's sense that we have achieved some sort of consistency. 'Far from being a mad, bits-and-pieces patchwork, the result is a strangely coherent and ultimately moving drama.'

Billington conjures a delightfully Jacobean image to convey the play's many Shakespearian resonances: 'The play is as full of echoes as a whispering gallery.' Ultimately, he thinks the play feels 'pseudo-Shakespearian', while noting that 'it proves that Cervantes had a profound effect on English cultural life'. His guess, like mine, is that there is more Fletcher than Shakespeare here, and, in trying to articulate why he has that impression, he suggests, 'at no point does the language achieve that blend of the high poetic and the quotidian that is his trademark'.

But in a rave review in the *Daily Mail*, Quentin Letts begs to differ, detecting the Bard both in some of the speeches of 'the lovelorn women' and in the second shepherd's assessment of the mad Cardenio. Letts cries, 'A yokel who says "I think his skull's as empty as a sucked egg" sounded like our boy' (though actually it's a line I pinched from Fletcher's *The Queen of Corinth*). But I am indebted to Letts for adding to the lexicon of words to describe the play's mixed origins, describing it as 'what the motoring trade would call a bitfer'.

Most of the critics would not venture any Shakespeare spotting. But Charles Spencer wrote: 'There are tantalising moments in which we seem to be hearing Shakespeare's own voice.' Of course, in fact, he's exactly right. But luckily none of the critics (nor any of the academics) noticed the lines I snuck in from *Hamlet*.

'So, what next, Greg?' someone asks, '*Love's Labour's Won*?'

Love's Labour's Won is regarded as Shakespeare's other lost play, but I don't think it has been lost.

While rehearsing *Love's Labour's Lost*, back in 2008, we became convinced that Berowne and Rosaline would morph into Beatrice and Benedick. Both couples feel themselves as outsiders; both enjoy sparring with each other. But in Act Five of *Love's Labour's Lost*, 'Jack hath not Jill'. The couple must put their relationship on hold 'for a twelve month and a day,' when Monsieur Marcade brings the unhappy news of the death of the Princess's father, at the end of the play.

In *Much Ado*, when Benedick and Beatrice meet again, he is not in her good books, and they continue the 'merry war' between them but with a more painful sense of an unresolved back history: 'I know you of old,' she sighs 'you always end with a jade's trick.'

So is *Much Ado* really *Love's Labour's Won*?

In *Palladis Tamia*, Francis Meres compiled a list of notable plays he had seen. This list includes the first tantalising reference to *Love's Labour's Won*. Meres includes several other plays by Shakespeare, whom he describes as 'the most excellent in both kinds for the stage' (i.e. comedy and tragedy):

his Gentlemen of Verona, his Errors, his Loves labors
lost, his Love labours wonne, his Midsummers night
dreame, & his Merchant of Venice.

Meres registered his list for publication in September 1598, the year *Love's Labour's Lost* was published. *Much Ado* was registered two years later, in 1600, but may of course have been playing in the theatre for some time before that, enough time for the plays to have been seen together and been regarded as a pair.

The argument against *Much Ado* being *Loves Labour's Won* is that a London bookseller called Christopher Hunt listed both *Love's Labour's Lost* and *Loves Labour's Won* in his stock three years later, in August 1603, after *Much Ado* had been published. And surely he would have used the title under which the play had been published.

But just as *Twelfth Night,* performed at about the same time, has the alternative title *What You Will,* then *Much Ado* could have been subtitled *Love's Labour's Won*?

Although David Tennant, playing Berowne, did remind me that actually *Love's Labour's Won* had been blasted into outer space when the witch-like Carrionites cast a spell on it, to bring about the end of the world; a plan foiled by Dr Who in the BBC TV series. So who knows?

60

Lot 460

Lewis Theobald's estate was sold at auction. The catalogue of that auction still exists in the Bodleian Library in Oxford. At his death, Theobald owned an astonishing twenty-nine Shakespeare quartos. Just let me put that into context. In libraries around the world, there are currently 107 copies of twenty-one plays by Shakespeare which were published in quarto editions before the closure of the theatres in 1642. Lewis Theobald owned nearly a third of that number. He owned more quartos than there are today in the Folger in Washington, the Bodleian in Oxford, the National Library of Scotland, and the University of Edinburgh put together. The British Library own ninety-three copies, most of which came either from David Garrick's collection, bequeathed in 1779, or from King George III's library, presented in 1823. They have all recently been put on the British Library website.

The quartos are very special things for anyone who loves Shakespeare. When the RSC were appearing at the Kennedy Center in Washington, the company were invited to visit the Folger Collection. We were asked if there was anything particular we wanted to see. With some trepidation I asked if they had a copy of the first quarto of *Titus Andronicus*. Tony and I had done the play in South Africa. 'Oh,' the librarian said rather proudly, 'we have *the only* copy of the first quarto of *Titus Andronicus*.' I felt quite light-headed holding this precious document, for this was the very first time Shakespeare had seen one of his plays in print, and this was the only copy left.

In the Bodleian catalogue of the auction of Lewis Theobald's estate, a price is scribbled next to each lot to record the sale. There is no price written next to lot 460.

Lot 460 was Theobald's collection of old plays. 195 of them, again in quarto editions, 'some of them so scarce as not to be had at any price, to many of which are manuscript notes and remarks by Mr Theobald, all done up neatly in boards in single plays'. Is it possible that the manuscript of *Cardenio*, the one in John Downes's handwriting perhaps, was among that lot?

Many people have gone in chase of lot 460.

It is possible that it went to one Thomas Seward, the father of the Swan of Lichfield, Anna Seward. Anna was a poet and novelist. If she left it in her estate, then it went to her daughter, Sarah, who married a man called Burrowes, and she went to live in the Burrowes family home in County Cavan, in Ireland, Stradone House. In 1921, in the last months of the war of the Irish Republic, Stradone House was burned to the ground by the IRA.

So if the manuscript of *Cardenio* survived the fire of the Globe Theatre in 1613, the Great Fire of London in 1666, the predations of Betsy Baker and her pan lining, and the Covent Garden Fire of 1808, it may have finally been incinerated by the IRA.

'The Defile of Despeñaperros in the Sierra Morena', from Gustave Doré's *Spain* (1876)

Epilogue
Si Quis?

Lost, in an instant, in a little word.

(*Cardenio*: Act Three, Scene Two)

History is full of lost masterpieces. Where is the portrait of Suleyman the Magnificent which Titian painted for the Duke of Mantua? What happened to Rubens' portrait of King James I's beloved George Villiers, the Duke of Buckingham, or Holbein's painting of the goldsmith, Hans von Zurich? Where is Rembrandt's *The Circumcision*?

The fate of the second book of Aristotle's *Poetics*, his theory of Comedy, is unknown. Indeed the plot of Umberto Eco's novel *The Name of the Rose* pursues that mystery, suggesting that it was suppressed by medieval monks. Comedy was too subversive for the Church.

Sophocles apparently wrote some 123 plays of which only seven survive, and we have fragments of another two dozen. That is hardly surprising as Sophocles was writing five centuries before Christ. Tony Harrison re-imagines in *The Trackers of Oxyrhynchus*, the fragment of a Satyr play by Sophocles, discovered in Egypt in 1907, and fragments of another turned up as recently as 2005, with the help of infrared technology previously used for satellite imaging.

Philip Henslowe's 'diary' (covering the years 1591–1609) lists intriguing lost plays about Nebuchadnezzar, Pope Joan, and Sir John Mandeville. Cervantes himself claims to have written between twenty to thirty *comedias* in his youth, of which only two are extant. A dozen Philip Massinger plays went up in Betsy Baker's conflagration

Humphrey Moseley, the 'stationer' who registered *The History of Cardenio* for publication in 1653, also claimed to have another play by Shakespeare called *Iphis and Ianthe*, or *A Marriage without a Man*, based on a story in Ovid's *Metamorphoses*, about a girl brought up as a boy, who falls madly in love with another girl. Would that we had that play.

Occasionally these works of art reappear. A Caravaggio turned up in a monastery in Ireland recently, a Turner at Bamborough Castle, and Brueghel's *Garden of Eden* was indentified hanging in a Devon country house. Pieces of lost music seem to turn up every other month. A lost work by Schumann recently reappeared in a German library, and a Bach funeral piece was found in a Kiev archive.

When Humphrey Moseley published the collected works of Beaumont and Fletcher in 1647, he had to apologise that one play was not included in the volume:

> One only play I must accept (for I mean to deal openly), 'tis a comedy called *The Wild Goose Chase*, which hath long been lost, and I fear irrecoverable, for a person of quality borrowed it from the actors many years since, and (by the negligence of a servant) it was never returned. Therefore I put this *Si Quis*, that whosoever hereafter happily meets with it, shall be thankfully satisfied if he please to send it home.

The Wild Goose Chase was then found and included in the second folio in 1679.

In 1500, Michelangelo made a bronze statuette of David for the Gonfaloniere of Florence, Piero Soderini. Vasari in his *Lives of the Artists* praises it. Tantalisingly there is a sketch by Michelangelo of the statue. Unlike his famous marble of David, here in a more typical pose, he stands on the head of Goliath. But would anyone be foolhardy enough to reconstruct the Gonfaloniere's statuette from this sketch? As foolhardy as reconstructing a lost Shakespeare play from an eighteenth-century adaptation? Maybe.

According to the *International Herald Tribune,* an expert at Christie's in London called Thomas Venning, who is a specialist in autograph letters and manuscripts, noted recently that the current record for a manuscript at auction is $31 million dollars, paid for a Leonardo codex in 1994. 'Were a Shakespeare manuscript ever to appear,' he said, 'it would very probably challenge it.'

But who knows? Let me put my own *Si Quis*? What if? Perhaps Shakespeare and Fletcher's lost play *Cardenio* will be rediscovered in a library in Turin, or a cardboard box in the attics of the Orrery family, or in Fulke Greville's empty tomb in Warwick. 'Whosoever happily meets with it, shall be thankfully satisfied if he please to send it home.' If it does reappear I may not be able to afford it, but I'll be first in line to see how it works onstage.

Acknowledgements

My thanks to:

Antonio Álamo, Emilio Hernandez and Ann Bateson; Chris Hickey at the British Council in Madrid; Professor José Manuel González in Alicante, and Juan Sanz Ballesteros in Alcalá de Henares; Professor Ralph Williams and the staff at Michigan University for their support in developing the script; Professors Brean Hammond, Gordon McMullan, Tiffany Stern and Valerie Wayne, for their different points of view

Michael Boyd for allowing me to chase a mad idea; my colleagues at the RSC for supporting the project, in particular Jeremy Adams, Jeanie O'Hare, Réjane Collard, Jane Tassell and Amanda Carroll; John Barton and Cicely Berry for their generosity and support; all the RSC actors and LAByrinth company who helped to workshop the play in Stratford and Michigan

The staff at the admissions office at the Bodleian Library in Oxford; Deborah Rea and Sue Hurley at the Stationers' Hall in London; Marcus Risdell at the Garrick Club

Mic Cheetham for encouraging the book, Nick Hern for his clear guidance in writing it, and Matt Applewhite for pulling it all together

Ellie Kurttz for the use of her photos; the production team, especially Niki Turner, Paul Englishby, Michael Ashcroft, Tim Mitchell, Mark Graham and Ben Brynmor, and the cast for bringing the play to life; and, finally...

Lewis Theobald for his *Double Falshood*.

Index

Adams, Jeremy xvi, xviii, 64, 71, 147
Aeneid (Virgil) xix, 166, 202
Álamo, Antonio 64, 71–3, 75–6, 109, 197–9, 214, 217, 239, 244
Alchemist, The (Jonson) 6, 115
All for Love (Dryden) 118
All is True (*Henry VIII*) 7–8, 16, 35, 57–9, 65, 91–3, 104, 194–5, 232
All's Well That Ends Well 6, 104, 140
Allam, Roger 152
Almagro Festival (La Mancha) xvi, 64, 130
Alphonso, Emperor of Germany 101
Anne of Denmark (Queen) 37, 47, 54–5
Antony and Cleopatra 81, 104, 113
Armitstead, Claire 232
Arnold, Lily 140
As You Find It (Charles Boyle) 173
As You Like It 104
Ashcroft, Michael 142, 168, 198
Astley, Nick 232
Aubrey, John 30, 84–5, 94

Bacon, Edmund 57
Bad Beginning Makes a Good Ending, A 6
Baker, Betsy 108, 249, 252
Bale, John 44
Ballard, Jamie 114
Ballesteros, Juan Sanz 136

Bandele, Biyi 129
Banqueting House (Whitehall) 15, 50, 69, 85–7
Barcot, Maya 200
Barquero, Luis Carro 224
Barton, Anne 43, 146
Barton, John 43–4
Bateson, Ann 123, 129–30, 132, 134, 136–7, 240
Beaumont, Francis 30–3, 50, 87, 102, 115, 118, 146, 252
Beggar's Opera, The (Gay) 219–20
Behn, Aphra 118, 129
Bennett, Ed 76
Berry, Cicely 76, 145
Best, Emily 114
Betterton, Mary 92, 151–2
Betterton, Thomas xx–xxi, 91–3, 98, 151–2, 158, 172, 217, 235
Billington, Michael 44, 146, 245
Blackfriars (playhouse) 16, 87, 90, 92
Bloom, Harold 189
Blount, Edward 104
Booth, Barton 154, 159, 179–81, 194–6
Booth (*née* Santlow), Hester 181, 186, 194–6
Borges, Jorge Luis 41
Boswell, Laurence xv
Bowman, John 22
Boyd, Michael 77, 98, 112, 113, 117, 146–7, 241

Boyle, Charles (4th Earl of Orrery) 171–3, 253
Boyle (*née* Howard), Margaret 42, 172
Boyle, Roger (1st Earl of Orrery) 172
Brenan, Gerald 143, 183–5, 197, 206
Bridewell Theatre (London) 230
Briggs-Owen, Lucy 157
Broken Glass (Arthur Miller) 234
Brooke, C. F. Tucker 229
Brynmor, Ben 199–200
Buck, George (Master of Revels) 16, 54
Buckingham, Duke of (*see* Villiers, George)
Bulgakov, Mikhail 118
Burbage, Richard 35, 58, 92, 221
Burgess, Anthony 12–13, 51
Bury Fair (Shadwell) 118

Calderón de la Barca, Pedro 137
Callow, Simon 164
Campion, Edmund 42
Canterbury Tales, The xv, 64
Captain, The (Fletcher) 6
Caravaggio 200–1, 252
Cardenio **Cervantes and Shelton** (*Don Quixote*) xv–xvi, 20, 40–43, 137, 175–7, 189–90, 192–3; **Shakespeare and Fletcher** 4–6, 14–17, 21, 24, 28, 33, 39, 48–59, 70, 78–82, 101–8, 147, 172–3, 217; **Davenant** xx–xvi, 84–5, 93–8, 101–3, 151–3, 217; **Theobald** (*Double Falshood*) xviii–xxi, 8–9, 19–21, 43–4, 66, 84, 96, 98, 114, 137, 151, 158–9, 162–7, 171–3, 177–81, 186–9, 193–6, 202–4, 208–20, 229–30, 233, 235, 249, 252–3; **Doran** (RSC) concept xv–xxi, 3–9, 23, 36, 168–70; design 67–70, 73, 123–44, 182–5, 226–8; 123–6, 143–4, 197–8, 206–7, 223–5, 234, 241; production 117–19, 228, 231, 234, 238–42; reception 241, 243–6; script 40–45, 63–8, 71–7, 109–12, 189–93, 205–7, 214–17; synopsis xi–xiii; workshop, casting, and rehearsal 113–16, 154–7, 163–4, 182–5, 189–93, 197–201, 205–7, 213–16, 221–5
Carleton, Dudley 79
Carlo Emanuelle (Duke of Savoy) 15–16, 53
Carlos II (King of Spain) 134–5

Carlos, Prince of Asturias (Don Carlos) 135
Carroll, Tim 155
Castillo, Raoul 114
Catalina Micaela (Infanta of Spain) 27
Cervantes Saavedra, Miguel de xv, xviii, 10–13, 42–3, 64, 67–8, 109, 115, 124, 128, 130, 133–7, 140, 178, 182, 190, 193, 198–200, 213–17, 239, 243–5, 252 (and see *Don Quixote* and *Cardenio*)
Chamberlain, John 79
Chances, The (Fletcher) 109, 111–12
Changeling, The (Middleton and Rowley) 70
Chapman, George 50, 118
Charles I 15, 54–5, 78–9, 85–7, 89–90
Charles II 90–2, 151–2, 172
Charles V (Emperor) xvii
Chaucer, Geoffrey xv, 11, 64,
Chesterton, G.K. 132–3
Chichester Festival Theatre 111–12
Christine-Marie (Princess of France) 55
Cibber, Colley 159, 179–81, 196
Cid, Le (Corneille) 19
City Madam, The (Massinger) 31–2, 156, 163, 223, 239
Classic Stage Company (New York) 189–90
Cobb, Alex 146
Cockayne, Sir Aston 32
Cockpit Theatre (London) 90–1
Coleridge, Samuel Taylor 94, 214
Collard, Réjane 20
Comedia de Don Quijote (de Castro) 19–20
Comedy of Errors, The 104, 247
Comical History of Don Quixote, The (D'Urfey) 21–2
Condell, Henry 30, 79–80, 104
Cook, Eric 114
Cooke, Thomas 204
Coriolanus 63–4, 96, 104
Coryate, Thomas 24–8
Courtyard Theatre (Stratford-upon-Avon) 76–7
Covent Garden Theatre (London) xix–xx, 235–7, 242, 249
Cowley, Abraham 102
Coxcomb, The (Fletcher) 110
Coypel, Charles-Antoine 21
Crago, Jacquie 222
Crashaw, Richard 102
Cromwell, Oliver 90, 172, 220

Crowther, Liz   200
Croydon Warehouse (theatre)   146
Cunningham, F.   35
Cure, Cornelius and William   46–7
Custom of the Country, The (Fletcher
    and Massinger)   109, 118
Cymbeline   104, 213

da Silva, António José   22–3
Davenant, William   84–95, 98, 102,
    151–3, 172, 217, 235
Davillier, Jean Charles   124–8, 132, 135,
    205
Davis, Mary   93
Day, Nicholas   185, 198–9
de Bouscal, Guyon Guérin   20, 23, 66
de Castro, Guillén   19–20, 23, 66
Defoe, Daniel   220
de Gheyn, Jacob   183–4
de Jersey, Peter   76
Dekker, Thomas   102, 108, 118
de la Cruz, Juana Inés   114
De Lalande, Michel Richard   21
Dennis, John   180
de Somogyi, Nick   210
d'Este, Alfonso (Prince of Modena)
    27
d'Este, Isabella (Princess of Modena)
    27
Destiny (David Edgar)   118
de Villa, Francisco, Marquis of St
    Michael (Savoyard Ambassador)
    54
Dibdin, Charles   200
Dodd, William   9
Dog in the Manger, The (Lope de Vega)
    71
Don Carlos (see Carlos, Prince of
    Asturias)
Don John (see John of Austria)
Don Quixote (Cervantes)   x, xiv–xvi,
    xx, 11–13, 16, 18–23, 35–6, 40–5, 51,
    66, 75–6, 110–11, 115–16, 118, 124–6,
    130, 136, 142–4, 172, 174–5, 193,
    198, 205, 207, 216–17, 244 (and
    see Cardenio)
Doran, John   196
Doré, Gustave   x, xiv, xxii, 18, 60, 74,
    120, 124–8, 135, 138, 144, 148, 174,
    205, 216, 250
Dorset Garden Theatre (London)
    172
Double Falshood (Theobald) (see
    Cardenio)
Downes, John   xx–xxi, 151–3, 173, 217,
    218, 235, 249

Drury Lane Theatre (London)   xx, 21,
    93–4, 154, 159–60, 179–81, 186–8,
    194–6, 200, 219, 231–2
Dryden, John   31, 96–7, 107, 118, 166
Duke's House (London):   first (see
    Lincoln's Inn Fields Theatre);
    second (see Dorset Garden
    Theatre)
Duncan-Jones, Katherine   34, 244
Dunciad, The (Pope)   202–4, 211
D'Urfey, Thomas   21–3

Edgar, David   114, 118
Edmundson, Helen   114
El Greco   27, 130–1, 140, 227, 234
Elizabeth I   14, 37–8, 42, 46–7, 135, 220
Elizabeth, Princess (Elizabeth Stuart,
    Electress Palatine)   14–15, 28, 39,
    49–52, 152
Elizabeth of Valois (Queen of Spain)
    27, 227
Emanuele Filiberto (Duke of Savoy)
    15–16
Enchanted Island, The (Davenant)
    96–7
Englishby, Paul   123–6, 207, 223–4
Epicoene (Jonson)   115
Ettridge, Christopher   185
Evans, Daniel   8
Evelyn, John   106
Exemplary Stories, The (Cervantes)
    109

Fair Maid of the Inn, The (Fletcher)
    109–10, 244
Fair Penitent, The (Rowe)   118
Fernández-Armesto, Felipe   176
Ferrabosco, Alfonso   5
Fielding, Emma   8
Fielding, Henry   187, 220
First Day's Entertainment, The   90
First Folio (Shakespeare)   30, 79–80,
    94, 103–4, 233
Flecknoe, Richard   90
Fletcher, John (life and career)   8,
    16–17, 19, 28–36, 39–41, 48, 57, 65,
    70, 73, 76, 79–80, 87, 98, 109–12,
    115–18, 190, 199, 203, 210, 213, 217,
    239–40, 244–6, 252 (and see
    individual plays)
Florizel and Perdita (Garrick)   97–8
Flower, Charles Edward   7, 10,
Folies de Cardenio, Les (Pichou)
    20–1, 66, 215
Ford, John   108, 118
Ford Davies, Oliver   76

Forman, Simon   47
Fortune Theatre (London)   87
Foscarini, Antonio (Venetian
   Ambassador)   17, 47, 49, 53, 55
Frederick V (Elector Palatine)   14–15,
   39, 49–52, 152
Fuente Ovejuna (Lope de Vega)   71
Fuerza de la Costumbre (de Castro)   19
Fugard Theatre (Cape Town)   234

Gabaleone, Giovanni Battista
   (Savoyard Ambassador)   5, 15–17,
   21, 24–7, 53–6, 240
Gainsborough, Thomas   82–3
Gainsborough, Earls of (*see* Baptist,
   Noel)
Galavan, Israel   197
Gale, Minnie   76
Game at Chess, A (Middleton)   78–9
Garrick, David   93–4, 97–8, 158–9,
   161, 248
George I   52
George II   xx, 194
George III   248
Gibbon's Tennis Court playhouse (*see*
   Vere Street Theatre)
Gilbert, Julian   169
Giordano, Luca   134–5
Globe Theatre (1599)   46–7, 57–9, 63,
   78–80, 92, 103–4, 108, 152, 236–7,
   242, 249
Globe Theatre (1613)   59, 78–9, 92,
   109, 152, 237
Globe Theatre (1997)   155
Godwin, Chris   163–4, 200
Gondomar, Count of (*see* Sarmiento
   de Acuña, Don Diego)
Gonzaga, Marguerite (Duchess of
   Mantua)   27
Gonzaga, Francesco (Duke of Mantua)
   27
González, José Manuel Fernandez de
   11, 67–8, 70, 239
Googe, Barnabe   182–5
Goold, Rupert   98
Gower, John   30
Goya, Francisco José de   140, 143, 182,
   228
Grady-Hall, Michael   183
Graham, Mark   141, 226–7
Grand, Jenny   170
Greene, Robert   43, 108, 118
Greville, Fulke   81–2, 253
Gulliver's Travels (Swift)   211
Gurr, Andrew   54, 233
Guthrie, Tyrone   154

Hadley, Michael   114
Hall, Peter   43, 118
Hamilton, Charles   146
Hamlet   35, 76, 91, 92–3, 153, 155, 165,
   170, 179, 191–2, 222, 232–3, 246
Hammond, Brean   207, 210, 235
Handel, George Frederic   194
Hands, Terry   66, 152
Harington, Sir John   14
Harlequin a Sorcerer   161
Harlequin, Dr Faustus   159–60
Harris, Henry   92
Harvey-Thompson, Alix   186–7, 190,
   194, 241–2
Hassell, Alex   155, 157, 168–70, 190, 233
Hayes, Felix   200
Haymarket Theatre (London)   22
Hemings, John   5–6, 30, 49, 58–9,
   79–80, 104, 236
Henri IV (King of France)   55
Henrietta Maria (Queen)   85–7,
   89–90
Henry Frederick (Prince of Wales)
   15–17, 24–8, 37–9, 46–8, 53–5, 91,
   134
Henry V   145, 210
Henry IV, Part One   6, 91
Henry IV, Part Two   6
Henry VI, Parts One, Two and Three
   43–4, 104, 113, 155
Henry VIII   16
Henry VIII   (see *All Is True*)
Henslowe, Philip   31, 252
Hernandez, Emilio   xvi–xvii, 64, 239
Herringman, Henry   107
Hickey, Chris   xviii
Hill, Chris   185
Hill, Dominic   156
History and Fall of Caius Martius, The
   (Otway)   97
Hoare, William   212
Hogarth, William   179–81, 208–9
Holbein, Hans   251
Hole, William   48
Homecoming, The (Pinter)   118
Hooper, Jim   76
Hope Theatre (London)   87–8
Houghton, Matti   200
House of Desires, The (Sor Juana)   114
Houston, William   63
Howard, Charles (1st Earl of
   Nottingham)   12, 115
Howard, Elizabeth   42
Howard, Margaret (*see* Boyle)
Howard, Theophilus (2nd Earl of
   Suffolk)   42, 172

Howard, Thomas (1st Earl of Suffolk) 41–2
Hunter, Kathryn   155
Hurley, Sue   101–3

Ingratitude of the Commonwealth, The (Tate)   96
Iphis and Ianthe   252
Ireland, William Henry   229–30
Irving, Henry   93, 159, 231
Island Princess, The (Fletcher)   8, 65, 116, 140

Jackson, John   161
Jaggard, William and Isaac   104
James I and VI   4, 6, 14–17, 27–8, 37–8, 41, 46–9, 53–6, 79, 85, 100, 193, 220, 251
James II (Duke of York)   152
Jew of Venice, The   102
Joao V (King of Portugal)   22
John of Austria, Don   132–5
Johnson, Rebecca   145
Johnson, Robert   5, 207
Jondon   239
Jones, Inigo   50, 69, 85–7
Jonson, Ben   6, 24, 31, 37, 43, 79–80, 87, 94, 102, 115, 118, 140
Juan Carlos I (King of Spain)   xv, xvii–xviii, 6, 134
Julius Caesar   104, 152, 179

Katherine of Aragon (Queen)   16
Kean, Edmund   93
Kemble, John   232, 236
Kent, William   219
Killigrew, Thomas   91, 118
King, Terry   215
King and No King, A (Beaumont and Fletcher)   6
King John   44, 104
King Lear   96
King's Men (company)   5–6, 29, 31, 34, 54, 57–9, 78–9, 91–2, 115
Kinnear, Rory   8
Kirchmaier, Thomas   182–5
Knight, Edward   54
Knight of the Burning Pestle, The (Beaumont)   115, 118
Knot of Fools, The   6
Kulick, Brian   189–90
Kyd, Thomas   118

LAByrinth (company)   114
Law Against Lovers, The (Davenant) 96–7

Lawson, Mark   243
Lee, Nicholas   224
Lennox, 2nd Duke of (*see* Stuart, Ludovick)
Lesser, Anton   8
Letts, Quentin   245–6
Ley, Charles David   68
Lincoln's Inn Fields Theatre (London) xx–xxi, 91–4, 151–3, 159–62, 172, 179–80
Lomax, Alan   206
London Academy of Music and Dramatic Art (LAMDA)   155
London Merchant, The (Lillo)   118
Long, Trevor   114
Lope de Vega, Félix Arturo   71, 137
Lope de Vega Theatre (Seville)   71
Lords' Masque, The (Campion)   50
Louis XV (King of France)   21
Lounsbury, Thomas   204
Love's Cure (Fletcher)   19
Love's Labour's Lost   17, 76, 247
Love's Labour's Won   246–7
Love's Pilgrimage (Fletcher)   109
Lovesick Maid, The (Brome)   102
Lowin, John   35, 58, 91–2
Lowndes, T.   xix
Lyly, John   118

Mabbe, James   199–200
Macbeth   91, 98, 104, 163, 179, 181, 195, 197, 222–3, 228, 232, 241–2
McGowan, Mark   185
Macías, Javier   224, 241
Mackintosh, Iain   159
McLuskie, Kate   81
McMullan, Gordon   7–8
Maiden's Holiday, The   108
The Maid's Tragedy (Beaumont and Fletcher)   146
Marat/Sade (Peter Weiss)   118, 156
Maria Anna (Infanta of Spain)   78–9
Maria Apollonia (Infanta of Savoy) 16–17, 24, 27–8, 53–6
Marie de Medici (Queen of France) 16
Market Theatre (Johannesburg)   130
Markham, Gervase   190–1
Marlowe, Christopher   100, 108, 118
Marr, Andrew   232
Marston, John   100, 118
Mary I   37, 51
Mary, Queen of Scots   46–8
Masque of Oberon, The (Jonson)   37
Masque of the Inner Temple and Gray's Inn, The (Beaumont)   50

Massinger, Philip   31–2, 35, 102, 108–9, 118, 156, 163, 252
Measure for Measure   96–7, 104
Meckler, Nancy   156
Memorable Masque of the Middle Temple and Lincoln's Inn, The (Chapman)   50
Merchant of Venice, The   98, 163, 197, 226, 247
Meres, Francis   246–7
Merry Devil of Edmonton, The   6, 103
Middleton, Thomas   70, 78–9, 100–3, 118, 146–7
Midsummer Night's Dream, A   10, 37, 76, 156, 247
Miguel/Will (José Carlos Somoza)   68
Miller, Hannah   155
Milton, John   102
Miserables, Los   142
Miss Julie (Strindberg)   185
Mitchell, Tim   123, 227
Molière   20
Monck, George   89, 91
Morris, Jan   143–4, 198
Moseley, Anne   107
Moseley, Humphrey   32, 101–7, 147, 172, 180, 252
Mountaineers, The (Colman)   22
Much Ado About Nothing   6, 51, 73, 96–7, 154, 247
Mustapha (Roger Boyle)   172

Nashe, Thomas   100
Necromancer, The   159–62
Neilson, Anthony   156
Newcastle, Duke of (*see* Pelham-Holles, Thomas)
Nixon, Pippa   115, 157, 164, 200, 228, 233
Noel, Baptist (4th Earl of Gainsborough)   82
Noh Theatre (Tokyo)   216
Nottingham, Earl of (*see* Howard, Charles)

Odyssey (Homer)   141
O'Hare, Jeanie   76, 147, 189, 224
Okonkwo, Chiké   200
Olazabal, Jason   114
Oldfield, Anne   177–8, 187, 196
Olivier, Laurence   92–4, 111–12
O'Neil, Bruce   223
Oroonoko (Behn)   129
Orphan, The (Otway)   172
Orrery, Earls of (*see* Boyle)
Osman the Great Turk   102

Othello   131, 155
Other Place, The (Stratford-upon-Avon)   141
Otway, Thomas   97, 159, 172
Overbury, Thomas   221
Ovid   100, 252

Padlock, The (Bickerstaffe)   200
Parson's Wedding, The (Killigrew)   118
Peake, Robert   26–7, 54–5
Peele, George   118
Pelham-Holles, Thomas (1st Duke of Newcastle)   219
Pepys, Samuel   93–4, 151–2, 220
Pericles   30, 80
Persiles y Sigismunda (Cervantes)   109
Philaster (Fletcher)   6, 17
Philip II (King of Spain)   27, 38, 51, 131–5
Philip IV (King of Spain)   79
Pichou   20–3, 215–16
Pizarro   237
Plutarch   97
Pope, Alexander   96, 162, 165–7, 202–4, 209–12, 219, 229
Porter, Mary   181, 186
Poulton, Mike   xv
Pourbus, Frans   27, 227
Priestley, J.B.   13
Purcell, Henry   22
Puritan Maid, Modest Wife and Wanton Widow, The   102
Purves, Libby   243–4

Queen of Corinth, The (Fletcher)   110, 246
Queen's Men (company)   43

Rafter, Denis   68
Ralegh, Walter   17, 37–8, 47
Rape of Proserpine, The (Theobald)   162
Rea, Deborah   100–2
Red Bull Theatre (Clerkenwell)   87, 90
Relapse, The (Vanbrugh)   159
Rhodes, George Ambrose   229
Rich, John ('Lun')   158–61, 179–80, 219
Richard II   96, 98, 158
Richard III   113
Risdell, Marcus   161
Rivals, The (Davenant; see *Two Noble Kinsmen, The*)
Rix, Oliver   155–6, 164, 168–70, 214, 241–2

Rodero, Cristina García   182
Rollo, Duke of Normandy (Fletcher)
    91–2
Roman Actor, The (Massinger)   31–2,
    35
Romeo and Juliet   97, 131–2, 139, 153
Rose, Clifford   146
Rowe, Nicholas   118
Rowley, William   70
Royal Court Theatre (London)   156
Royal Shakespeare Company (RSC)
    xi, xv–xvi, xviii, xxi, 7, 19–20, 29,
    43–4, 63–4, 68, 75–7, 113–19,
    139–41, 145–7, 155–7, 163–4, 185,
    197–201, 213–17, 221–5, 238–9, 248
Royal Shakespeare Theatre (Stratford-
    upon-Avon)   7, 63–4, 76, 117–18,
    130, 139, 145–7, 163, 228, 240–1
Rubens, Peter Paul   85–7
Rule a Wife and Have a Wife
    (Fletcher)   159
Rupert Prince (Count Palatine)   89
Rylance, Mark   155

Sagovsky, Kate   223
Salmacida Spolia (Davenant)   85–7
Sarmiento de Acuña, Don Diego
    (Count of Gondomar, Spanish
    Ambassador)   55, 78–9
Savall, Jordi   124
Scheemakers, Peter   219
Scott, Elisabeth   63
Seary, Peter   171–2
Second Maiden's Tragedy, The
    (Middleton)   118, 146–7
Sejanus (Jonson)   43, 140
Seward, Anna   249
Seward, Thomas   249
Shakespeare Memorial Theatre
    (Stratford-upon-Avon)   7, 10,
    63, 91
Shakespeare, Edmond   31
Shakespeare, Susannah   89
Shakespeare, William (*life, career, and
    reputation*)   xv, xviii–xx, 6–17,
    28–36, 39–43, 48, 57–9, 64, 67–8,
    70, 73, 79–98, 103–4, 115, 118, 131,
    136, 154, 164–7, 172, 176, 187–92,
    195, 202–4, 209–13, 219, 223,
    229–33, 239–40, 243–9, 252 (*and
    see under individual plays*)
Shaw, George Bernard   213
Shelton, Thomas   16, 35–6, 40–5, 76,
    115–16, 136, 147, 172, 189–92, 207,
    217, 244
Sher, Antony   116, 130, 234, 248

Sheridan, Richard Brinsley   230
Shirley, James   102
Shulman, Nicola   232
Sicilian Usurper, The (Tate)   96
Siddons, Sarah   231–2, 235–6
Sidney, Philip   81
Siege of Rhodes, The (Davenant)
    90–1, 102, 151–2, 172
Singer (Peter Flannery)   118
Soloski, Alex   189
Sonnets, The   34, 176
Sophocles   251
Sor Juana (*see* de la Cruz, Juana Inés)
Sosanya, Nina   76
Southampton, Earl of (*see*
    Wriothesley, Henry)
Spencer, Charles   244–6
Stede, John   218
Stern, Tiffany   239–40
Stewart, Patrick   113
Stowe, John   87
Stuart, Ludovick (2nd Duke of
    Lennox)   55
Stubbings, Marion   200–1
Suckling, John   102
Suffolk, Earls of (*see* Howard)
Suzman, Janet   63, 145
Swan Theatre (Stratford-upon-Avon)
    xi, xxi, 7, 63, 77, 116, 117–19, 123,
    139–41, 142, 221, 225, 226–9,
    240–1, 245
Swift, Jonathan   211–12

Tamer Tamed, The (Fletcher)   7–8,
    29, 54, 65, 142, 164
Taming of the Shrew, The   7, 104, 164,
    177
Tate, Nahum   96
Taylor, Gary   64–6
Taylor, Joseph   35, 91–2
Taylor, Paul   243
Teatro Albéniz (Madrid)   64
Teatro Español (Madrid)   xv
Tempest, The   6, 15, 91, 96–8, 104,
    155
Tennant, David   76, 247
Theatr Clwyd   66
Theatre Royal (Bath)   231–2
Theatre Royal, Drury Lane (*see* Drury
    Lane Theatre)
Theobald, Lewis (*life and career*)
    xviii–xxi, 7–9, 21–2, 82–4, 93,
    96–8, 151–3, 158–62, 165–7, 171–3,
    179–81, 187, 194–6, 202–4, 208–12,
    218–20, 228–30, 233, 235, 248–9
    (*and see Cardenio*)

Timon of Athens 104
Tirso de Molina 137
Titus Andronicus 130, 248–9
Thorndike, Sybil 30
Tourneur, Cyril 108
Trackers of Oxyrhynchus, The (Tony Harrison) 251–2
Turner, Niki 123–4, 129–32, 137, 139–41, 143–4, 226–7
Twelfth Night 104, 191–2, 247
Two Gentlemen of Verona, The 104, 117, 247
Two Noble Kinsmen, The 50, 93

Union Theatre (Southwark) 199

Vaughan, Henry 102
Velázquez, Diego 133
Venice Preserved (Otway) 159
Vere Street Theatre (London) 91
Verstegan, Richard 42
Very Woman, A (Fletcher and Massinger) 109
Vida do Grande D. Quixote de la Mancha (da Silva) 22–3
Villiers, George (1st Duke of Buckingham) 79, 251
Volpone (Jonson) 31
Vortigern (Ireland) 229–30

Walcott, Derek 141
Walter, Harriet 113
Warburton, John 107–8
Warburton, William 209
Wars of the Roses, The 43–4
Wayne, Valerie 115–16, 225
Weber, Henry 110

Webster, John 38, 118
Wells, Stanley 164
West, Timothy 63
Wheeler, Duncan 75, 217
Wilby, Jaki 197–8
Widow's Prize, The (William Samson) 102
Wild Goose Chase, The (Fletcher) 34–5, 252
Wilkins, George 32
Wilks, Robert 154, 179–81, 186–8
Williams, Ralph 113–14
Williams, Mr 181, 194–5
Wilmott, Phil 199
Winter's Tale, The 6, 47, 97–8, 104, 105, 146, 188
Wit in Madness (Brome) 102
Woman's Mistaken, The (Drew Davenport) 102
Woman's Prize, The (see *Tamer Tamed, The*)
Women Beware Women (Middleton) 103
Wood, Michael 207
Wotton, Henry 57–8
Wren, Christopher 105
Wriothesley, Elizabeth 82
Wriothesley, Henry (3rd Earl of Southampton) 82, 115
Wyatt, Thomas 232

York Mystery Plays 68

Zoffany, Johan 159
Zuñiga, Balthasar de (Spanish Ambassador) 78
Zurburán, Francisco de 139, 200–1